# THE RITE OF URBAN PASSAGE

**Articulating Journeys: Festivals, Memorials and Homecomings**
*General Editors:*
Tom Selwyn, SOAS University of London
Nicola Frost, Devon Community Foundation

The landscape of contemporary mobility stresses ideas of home, return, com-memoration and celebration. Groups seek to mark changing elements of his-torical and cultural importance through architecture, narrative and festivity. Migrants and their descendants frequently travel between 'homes', reinventing and reshaping as they go. Such events can themselves attract travellers and pilgrims with their own stories to tell. Engaging with more substantive ethno-graphic features and linking back to classical anthropological and philosophical concerns, this series contributes to a new understanding of the Other encoun-tered away from home but also of the Self and home.

**Volume 1**
Waiting for Elijah
Time and Encounter in a Bosnian Landscape
*Safet HadžiMuhamedović*

**Volume 2**
The Rite of Urban Passage
The Spatial Ritualization of Iranian Urban Transformation
*Reza Masoudi*

# THE RITE OF URBAN PASSAGE

## The Spatial Ritualization of Iranian Urban Transformation

Reza Masoudi

berghahn
NEW YORK · OXFORD
www.berghahnbooks.com

First published in 2018 by

Berghahn Books

www.berghahnbooks.com

**Library of Congress Cataloging-in-Publication Data**

Names: Masoudi, Reza, author.
Title: The rite of urban passage : the spatial ritualization of Iranian urban
    transformation / Reza Masoudi.
Description: New York : Berghahn Books, [2018] | Series: Articulating
    journeys : festivals, memorials, and homecomings ; 2 | Includes
    bibliographical references and index.
Identifiers: LCCN 2018008951 (print) | LCCN 2018016895 (ebook) |
    ISBN 9781785339776 (ebook) | ISBN 9781785339769 (hardback : alk. paper)
Subjects: LCSH: Tenth of Muḥarram--Iran--Dizfūl. |
    Islam--Iran--Dizfūl--Customs and practices. | Shiites--Iran--Dizfūl. |
    Urbanization--Iran--Dizfūl--History--20th century. | City
    planning--Social aspects--Iran--Dizfūl--History--20th century. |
    Dizfūl (Iran)--Social life and customs.
Classification: LCC BP194.5.T4 (ebook) | LCC BP194.5.T4 M37 2018 (print) |
    DDC 297.3/6--dc23
LC record available at https://lccn.loc.gov/2018008951

**British Library Cataloguing in Publication Data**
A catalogue record for this book is available from the British Library

ISBN 978-1-78533-976-9 hardback
ISBN 978-1-80073-649-8 paperback
ISBN 978-1-78533-977-6 ebook

https://doi.org/10.3167/9781785339769

*To Kian and Azita, my son and wife*

# CONTENTS

# Figures

# MAPS

# ACKNOWLEDGEMENTS

This book is a result of my long-term focus on religious rituals as part of urbanization process. This idea stems from my PhD research that had the full financial support of my father-in-law, Majid Ghandi-zadeh Dezfuli, who has always been my true mentor and friend. The manuscript of book was partly prepared during my Writing Fellowship at the Max Planck Institute for Religious and Ethnic Diversity (MPI-MMG), Göttingen, Germany. I am grateful to Professor Peter Van der Veer, the director of MPI-MMG, for this generous fellowship. I have to express my gratitude to Professor Tom Selwyn for his full support ever since he was my PhD examiner in 2009.

# PREFACE

## The Retrospective of this Book

This book is the outcome of a usual academic process. However, it is rooted in a lifelong personal curiosity about the dynamics of urban culture. I am not sure why this curiosity has stayed with me, but I can briefly narrate its history.

When I was ten years old, I was exposed to the oral cultural history of my hometown in a way that was unusual for my generation. Every evening, I had no choice but to listen to the narratives of elderly members of my family that made our long, dark and fearful evenings bearable. It was 1980, when the Iran-Iraq war stormed the country with my hometown, Dezful, near the border. Dezful became one of the most bombed cities during the war. There was a power cut every evening to keep the city in absolute darkness because of airstrikes; there was no way to watch TV. We spent our long evenings listening to our parents and grandparents tell stories about the city and their traditional way of life, stories that were otherwise edged out by television. The war dragged our evening lifestyle back to earlier times. This experience made a substantial impact on my interest in the oral history of cities and cultures.

One of the most interesting stories was about the traditional Muharram rituals and the rearrangement of Muharram processions. Years later, I revisited this subject for my final design project and dissertation to complete my master's in architecture at the University of Tehran in the mid-1990s. I intended to design the site of an old cemetery around the tomb of Roodband, which had been the focal point of the Dezful Muharram processions ever since their rearrangement in the very early 1950s. This site became the heart of the city during Muharram commemoration, the most important socio-cultural annual event. Nonetheless, this site was not an important place for the everyday life of the city, and was ignored by modern urban planners, remaining an empty arena at the margins of the old city. The site is on the east bank of the River Dez, with a striking view over the river. My aim was to design the site in such a way as to reposition it as the cultural heart of the city,

**FIGURE 0.1** The cemetery around the tomb of Roodband. The tomb is in the background. Dezful, 1996. Photo by the author.

considering that a new bridge over the river was about to change the position of this site in the urban configuration. Soon, I realized that this was not simply a normal urban design project, and that the question of ritual and city was far more complex than what I had learned about cities in a school of the built environment. My dissertation received the award for the Dissertation of Year in Art and Architecture, but the theoretical curiosity about the relationship between city and ritual stayed with me for years and fundamentally shaped my academic career. This book is certainly the result of this curiosity, but it has by no means exhausted my inquiry about ritual, space and cities.

The journey from the built environment discipline to social anthropology and ritual studies was not a short one. This was an academic voyage via a diploma, my second master's degree, my PhD and post-doctoral research projects. My old and new colleagues may conceive this journey as a break from one discipline and into another. However, from my point of view it was a seamless journey of following a theoretical curiosity, without regard to the established disciplinary boundaries.

Since the nineteenth century, human knowledge has predominantly been developed and produced through the division of academic disciplines and establishment of respective scientific methods. However, during the second half of the twentieth century this was called into question, leading to interdisciplinary teaching and study. In *Against Method* (1993; orig. 1975), Paul Feyerabend (1924–1994) rejected the existence of a universal scientific method. As a philosopher of science, he made a case for an anarchistic approach in science. Feyerabend argued that the great scientific findings are often achieved when someone ignores general standard procedures and goes beyond the established scientific methods. He even stated that science is essentially an anarchic enterprise. In the opening statement of his introduction he wrote 'that anarchism, while perhaps not the most attractive political philosophy, is certainly excellent medicine for epistemology, and for the philosophy of science' (1993: 9). On the other hand, there has been concern about professionalizing academic disciplines, which effectively reduces academic disciplines into certain techniques or methods, such as reducing anthropology into ethnography, or history into historiography. In his talk at UC Berkeley, Hayden White mentioned that the field of history has been professionalized, thus this discipline is not often revolutionized from within. This circumstance, he argued, even pushes great thinkers out of academia: Nietzsche resigned from his position at the University of Basel and Marx never received an academic appointment. Often, someone from the periphery of the field of history, such as literature, contributes to a new discourse in this discipline (White, 2014). This situation has created the desire to engage in interdisciplinary studies, and scholars in science, social sciences, art and humanities very often borrow concepts and ideas from each other. Surprisingly, there is no common understanding about key concepts among scholars of different disciplines. The borrowed terms and concepts – such as myth, language, space, landscape and place – very often lose their meanings across disciplines and become metaphors. I am frequently surprised to see how a concept from one discipline transforms into a metaphor or complex concept with a different connotation in another field of study. I would argue that this is partly due to the effects of the 'Chinese whisper game' or the game of 'telephone', in which ideas and concepts are further distorted as they are passed 'down the line'. In an interview, Hayden White explained that it is rather difficult to initiate a concrete interdisciplinary collaboration, since there is no longer a common language or even a theory among humanists (White, 2013). In this intellectual landscape, some scholars have been able to make substantial contributions by proposing and developing a theoretical framework that integrates diverse and fragmented understandings of a key concept, as Lefebvre (1991; orig. 1974) did with the notion of space in *The Production of Space.*

The contribution of the present book is not the result of borrowing ideas and concepts from other disciplines. Rather, it reflects my personal journey across disciplines throughout my academic training and research career. In other words, this book is not the result of a migration of concepts, but the disciplinary migration of its author.

# INTRODUCTION

This book is entitled *The Rite of Urban Passage*, inspired by van Gennep's classic book, *The Rites of Passage*. The reason behind this was not to have a catchy title nor to imply that this book is greatly influenced by van Gennep. The title of the book should be read as a set of keywords referring to 'Muharram rituals', 'the Iranian city', and 'the process of modern urban transformation'. I actually coined 'the rite of urban passage' to describe the re-arrangement of Muharram procession routes in the city of Dezful in the early 1950s. I explain in chapter four that this historic event was a ritual per se, that signified a major change in the social constitution of Dezful during the Iranian modernization. The re-arrangement of processions ritualized the passage of the urban society from the traditional constitution into a new social make-up. Thus, 'the rite of urban passage' discursively implies the dynamics of Muharram rituals and urban transformation. The investigation into Muharram procession dynamics during the Iranian modernization was the starting point of this book, yet the investigation unfolded in a much broader historical and theoretical landscape. Ultimately, this book is not just about Iranian cities or Muharram rituals, by which Shi'i Muslims annually commemorate the tragic martyrdom of Hussein ibn Ali in the seventh century. It offers an alternative approach to investigating the process of urban transformation and develops a fresh spatial approach in ritual studies.

The chapters of this book are developed in two main parts. The first part includes chapter one, which formulates the ritual as a spatial practice, and chapter two, which offers a spatial reading of the evolution of Muharram rituals throughout Shi'i history. Through this alternative history, the idea of the 'spatial manifestation' of ritual is formulated. This idea is one of the theoretical components of ritual theory that is developed in this book. The second part predominantly focuses on 'the spatial organization' of Muharram processions, throughout chapters three, four and five. These chapters extensively investigate the social and spatial logic of Muharram processions before and after urban transformation, as well as the complex process of changing procession routes. The overarching aim of these chapters is to carefully examine the process of urban transformation through the prism

of ritual. Muharram rituals are considered as part of an urban process by
which the traditional Iranian cities transitioned into a new era. Although the
second part of the book presents first-hand ethnographic and oral history
materials, its main contribution is to show an alternative approach to urban
studies. Each chapter contributes to developing the idea of this book that
is to entwine urban and ritual studies, and the discussions in each chapter
are structured so they can be read as independent texts. In other words, this
book has a kind of fractal structure: while each segment is a component of a
larger system, it can also be individually recognized in its own right.

Chapter one is a theoretical review of the framework of ritual studies
and the paradigm shifts that have taken place in this field of research. This
chapter does not offer a broad, general and extensive literature review in
ritual theory; rather, it outlines the theoretical framework of this research,
considering Muharram commemoration as a changing social-spatial collective performance. Although there is extensive discussion around the idea of
the religious ritual as a changing social practice, the heart of this chapter is a
section on the relationship between ritual, place and space. The discussion
distinguishes 'the place of ritual' from 'the ritual spatiality'. This idea is the
theoretical foundation of chapter two, which explores the spatial genealogy
of Muharram rituals.

Chapter two introduces the tragic battle of Karbala when Hussein ibn
Ali, the grandson of the Prophet Mohammad, and his few companions were
brutally massacred in the Muharram of 680. This historic tragedy unfolded
after the political dispute over the legitimacy of the Umayyad Caliphate. The
discussion then explains how this historic tragedy has since transcended
into meta-history. From the Shi'i point of view this tragedy is not merely
one of the historic events that established the Shi'i–Sunni division, but the
Shi'i myth around which their creed and rituals are constituted. After this
general introduction to the Karbala tragedy, chapter two extensively reviews
the development of Muharram rituals throughout history. In parallel, the
establishment of Shi'i religious buildings, such as *husseinyeh* and *tekyeh*, is
also discussed. The main contribution of this chapter is to offer a spatial
reading of the history of Shi'i rituals, dealing with the spatial evolution of
rituals. It shifts the focus from what participants do during rituals or where
they practise it, to how rituals are spatially manifested. The key point is the
shift of attention from action to spatial manifestation. As I shall discuss,
the rituals are either manifested in concentrated or dispersed forms (such
as the service session and the procession) that produce fundamentally different social engagements. The spatial reading of Muharram ritual history
shows that the evolution of a concentrated ritual into a dispersed one, or
vice versa, is the process by which the new rituals were often invented. This
chapter does not solely address Muharram rituals in Iran, but explores the

development of rituals in its broad historical and geographical landscape. Nonetheless, the main aim is to investigate the broad historical background of rituals practised in Iran.

The second part of the book, throughout four chapters, specifically looks at Muharram processions in the city of Dezful in the southwest of Iran. It concentrates on the social and spatial logic of the processions and how they have changed during the twentieth century.

Chapter three focuses on the social logic of Muharram processions in their traditional format. This chapter begins with a discussion about traditional Iranian urban society that was constituted based on the Heydari and Nemati parts, described as social moieties by Perry (1999). Heydari-Nemati as a social organization was constituted based on the traditional ruling system in which each borough was ruled by an elite family, aka landlord families. The local elite families teamed up in two socio-political groups that competed for greater power in the city, therefore the city was governed by a polarized system. In this political landscape, the urban boroughs divided into two rival groups, Heydaris and Nematis. The discussions in this chapter review the historical background of the Heydari–Nemati division, and explains how this division is reflected in urban realities in general and Muharram processions in particular. This chapter also discusses the other features of urban society, articulating how local communities are socially constituted within each urban moiety. These discussions reveal that Muharram processions were the primary medium of practising and negotiating the social division, cohesion and solidarity by which local communities are constituted as urban society. The social investigation, through the lens of Muharram rituals, reveals that the traditional social struggle occurred among urban communities, not social classes. The social moieties of Heydari and Nemati predominated the logic of these urban negotiations. This investigation reveals the nature of this unique urbanism that cannot be fully articulated by conventional ideas that explain urban processes as being merely based on the idea of 'class struggles' and 'everyday life'.

Chapter four, 'The Rite of Urban Passage', investigates the complex landscape of the transformational period of Iranian cities since the 1920s, when the modern Pahlavi dynasty was established. This chapter begins with a depiction of the broad landscape of the Iranian modernization and then zeroes in on the city of Dezful. The discussions investigate the physical and very complex socio-political transformations of this city. In this chapter, I argue that although the physical transformation of the city is the most visible manifestation of urban modernization, the end of the Heydari–Nemati division encapsulates the urban transformation. This was not a smooth process; it was a socially tense and violent period. The establishment of new procession routes signified the end of urban violence and the abolition of traditional social divisions. I argue that the re-arrangement of processions is also a ritual, and I call it 'the rite of urban passage'. The rite mediated the passage from the traditional urban society to a new social make-up. This chapter examines the complex relationship between rituals and urban violence and conciliation. While chapter four focuses on describing the social and political context of urban transformation and re-arrangement of Muharram processions, chapter five examines the spatial complexity of re-arranged procession routes.

Chapter five analyses 'the spatial organization' of the transformed Muharram processions. The processions were historically organized in each part of the city because of the traditional Heydari–Nemati division. The processions were then reorganized to ritualize social integration. However, the new processions are more complex than merely representing the integration of the two moieties. They mediate practising the new social make-up, in which Heydari and Nemati parties are integrated, simultaneously keep alive the idea of traditional social division. I formulate how the spatial organization of processions constitutes a lived/performed space, or ritual space, in which the past and present are discursively performed, revealing a sophisticated way of performing urban history. Moreover, I differentiate 'the spatial organization of processions' from 'performed ritual space', then conceptually formulate 'performed ritual space' as a 'topological space' in which past and present can be simultaneously performed. These discussions bridge ritual and urban studies, demonstrating how these two fields can contribute to theoretical development in other disciplines.

One of my arguments in chapter five is that the spatial organization of processions will change only when the urban society is fundamentally transformed. The urban society may not fundamentally transform, but it is a changing institution. Therefore, the question is: how does a ritual that is essentially supposed to reflect social reality represent the gradual social dynamics? Chapter six is dedicated to answering this question by looking at the reinvention of the shawl exchange custom during Muharram in the city of Dezful in recent years. This chapter is not aimed at enhancing our knowledge about 'the spatial dynamics' of Muharram rituals, but it captures the process of maintaining the relevance of Muharram commemoration in a changing society.

The concluding chapter lays out the full picture of the framework of spatial study of rituals as developed in this book, and formulizes the idea of ritual space. The formulation of the framework for studying the spatial dynamics of rituals is based upon two components: 'the spatial manifestation' and 'the spatial organization' of the ritual, as discussed in the book. The concluding discussion will explain that 'the spatial dynamic' of rituals is driven by two independent but parallel processes: the evolution of ritual manifestation and the transformation of the spatial organization of ritual. The discussion will then formulate the notion of ritual space on a more conceptual level. Finally, I will explain how this new idea of ritual space differs from key conceptual ideas that have been discussed, such as those offered by Lefebvre and J.Z. Smith, and how this book contributes to the field of ritual and urban studies.

# PART I

═══

# THE SPATIAL MANIFESTATION OF RITUAL

The first part of the book discusses the spatial aspect of ritual and introduces the idea of 'the spatial manifestation of ritual', one of the theoretical components of ritual theory that is developed in this book. Chapter one establishes the theoretical component of the idea, articulating ritual as a profoundly spatial practice. This idea provides a theoretical foundation for a spatial reading of the history of Muharram rituals. Then chapter two contextualizes the notion of spatial manifestation throughout the historical development of Muharram rituals. These discussions not only offer a new theoretical outlook in ritual studies, but also provide a platform for locating ritual at the centre of attention in urban studies.

# CHAPTER 1

# TOWARDS A FRAMEWORK FOR SPATIALLY STUDYING RELIGIOUS RITUALS

Ritual studies have been conventionally located in the discipline of religious studies and anthropology; however, rituals have received the attention of diverse social science disciplines in recent decades. This disciplinary expansion in ritual studies is partly due to the paradigm shift in ritual studies that has stretched the conceptual implication of rituals. This is also due to an increase in interdisciplinary studies that have turned to rituals as a key to understanding religious, social, cultural and political changes. This development in ritual studies has diversified the notion of ritual and turned it into a key concept that resists strict definition. Therefore, instead of attempting to define the ritual, the first section of this chapter discusses the ritual framework that developed based on paradigm shifts in ritual studies. The second part of this discussion will address one of the important recent shifts in the notion of ritual: the shift from perceiving rituals as a set of fixed actions to seeing them as changing performances. This discussion expresses the fact that rituals are not formulaic and passive representations of community myths or social reality. Rituals are dynamic collective performances that are active parts of social and religious changes.

The second section will address the key subject of this chapter: the question of rituals, place and space. This section will review how ritual theories have engaged with the idea of territory and place, then discuss Davis Parkin's idea that formulates ritual as a spatial system. This discussion will address in particular the ambiguity between the place of ritual and ritual spatiality, an idea that provides a platform for the following chapter, which formulates the idea of the spatial manifestation of rituals.

## The Framework of Ritual Studies

The definition of ritual has changed throughout the history of social science, reflecting the shifts in ritual studies. Tala Asad (1993: 56–62) carries out a simple but interesting survey about the entry of 'ritual' throughout the different editions of the *Encyclopaedia Britannica*, first published in 1771. All editions up to the seventh, published in 1852, described ritual as the instruction of performing religious ceremonies; the entry then became obsolete and was removed from subsequent editions. The entry for 'ritual' was reintroduced and expanded in the eleventh edition, published in 1910. Interestingly, it is only in this edition that 'ritual' is defined as a 'symbolic performance'. In this edition, 'ritual' is described not solely as a religious practice, but as a cultural phenomenon that has psychological and socio-logical functions. Asad explains that 'ritual' not only reappeared but was considered as 'something quite new', different from previous editions. It is not strictly confined to religious routines, but is extended to observances that do not have a religious character. While psychological studies address the divine or emotional experience of individuals during rituals, sociologists and anthropologists predominantly focus on the collective experience of rituals.

The classic approach of the nineteenth century considered the ritual as a necessary but secondary expression in religion and belief systems. This was the approach of many scholars such as Max Müller, Edward Tylor and Herbert Spencer,[1] who paid attention to emotional sacred experience as the foundation of developments of religious creeds. In this approach, ritual is a passive expression of belief systems; it is often seen as a fixed set of formalized routines to be observed in celebrating religious ceremonies. Catherine Bell (1992: 3, 13–15, 1997: 27–28) has reviewed the paradigm shift in the history of ritual studies. She argues that the first shift from the classic understanding of ritual is rooted in the works of Fustel de Coulanges[2] and Robertson Smith,[3] who considered the ritual as more basic than belief and integral to the social dimensions of religion.

Numa Denis Fustel de Coulanges was a French historian who explored the social constitution of Greek and Roman cities in his classic book *The Ancient City: A Study on the Religion, Laws, and Institutions of Greece and Rome* (trans. 1963; orig. 1864). He explained:

> we must not lose sight of the fact that, among the ancients, what formed the bond of every society was a worship. Just as a domestic altar held the members of a family grouped around it, so the city was the collective group of those who had the same pro-tecting deities, and who performed the religious ceremony at the same altar. (Fustel de Coulanges, 2001: 121)

Although he reformulated the idea of rituals as a social practice, he also notes that the notion of religion differed from what it means to us today: it implied 'a body of dogmas, a doctrine concerning God, a symbol of faith concerning what is in and around us' (Fustel de Coulanges, 2001: 139). He explained that almost everything in ancient times was connected to religion, from the founding of a city, the consecration of a temple, to the arrangement of a public assembly and the deploying of an army to a battle (Fustel de Coulanges, 2001: 114, 115, 136).

Fustel de Coulanges and Robertson Smith made important contributions in placing ritual studies within social science disciplines. They showed the primacy of ritual and considered it as more basic than creeds in elucidating the social dimension of religion. However, Durkheim comprehensively formulated the construction of social solidarity as the elementary function of religious practice, and described 'religion as an eminently social thing'. He stated that 'religious phenomena fall into two basic categories: beliefs and rites' (Durkheim, 1995: 33), thereby he extensively explored rituals in *The Elementary Forms of Religious Life.*[4] Durkheim established that beliefs and rituals play a fundamental role in creating social solidarity and constituting human society. Based on the foundation established by Fustel de Coulanges, Robertson and Durkheim in particular, Henri Hubert and Marcel Mauss inverted the earlier approach that the ritual is a necessary but secondary expression in religion. In *Sacrifice: Its Nature and Function,*[5] they showed how collective performances and social activities drive religious belief systems (Hubert and Mauss, 1981). In the opening of this book, they state that *Sacrifice* is aimed at scientifically defining the nature and social function of the rite of sacrifice. Although they admitted being in debt to the ideas of Tylor, Robertson Smith and Frazer, they rejected the approach of the English anthropological school which focused on the genealogical evolution of rituals and the theological exaggeration of Smith's doctrine (Hubert and Mauss, 1981: 7–8). They developed their idea by rejecting the 'chronological comparative' and 'historical evolution' (Smith's focus) and instead focusing on how sacrifice functions.[6] This led them to formulate two fundamental processes that range across all type of sacrifices: sacralization and de-sacralization, which are driven by social matters and forces. Therefore, although they indicated that their book has a functionalist approach, their work introduced a functional-structural analysis of the sacrificial system and departed from Durkheimian functionalism.

Durkheim influenced a major shift in ritual studies by highlighting the social function of rituals. However, the Durkheimian notion of ritual is solely associated with religious rituals and the framework of religion and the sacred. This was partly due to his primary goal of scientifically articulating the social function of religion, wherein he argues that it consists of intellectual conceptions of beliefs and rituals (Durkheim, 1995: 34, 99). As Bell (1997: 38–39) has shown, anthropologists such as Arnold van Gennep and Max Gluckman pushed the idea of ritual beyond its Durkheimian definition and recognized the ritual as a social practice.

In his classic book *The Rites of Passage*,[7] Arnold van Gennep articulated that rituals not only create and maintain social solidarity, but also drive and regulate the pattern of human social life. He begins with the idea that 'the life of the individual in any society is a series of passages from one age to another, from one occupation to another, and from one place to another'. He argued that the essential purpose of ritual is 'to enable the individual to pass from one defined position to another' (van Gennep, 1960: 3). Then, through an exploration of large numbers of customs and rites, he demonstrated how rituals enable people to pass from one life stage or status to another, from birth, childhood and adulthood to marriage and death. His work was influenced by Durkheimian functionalism, but more significantly he focused on the internal pattern of rituals, on the structure of rituals. He formulated the process of each passage as comprising three stages: 'preliminal', 'liminal'[8] and 'postliminal' stages that he also called 'separation', 'transition' and 'incorporation'. Although van Gennep concerned himself with symbols in rituals, he explored the underlying function and structure of rituals as well. As Morris notes, what van Gennep indicated is 'the underlying pattern common to all transition rituals' (Morris, 1987: 247). He demonstrated the significance of liminal or transitional status for passage from one position to another. This is a status when everyday role and norms are altered or ignored, when totally different roles are imposed upon those individuals who are in a transitional status. His work also argues that due to the socio-cultural significance of liminal stages, those rituals that formalize liminal states are usually more developed than rituals that ratify the other two stages. For example, the pilgrimage to Mecca involves a series of rituals. Pilgrims are separated from everyday status by the rite of wearing *Ihram*. They undertake the main part of the pilgrimage during a liminal state when everyday norms are altered. For example, clipping nails and trimming hairs is not allowed, pilgrims' marriages are temporary suspended, and the gender segregation even during praying is disregarded. The Haj ritual ends in the rite of sacrifice, and pilgrims are incorporated back into normal status through a set of rites such as trimming and shaving hair. While van Gennep identified and formulated the liminal state, it was Victor Turner who extensively investigated and discussed the significance of liminal state.

The British anthropologist Max Gluckman (1911–1975) brought two key insights to ritual studies by modifying the Durkheimian idea of ritual. He also argued that van Gennep's rites of passage was more applicable in the tribal social context than in modern urban society. Gluckman argued that

Durkheimian functionalism formulates ritual as a mechanism to produce social cohesion and solidarity, but neglects the sheer contribution of rituals to regulating social conflicts and tensions that play critical roles in constituting social structure. He addressed this subject in two ways: first, he argued that rituals affirm a set of complex social relationships that are not limited to social solidarity. He explained that a member of society belongs to not one but several social groups. The individual is associated with different fellows; they are allies in one set of relationships but can be enemies in another (Gluckman, 1962: 40). Therefore, 'the members of the congregation assembled in unity there, were enemies of one another in many other situations' (1962: 41). Secondly, he argued that Durkheim ignored the social conflict and tension built into the structure of any society. Gluckman states: 'Every social system is a field of tension, full of ambivalence, of co-operation and contrasting struggle' (1963: 127). He showed that rituals are mechanisms to channelize tension and mediate protest and rebellion. He particularly discussed 'rituals of rebellion', a practice to temporarily overturn the normal rules of authorities, a formal symbolic expression of tension and conflict embedded in the social structure of power, in a way that permits the restoration of a functioning social equilibrium.

Gluckman sincerely admired the works of van Gennep and Radcliffe-Brown; however, he argued that the rituals that van Gennep investigated are incompatible with the structure of modern urban society. Gluckman (1962) argues that tribal societies have a greater elaboration of ceremoniousness in all their relationships than modern society. He suggested that tribal society is highly ritualized as individuals simultaneously play several social roles that are not isolated from each other, therefore 'the relationships between the members of these groups serve a multiplicity of purposes' (1962: 26). This social status creates a complex moral landscape in which the multiple social roles of an individual (such as being a son, brother, father, husband and chief) entwine, and an action in one role will affect the other roles. Therefore, Gluckman argued that 'it is this compound of moral evaluation, and the spreading effect of breach of role, which accounts for the way in which various roles are ritualized, and why rituals are attached to so many changes of activities, in tribal society' (Gluckman, 1962: 29). In modern social society however, Gluckman argued that it is not only social roles of individuals but also social conflict are fragmented and segregated. Modern society has conflicts similar in nature to those of tribal society, but they are dispersed through different ranges of social relationships that are not entwined. This status fragments social relations and isolates ranges of social conflicts from one another. Therefore, he argued that 'ritual, and even ceremonial, tend to drop into desuetude in the modern urban situation where the material basis of life, and the fragmentation of roles and activities, of themselves segregate social roles' (Gluckman, 1962: 38). Therefore he argued that rituals and even ceremonies have lost ground in modern urban society.

I am in agreement with Gluckman that the role of rituals in regulating individuals' social relations declines in urban society. However, I challenge his point that rituals are generally losing their significance in modern urban society. While the social relations of individuals are important components in the constitution of tribal society, the social relations between communities play critical roles in the constitution of urban societies. It is often argued that modern cities are becoming secular landscapes. However, in recent years the role of religious rituals is increasingly manifesting itself as an important social practice to shape and transform urban society (e.g. see Van der Veer, 2015).[9] In my chapter about Mumbai in *Handbook of Religion and the Asian Cities*, I have argued that urbanization is not simply about the migration of people to a city. It is intrinsically about encountering the diverse ethnic, religious and political groups that cohabit in a place and negotiate their social relations. In this study, I investigated how Muharram rituals played an important role in negotiating and constituting relationships between communities that poured into Mumbai in a very short time. In this context, Muharram rituals appeared as part of an urbanization process that shaped Mumbai as a cos-mopolitan city during the last two centuries (Masoudi Nejad, 2015a). In the following chapters of this book, I shall discuss in extensive detail that rituals have by no means lost ground in urban context; they play a critical role in the practice of social relations among urban communities. However, my dis-cussions are obviously not about the everyday social relations and practices, but focus on the liminal time of Muharram commemoration. Although the liminal period of ritual is temporal and short, I will demonstrate that it has a perpetual impact on shaping and changing social relations by which urban society is constituted. I have discussed and developed this idea partly under the influence of Victor Turner.

'Van Gennep's work on the structure of ritual and Gluckman's on the ritualization of social conflict were developed into a powerful analytical model by Victor Turner (1920–1983)' (Bell, 1997: 39). A former student of Gluckman, Turner was influenced by van Gennep and initially focused on the notion of liminal stages in *The Drums of Affliction* (Turner, 1968). He then extensively investigated the significance of the liminal state in *The Process of Ritual: Structuralism and Anti-structuralism* (Turner, 1969).[10] In these works, although he combined social functionalism with symbolic structuralism, he pushed his inquiry beyond functional and structural questions. Instead of focusing exclusively on the structure of rituals, as van Gennep did, Turner described the interrelationship between rituals and the cycle of crises in the social structure of communities. He has shown that rituals not only create unity, but also controlled tension and conflict to restore social equilibrium or create a new social structure. He formulated this process based on the cycle of departure from a social structure to anti-structure and back to (new) structure.

The liminal time of rituals is a departure not only from everyday norms and roles but also from normal social structure, a status that Turner calls *communitas*. He noted that 'for me, *communitas* emerges where social structure is not' (1969: 126). *Communitas* is a Latin term that Turner preferred over *community* in order to distinguish this modality of social relationship from everyday social solidarity (Turner, 1969: 96). *Communitas* implies the feeling of solidarity during the liminal period of rituals, when participants in rituals step outside their prescribed social position and gain a social status they do not have normally. The significance of the transitional/liminal moment is in suspending or inverting social hierarchy and organization. Turner explained that *communitas* is not the status of chaos or disorder, it is an alternative and temporal form of social solidarity. In Turner's outline, liminality and *communitas* are both components of anti-structure (1974: 273–74). In articulating 'anti-structure', Turner writes:

> I have used the term 'anti-structure', ... to describe both liminality and what I have called '*communitas*'. I meant by it not a structural reversal ... but the liberation of human capacities of cognition, affect, volition, creativity, etc., from the normative constraints incumbent upon occupying a sequence of social statuses, enacting a mul-tiplicity of social roles, and being acutely conscious of membership in some corporate group such as a family, lineage, clan, tribe, nation, etc., or of affiliation with some pervasive social category such as a class, caste, sex or age-division. (Turner, 1982: 44)

Turner emphasized that social structure is only one of the systems that constitute society; *communitas* is another. Society is sustained by both social structure and *communitas*; he argued that in the absence of *communitas*, social structure would be over-bureaucratized and rigidified (1969: 129). Therefore, he considered anti-structural status as a temporal period but a necessary part of sustaining social organization. The significance of the anti-structural situation lies in the potential it offers for restructuring and renewing social structure and power relations.

Turner formulated two kinds of liminal states. The first type of liminality characterizes rituals of 'status elevation', through which the ritual subject or novice is irreversibly conveyed from one state or position to another. Rituals of status elevation, such as marriage or the Haj pilgrimage to Mecca, permanently change the social position of individuals. The rituals of status elevation not only facilitate the changing of individuals' social position in society, but also mediate the possibility of restructuring social constitution. The second type of liminal state is produced by cyclical or calendrical ritu-als; these are rituals of status reversal. This means that the previous social structure is restored after cyclical rituals (Turner, 1969: 167). An example of this kind of liminal state is the liminality during the annual commemoration of Muharram. Urban communities practise their social solidarity through Muharram rituals, when ritual participants gain an alternative social status and authority. For example, uninfluential individuals can claim an important position in *communitas* during Muharram. However, this temporal social privilege ends after the commemoration, when the community's social structure is restored, and individuals return to their everyday social position (see chapter six).

Despite extensive theoretical development in formulating social aspects of rituals, the notion of ritual exclusively addresses religious performance, including Turner's ritual definition (see Turner, 1967: 19; 1968: 15). However, Platvoet (2004) explains that by the end of the colonial era, the exclusive definition of ritual changed as a result of dramatic shifts in anthropological studies. He argues that in the post-colonial era many anthropologists were forced out of former colonies and had no choice but to study their own secularized societies. This led to interactions between anthropologists and scholars in other disciplines such as sociologists, political scientists and ethnologists. For example, Erving Goffman (1956, 1961, 1966, 1967) extensively studied everyday social encounters in public spaces in secularizing societies. He focused on the ritualistic or normative order that prevails in personal behaviours in everyday social interactions in his seminal book *Interaction Ritual: Essays on Face-to-Face Behaviour*. Goffman's work implies a shift in what can be considered a ritual. Platvoet suggested that the publication of *Secular Ritual* (Moore and Myerhoff, 1977) signifies that ritual no longer exclusively refers to religious acts. This conceptual development suddenly expanded the circle of ritual. Bell explained that on the one hand, ritual is not a clear and closed category of action. On the other hand, the ambiguity of the ritual category is worsened by the attempt to consider many forms of social behaviour as ritual (Bell, 1992: 74). Today, a wide range of human activities are considered 'rites' or 'rituals',[11] including praying, funerals, window-shopping, preparation for surgery and even online activities such as posting a photo to Instagram.

Nowadays, it is often difficult to characterize a practice as either an everyday routine or a ritual performance. Therefore, ritual is broadly defined as a symbolic repeatable action to distinguish it from everyday instrumental behaviours (e.g. Asad, 1993: 55). Interestingly, Calhoun defines 'ritual' as 'repeatable patterns of behaviour that carry complex meanings, especially when shared within a group and related to basic themes of group culture'. However, immediately after this definition he notes that 'the study of ritual is at the heart of much anthropological research and, like so many key terms, resists strict definition' (Calhoun, 2002: 417). Nonetheless, rituals are often conceived of and defined as a timeless set of fixed and formalized acts or performances that are repeated. For example, the *Cambridge Dictionary* still defines ritual as 'a set of fixed actions and sometimes words performed regularly, especially as part of a ceremony'. However, and rightly, Bell explains that 'formality, fixity, and repetition are not intrinsic qualities of rituals' (Bell, 1992: 92).

Kreinath has explained that 'the topic "dynamics of changing rituals" may seem paradoxical at first glance since rituals derive much of their authority and power from presenting themselves as unchanging and timeless. Nevertheless, it has become clear that rituals as events in time change constantly in the process of historical time' (2004: 267). Kreinath's point reflects the core idea of ritual studies, published in *The Dynamics of Changing Rituals*. These studies have investigated the dynamics of rituals in different social and historical contexts. For example, Odenthal has examined the dynamic of liturgy in Catholic Church history. He has pointed out that 'liturgical reforms always respond to a paradigm shift; to new challenges and changes in society and the church' (Odenthal, 2004: 218). An overall review of the studies in *The Dynamics of Changing Rituals* shows that ritual changes may be concerned with different aspects, such as function, form, meaning and acted performance. These studies have demonstrated that although one aspect of a rite might change, other aspects may remain unchanged. For instance, while the performance and form of a ritual can be preserved, its social connotations can be changed. Moreover, Kreinath et al. (2004) particularly highlight the significance of distinguishing changes 'in' and 'by' ritual. 'On the one hand, rituals can change in their performance in reaction to changes in the respective social and cultural contexts. On the other hand, new rituals can arise as a consequence of rapid social changes' (Kreinath et al., 2004: 3). For instance, Stausberg (2004) shows that due to the socio-economic changes among the Parsi-Zoroastrian community, their traditional rituals were restructured and new rituals were established in response to the needs of this orthodox and elite community in India. More importantly, rituals are not a passive reflection of religious or socio-political changes, they can be an active part of changing processes. The social tensions and conflicts during the liminal time of rituals can be the source of social and political changes. For example, in 'Ritual of War', Platvoet (2004) argues that hidden and institutionalized violence in rituals has an impact in societies, not only in plural societies with histories of communal violence like India, but also in homogenized societies.

## Towards the Idea of Ritual Spatiality

Arnold van Gennep not only formulated how rituals facilitate social passage, but he also discussed 'territorial passage', wherein mankind has formulized passage through and access to exclusive territories and spaces via rituals. He argued that 'the spatial separation of distinct groups is an aspect of social organization' (van Gennep, 1960: 192). Therefore, individuals do not have the unconditional right to access exclusive spaces. He explained that not only do rituals mediate the passage from profane to sacred spaces and across political borders, but also that access to certain parts of home or the work place is regulated by rites.

Prior to van Gennep, Durkheim and Mauss in *Primitive Classification* (1963)[12] extensively discussed the Zuni spatial system by which their society is structured and their settlement is organized. The Zuni tribe assigns all things and facts in the universe to their spatial system that is defined by seven regions: north, south, west, east, zenith, nadir and the centre.[13] In this book, Durkheim and Mauss addressed the spatial organization of primitive societies and the way in which they practise their social relations in this spatial arrangement. The Zuni spatial system, as described by Durkheim and Mauss, reflects Leibnizian relational space, in which the space does not exist as an object. Instead, the relational system constitutes parts as a whole.[14] Durkheim and Mauss drew attention to the spatial understanding of the structure of societies for the first time (e.g. see Lévi-Strauss, 1963: 290). However, as Bell (1992) has noted, it was van Gennep who directed the attentions of anthropologists to the idea of space, place and territory in ritual studies, influencing anthropologists such as Eliade, Victor Turner, Rappaport and Jonathan Z. Smith.

Mircea Eliade (1907–1986) was a Romanian historian of religion and a professor at the University of Chicago. He is well known for his theories of the sacred–profane dichotomy; he argued 'that *sacred* and *profane* are two modes of being in the world, two existential situations assumed by man in the course of his history' (1959: 14; italics in original). Eliade defined profane space as homogenous, neutral and unstructured, thus chaotic and vague. In contrast, sacred space is structured and oriented by 'the centre of the world'. Sacred space has existential value for the religious man, since without it nothing can begin and be done in the chaos of homogeneity of profane space. It is only in the sacred world that the religious man has a real existence (e.g. see Eliade, 1959: 20–23, 64). In this framework, the ritual has cosmological significance since it constructs sacred space as a reproduction of cosmos. Thus the ritual effectively reproduces the work of the gods (Eliade, 1959: 22, 29). As mentioned, there is other scholarship that investigates the role of ritual in defining and controlling the natural environment. For example, Turner investigated the idea of territory in his famous case study, the Ndembu, by showing how hunters define and control their territory by rituals (Turner, 1975: 69). Rappaport has explained that rituals not only define the relationship between individuals in society, but also formulize the relations of human society and ecology. He showed how rituals define and control landscape and regulate the distribution of natural resources (Rappaport, 1968, 1979).

J.Z. Smith (1987) has significantly contributed to the investigation of the relationships between religious myth, ritual and place. Building on classic works, such as Durkheim's and Eliade's, Smith articulated the role of ritual in making sacred places by imbuing them with an ultimate quality that cannot be found in profane places. He developed his idea through a careful and critical re-reading of classic studies on Australian tribes, particularly Eliade's, as well as biblical and classic texts, to examine two sacred sites in Jerusalem. In this investigation, he predominantly focused on the sacralization of place. He extensively applied Eliade's notion of sacred–profane and pure–impure and also used the directional system to articulate sacred places. However, he remained truly critical of Eliade's description of Australian aboriginal myths and rituals. Smith overemphasized the significance of ritual in a way that mirrors Eliade's idea that ritual has cosmogonic value in configuring an orientation system and constructing sacred space (e.g. see Eliade, 1959: 22, 29). However, he rejected Eliade's proposal of a universal pattern of cosmological systems as based on creating 'centres' across diverse civilizations. What is particularly interesting about Smith's work is that he discredited location and architecture (the built environment) as the primary source of divine and sacred qualities. Smith argued that the sacredness of holy places is not an inherent terrain, but a mythical and cosmological quality produced by rituals. He argued that the sacred places across Australia, India and the Near East are either accidental or simply happened to be chosen by kings or gods for building temples, reflecting positions of power. For example, he argued that

> In the Near East, whether temple building be by gods or by kings, one gets a much greater sense of the arbitrariness of place. A temple is built where it happens to have been built. A temple is built at the central place, the place where a king or god *happens* to have decided to take up residence. Perhaps this is because temple here is always a royal function, and the power of kingship is such that it constitutes a place as central sheerly by being *there*. (Smith, 1987: 22; italics in original)

On sacred places in Jerusalem, he also wrote: 'There is nothing inherent in the location of the Temple in Jerusalem. Its location was simply where it happened to be built. ... There is no biblical aetiology for the location of Jerusalem's temple .... It could, in principle, have been built anywhere else and still have been the same' (Smith, 1987: 83–84). It is clear that Smith's claim about the accidental characteristics of sacred places in Jerusalem cannot be considered a universal principle. There are endless numbers of sacred places that are built at unique locations defined by physical geography. However, the importance of Smith's argument is in how it shifts the attention from physical geography to a kind of phenomenological geography that prioritizes a human experience predominantly shaped by rituals. It is only in this line of investigation that he also paid attention to the layout and hierarchy in the architecture of temples. In examining cognitive perceptions of sacred places, Smith formulated how rituals and the architecture of temples function hand in hand to construct, rectify and replicate the system of sacred–profane, pure–impure and the hierarchy of power and status.

Although he explained the orchestration of rituals and temples, he envisaged the built environment (architecture) as secondary to the ritual; the built environment is a stage on which rituals are performed. Interestingly, Smith explained that rituals are a mechanism not only to produce holy places, but also 'to replace' and replicate sacred places. He argued that 'the Temple was a synchronic structure. The place could be replicated in a system of differences transferred to another realm or locale' (1987: 86). However, he explained that the location of some sacred sites is not arbitrary, as they correspond to the geography of myth. For example, the Church of the Holy Sepulchre could not have been built anywhere else, as its site had to correspond to the gospel narrative. This statement does not mean that Smith wanted to give all the credit to the location or physical geography; the argument articulates the significance of myth (e.g. see Smith, 1987: 84–86). However, he refused to prioritize myth over ritual. He saw myth and the built environment as part of the ritual orchestra. For example, he argues that 'ritual is, first and foremost, a mode of paying attention. ... It is this characteristic, as well, that explains the role of place as a fundamental component of rituals: place directs attention' (1982: 103). He also argued that the attention generated by rituals transforms the ordinary into the extraordinary and sacred.

I would argue that Smith's main agenda seems to be the prioritization of ritual in the process of sacred place-making, an idea formulated with great care. However, as his investigation was based on religious, ancient or classic texts, his entire investigation focuses on the role of ritual in producing sacredness. Therefore, he limited rituals to religious discourse and failed to see the social dimension of rituals. Many rituals are based on a religious myth, therefore we recognize them as religious rituals. However, as I shall discuss throughout chapters three, four and five, rituals are often heavily charged with social agendas that have nothing to do with the ritual myth. Social agendas commonly push religious agendas and myth into the background of the ritual. Moreover, Smith's perspective cannot be used to articulate many rituals that are not aimed at addressing the sacred–profane delineation, such as London's Notting Hill carnival. The second and more crucial problem is that Smith mainly discussed the process of place-making by investigating ritual 'in' religious places. His argument lacks a conceptual formulation on the interaction between ritual, myth and place.

The aforementioned studies maintain a stereotypical focus on the inter-relationship between ritual and place. They predominantly aim to under-stand the role of ritual in regulating and formulating access to places, the ritualization of the built/natural environment, and defining sacred space. However, David Parkin took a different approach and articulated the idea of ritual as a 'spatial system'. He discussed this idea in *Sacred Void* (1991) and 'Ritual as Spatial Direction and Bodily Division' (1992), works focused on the role of rituals and beliefs in defining relationships among communities that inhabit three different ecological and cultural territories in Kenya. The three communities follow different religions: indigenous African creeds, Islam and Christianity. While *Sacred Void* is predominantly an ethnographic work, Parkin (1992) offers more theoretical clarification about ritual as a spatial practice through a discussion of the problems of ritual–myth ambi-guity – a classic anthropological enquiry.

Anthropologists from Lévi-Strauss to Lewis have tried to distinguish myth and ritual by focusing on the notion of action. Lévi-Strauss explained that myths are often seen as the ideological projections of a rite; however, some anthropologists have reversed the direction of this relationship and regard ritual as a kind of dramatized illustration of the myth. He concluded that regardless of the nature of the myth–ritual relationship, 'the myth exists on the conceptual level and the ritual on the level of action' (Lévi-Strauss, 1963: 232). Similarly, Lewis sees rituals as actions, distinguishing them from beliefs, symbols and myths which are mental concepts (Lewis, 1980: 10–11). Lévi-Strauss also explained that the linguistics and speech is inseparably part of a social action. Therefore, he stated that ritual is neither fully a statement nor an action; this statement is echoed by Tambiah (1979), Lewis (1980) and Bloch (1986). Parkin (1992) agrees with the statement that speech is part of social action. Yet he argues that due to the conceptual indistinctness of 'action', considering rituals as actions does not solve the problem of myth–ritual ambiguity. Therefore, instead of 'action', Parkin steers toward 'ritual spatiality'. He explains that rituals are held in order to privilege physical action in contrast to myth, which privileges the words (Parkin, 1992: 12). He notes that:

> Words may be important elements of ritual performance, sometimes critically so. But while words may stand alone in myth unaccompanied by gesture, they are dependent on the directional movements that make up ritual. It is in this sense that ritual, full

of spatial movement and gesture performance, could make the evolutionary transition to drama and theatre, based at first primarily on mime rather than on dialogue. (Parkin, 1992: 17)

Thus, as a 'minimal definition' Parkin states that 'ritual is formulaic spatiality carried out by groups of people who are conscious of its imperative or compulsory nature and who may or may not further inform this spatiality with spoken words' (1992: 18). In other words, while ritual can manifest without words, it cannot be identified without its spatiality. Therefore, he argued that 'formalized activities without words are ritual while words without action are myth' (Parkin, 1992: 18). With this as a foundation, ritual is articulated as the spatial manifestation of myth. If we reverse the myth–ritual relations, as Lévi-Strauss (1963) suggested, then myth can be defined as a transcription of a spatial performance.

Parkin approached ritual by paying attention to bodily movements and directional postures, and explained that ritual is manifested as a space through collective body performances and repertoire. In this framework, he suggested that 'movement' should be conceived on physical and metaphorical levels. For example, he notes that 'the rites of passage' are associated with directional movements; however, some rituals, such as funerals, regulate metaphoric journeys even when the body remains in one position (Parkin, 1992: 22). Although he did not conceptually discuss the relationship between body movements and ritual spatiality as such, it seems 'ritual space' does not correspond to the Newtonian idea of 'absolute space' that is a pre-existence entity. Rather, it is a 'relative space' that emerges based upon body performances. As I shall discuss in chapter five, such space and body movements coexist but they are not collapsible into one entity.

Parkin's main theoretical concern was to conceptualize the sacred and its relation to the notion of space. What differentiates his approach from that of his scholarly ancestors is the shift in attention from 'the place' of rituals to the notion of 'space' and 'the spatial aspect' of funerals and other rituals practised by different communities in three different cultural and ecological territories in Kenya. This approach shifted his focus from the content and the location of rituals to the common spatial logic of rituals, leading him to consider the ritual to be an intrinsically spatial performance. Parkin did not conceptually discuss the notion of space in detail and simply stated 'I see space as understood in three ways: as a fixed centre amenable to being regarded as absolutely sacred; as a relational pattern of ecological zones and human movements; and as an indeterminately regarded amorphism, without centre, boundary or even content' (Parkin, 1991: 7). It is clear that these three kinds of space address different notions of space, and Parkin's proposition shows that he did not intend to bridge and integrate these three spaces. For Parkin, there are fixed sacred spaces that function as the tradi-tional capital or centre of an indigenous society. These sacred spaces have inviolable boundaries, described by Parkin as follows: 'rather like Newton's void having existence without objects in it, it does not need persons in it for it to remain sacred and central, and indeed it is often empty or almost empty for long periods' (Parkin, 1991: 8). On the other hand, the second kind of space that Parkin has mentioned is clearly based upon Leibnizian relations of space.

Although Parkin did not offer a single and concrete idea about space, his spatial approach allowed him to investigate sacred centres, rituals, human movements, and cultural and ecological territories in one conceptual frame-work. I would argue that within the field of ritual studies, for whatever reason, the significance of Parkin's idea of ritual spatiality remains underestimated, and it has not been advanced further, by him or other scholars. Therefore, his scholarship is predominantly known by those who are focused on the anthropology of East Africa. Considering my own regional focus, it was ser-endipitous that I came across one of his book chapters and then investigated his work. Also serendipitous was the fact that we were both fellows at the Max Planck Institute (MPI-MMG) in Göttingen at the same time and I was able to discuss with him the influence of his work on the development of my arguments. Parkin's theories became an important foundation from which I spatially investigate Muharram rituals, and they have helped me to develop my own conceptual framework that I will formulate in following chapters.

## Conclusion: The Proposition of this Study

This literature review outlines the theoretical framework for my study. Muharram commemoration is an annual religious event, but I do not approach it from conventional religious studies that predominantly focus on the question of the sacred–profane, nor do I ignore and underestimate the religious significance of Muharram rituals. In the following chapters, I investigate Muharram rituals as an urban religious practice. The annual commemoration of the Ashura tragedy during Muharram is foundational for Shi'i Muslim creeds, and this annual event is heavily charged with social agendas that define the relationships between urban communities. Therefore, I refuse to characterize Muharram rituals based on the arbitrary religious–secular division. I would argue that Muharram commemoration is one example that blurs the religious--secular dichotomy.

Muharram rituals, like other rituals, simultaneously construct solidarity among members of a community and create a symbolic boundary between them and 'other' communities. Therefore, while rituals construct and maintain social solidarity, they also exaggerate social tension between urban communities. In fact, in contrast to the Durkheimian notion of ritual that focuses on the role of rituals in creating social bonds, social historians of Iran, the Middle East and India predominantly blame religious rituals for inflaming social tensions and conflicts. These are two extreme positions that emphasize either social solidarity or social conflict. In chapters three and four I extensively investigate how Muharram rituals are collective performances for practicing complex social relationships that cannot be simplified into dichromatic statuses and conditions such as solidarity–division, or conflict–conciliation.[15]

Turner and Gluckman, like many other scholars, mainly focused on how rituals regulate social relationships between individuals in communities. My study focuses on the relationships between communities in urban society. Although in chapter six I do, to some degree, discuss how Muharram rituals define an individual's social position, the discussions mainly articulate the role of Muharram processions in shaping and reshaping social relations between communities that constitute urban society. These discussions will elaborate on my disagreement with Gluckman, who argues that rituals are losing their social function in modern urban society.

My final and most important proposition is to investigate the spatial dimensions of Muharram rituals. This investigation unfolds on two different levels and formulates the conceptual components of my spatial idea of ritual. The following chapter formulates 'the spatial manifestation of rituals': how rituals spatially manifest regardless of their place and performed actions during rituals. This approach also offers an alternative reading of the historical dynamics of Muharram rituals. The second component is 'the spatial organization' of Muharram processions, primarily investigated in chapters three and four, and conceptually formulated in chapter five.

## NOTES

1. Friedrich Max Müller (1823–1900) was a German Orientalist; Sir Edward Burnett Tylor (1832–1917) was an English anthropologist; and Herbert Spencer (1820–1903) was an English philosopher and sociological theorist.
2. Numa Denis Fustel de Coulanges (1830–1889) was a French historian; his ideas on this subject are mainly introduced in *The Ancient City* (trans. 1963; orig. 1864). He declared that the 'city had been founded upon a religion, and constituted like a church' (Maddox, 2008).
3. William Robertson Smith (1846–1894) was a Scottish theologian and Semitic scholar (Livingstone, 2006).
4. *Les Formes élémentaires de la vie religieuse: le système totémique en Australie* was originally published in 1912.
5. *Sacrifice: Its Nature and Function* was originally published in 1898.

6. One of the main criticisms that Durkheimian functionalism received was that it failed to take into account historical changes.
7. *Les rites de passage* was originally published in 1908 in French. It was published in English for the first time in 1960.
8. 'Liminal: Latin *limen*, meaning threshold' (Bowie, 2000: 163).
9. *Handbook of Religion and the Asian Cities: Aspiration and Urbanization in the Twenty-First Century* (Van der Veer, 2015) is a major edited volume dedicated to discussing the significance of religious practices in Asian mega cities.
10. Turner followed up this subject in his many other works, including *Drama, Fields, and Metaphors* (1974), 'Frame, Flow and Reflection: Ritual and Drama as Public Liminality' (1979), and *From Ritual to Theatre* (1982).
11. According to Fritz Graf (1998), ritual is composed of several single acts known as a rite.
12. *De quelques formes primitives de classification* was originally published in 1903.
13. Other ideas associated with this group are those of Charles Keyes (1975). He has explained the link between space and time in defining twelve regional centres based on the calendar idea by traditional Buddhist pilgrimage in Thailand. Keyes's idea partly echoes what Durkheim and Mauss explained in *Primitive Classification*.
14. For more, see chapter five.
15. See also Masoudi Nejad, 2014, 2015b.

CHAPTER 2

# THE SPATIAL GENEALOGY OF MUHARRAM RITUALS

The Muharram rituals observe the martyrdom of Hussein, a grandson of the Prophet Mohammad, and his companions in the tragic battle of Karbala on Ashura day. The commemoration of Muharram constitutes several rituals and rites established throughout history in different cultural regions across the world. From the Shi'i Muslim point of view, this tragedy is not merely a historical battle; this is an event that shapes the history of mankind before and after. The history of Muharram rituals is relatively well explored; however, the study at hand calls for a new reading of this history: a spatial reading. Studies on the history of Muharram rituals, such as the seminal work of Nakash, are predominantly based on either the notion of action theory (focusing on what is performed during the commemoration) or on where the rituals take place. This chapter shifts the focus from what participants do during rituals or where they practise the rituals, to how rituals are spatially manifested. The discussion also focuses on exploring the evolution of ritual manifestations throughout history. This spatial reading is a 'narrative structure' (White, 1975)[1] that explores how Shi'i Muslim rituals developed and evolved.

The discussion here follows that of the previous chapter where I elaborated the ritual as a spatial phenomenon. As discussed, David Parkin (1991, 1992) argues that the problem of ritual–myth ambiguity would not be solved by considering the ritual as an action. For example, Lévi-Strauss, like many others, argued that 'the myth exists on the conceptual level and the ritual on the level of action' (Lévi-Strauss, 1963: 232). Parkin, however, argues that the ritual is distinguished from the myth as the ritual cannot be identified without its spatiality, while the myth cannot be identified without its words. The advantage to Parkin's idea is that it replaces the notion of action with spatiality. Within this framework, I defined the rituals as the spatial manifestation of myth. In this chapter, I articulate how the Muharram rituals are spatially manifested and formulate the evolution of ritual manifestation throughout Shi'i history.

The diverse Shi'i rituals are conventionally categorized according to the actions performed during the rituals, such as chest-beating and flagellation. However, the spatial reading of Muharram rituals focuses on how these performances are spatially manifested and whether rituals are spatially concentrated in a single place or dispersed throughout the city. The discussion shows how the evolution of a concentrated ritual into a dispersed one, or vice versa, is born of the processes by which the new rituals were invented. I shall also elaborate that this process is politically driven and does not have a significant correlation with the development of Shi'i religious buildings.

## The Tragedy of Karbala on Ashura Day

Ashura is literally derived from the Arabic term *a'shara*, meaning ten, and *al-a'sher*, meaning tenth. Ashura itself is the name of the 10th of Muharram, the first month of the Arabic lunar calendar, indicating the significance of Ashura day in the tribal culture of Arabian Peninsula. 'Very early Islamic tradition has claimed for that day high status: it was said that on it many supernatural events took place' (Ayoub, 1978: 149). Ashura day is associated with many myths in the history of the Middle East, the birthplace of the Abrahamic religions. It is claimed that Ashura is the day when God forgave Adam, Noah's Ark reached dry land, God split the Red Sea for the children of Israel, and God accepted David's repentance (e.g. see Ayoub, 1987: 874; 1988: 59; Rizvi, 1986: 287). Nonetheless, Ashura day is particularly observed by Shi'i Muslims as the tragic day when Hussein was martyred in the battle of Karbala in the late seventh century, following a political dispute over the legitimacy of Umayyad authority.

While the theological division between Sunni and Shi'i Muslims developed over time,[2] the division initially originated in a political dispute over the successor of the Prophet Mohammad (d. 632). Some argue that the division even has roots in the old enmity between the Hashemite clan of Mohammad and the Umayyad Caliphate of Mu'awiyah who had refused the prophecy until nearly everyone else in Mecca had converted to Islam (e.g. see Afary, 2003: 11). As Kasravi (1944) has explained, the second half of the first century of Islam (the sixth century) was a time of struggle for political power after the death of the Prophet. The political dispute escalated sharply over the successor of the fourth Caliph, Ali ibn Abi-Taleb, who was a cousin and son-in-law of the Prophet. Ali, like the second and third Caliph, was assassinated; then Mu'awiyah, the governor of Syria who had already revolted against Ali, claimed authority over Muslim society and established the Umayyad Caliphs (662–750). Muslim society was then clearly divided into two main parts: the Shi'i of Ali (meaning the party of Ali) who supported Ali's family, and the Sunni part who accepted Mu'awiyah as the Caliph. The Sunni community believed that the Prophet's successor should be elected as Caliph according to ancient Arabic tribal tradition, so they are known as Sunnis, the traditionalists. In contrast, the Shi'i Muslims argued that the Muslim community should not be led by a Caliph, but by a spiritual leader known as *imam* (leader) who possesses a divine right to authority in both spiritual and temporal matters. Therefore, Shi'i Muslims do not recognize the authority of the first three Caliphs; from the Shi'i point of view Ali is not the fourth Caliph but rather the first *imam*. The Shi'i community claimed that the rightful successors of Ali are the descendants of Ali and Fatima, the Prophet's daughter.

When the first Umayyad Caliph died and was succeeded by his son, the Shi'i–Sunni division grew deeper over the authority of the second Umayyad Caliph, Yazid. Ayoub (1987), a scholar who sincerely holds Shi'i belief, argues that after the death of Mu'awiyah, his son Yazid succeeded him by hereditary appointment rather than by election or popularity. Therefore, he argues that the authority of the second Umayyad caliph was not even based on the tribal tradition, but on the rule of family monarchy. Tabatabaei also argues that Mu'awiyah transformed the Caliphate into a hereditary monarchy and therefore even the Sunni community 'distingush[es] between the "rightly guided caliphs" (khulafa rashidun) who are the first four caliphs ..., and the others who began with Mu'awiyah and who did not possess by any means the religious virtues of the rightly guided caliphs' (Tabatabaei, 1975: 61). When the second Umayyad came to power, a Shi'i community in the city of Kufa, where Ali ruled, urged Hussein to lead them in revolt against the Umayyad rule.[3] Journeying from the city of Medina to Kufa, Hussein arrived and encamped on the plain of Karbala where he faced Yazid's army. Hussein and his few companions were denied access to the water of the Euphrates in the burning desert of Karbala as they continued to fight and rejected the political legitimacy of Yazid. They were slaughtered one by one until Hussein himself was murdered in cold blood on the day of Ashura, 13 October 680.[4] Hussein's body was trampled by horses and his head cut off and sent in the company of his family members to Yazid's court in Damascus (see Howard, 1990: 163). As Crow (1986: 72) has noted, the death of Hussein shocked Muslim society and triggered many revolts and movements across the region.

From the Shi'i point of view, the battle of Karbala is more than a historic battle over a political dispute, and the event has transcended into 'meta-history' (Chelkowski, 1988: 263). The Shi'i slogan – 'Every day is Ashura,

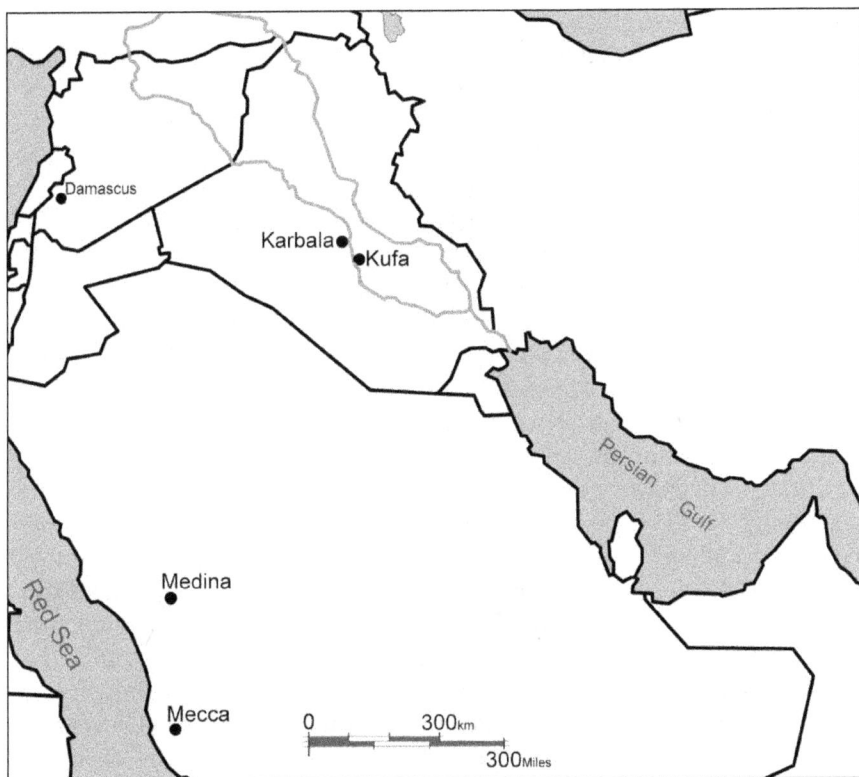

**MAP 2.1** The geographical location of Mecca, Medina, Karbala, Kufa and Damascus. Map by the author.

and everywhere is Karbala' – implies that the battle of Karbala is an eternal battle between justice and injustice, wrong and right, that is dispersed across time and space. The tragic battle of Karbala is indeed 'the Shi'i myth'. Myth is classically known as an invented story; however, as Calhoun (2002) explains, a myth is a story that 'contribute[s] to the elaboration of a cosmological system and to a cohesive social identity'. The tragedy of Ashura is 'the Shi'i myth', since the battle of Karbala is regarded by Shi'i Muslims 'as a cosmic event around which the entire history of the world, prior as well as subsequent to it, revolves' (Ayoub, 1978: 141). Michael Fischer argues that the tragedy 'provides a way of clearly demarcating Shi'ite understanding from the Sunni understanding of Islam and Islamic history' (1980: 21). As Ayoub (1978) has comprehensively elaborated, the tragedy of Karbala is considered by Shi'i Muslims to be the greatest suffering and redemptive act in history. The memory of the tragedy has profoundly influenced Shi'i creed and rituals to such a degree that Canetti stated: 'No faith has ever laid greater emphasis on lament' (Canetti, 1962: 153). Fischer (1980) has gone further and argued that the memory and commemoration of the Karbala tragedy has produced 'the Karbala paradigm' by which Shi'i culture is constituted.

Shi'i Muslims developed numerous rituals throughout history to observe the tragedy of Ashura. The rituals originated mostly in Iraq, were highly enriched in Iran during the Safavid era (sixteenth to eighteenth centuries), and then spread and diffused across the Indian subcontinent (Calmard, 1996). The Shi'i faith has a background in the Deccan of India prior to the establishment of the Safavid dynasty of Iran (see Matthee, 2006). Nonetheless, as Howarth (2005) notes, the Safavids not only initiated the most flourishing Shi'i cultural era in Iran but were also one of the primary forces in spreading the Shi'i faith to India. Later during the colonial era, Indians greatly contributed to spreading the rituals to as far as East Africa and the Caribbean islands of Trinidad (see Korom, 1994, 2003).

There is a delicate string that interconnects the history of Muharram rituals throughout Egypt, Syria, Lebanon, Yemen, Iraq, Iran, India and beyond. However, as Nigel Thrift argues, 'no social process unfolds[s] in the same way across different places, raising the significance of context in explanation to a central position' (Warf, 2004: 298). Like other socio-religious practices, the Shi'i rituals were also diffused and localized, constituting their own social meaning across such a vast geography. Therefore, although some theologians and scholars[5] see the commemoration as being solely a lamentation event, the Muharram rituals cannot be reduced to a single intention.

The commemoration of Ashura is practised across a vast cultural territory, based on numerous rites and rituals, many of which are local performances that are appropriated and reinvented to observe Ashura. What I would like to emphasize here is that there is a difference between 'the theological idea of Muharram observation' and 'the Muharram rituals as a socio-cultural practice'. Muharram is often the most significant socio-religious time for Shi'i communities, as well as non-Shi'i communities who observe the event. Fischer (1980) has argued that the commemoration provides a paradigm by which Shi'i culture is constituted. However, the commemoration has never been solely shaped by the established theological prescription for the commemoration. Rather, the very diverse socio-cultural systems of Shi'i communities are encapsulated in the rituals that they constantly invent, appropriate and perform during Muharram.

## A Shift from the Action to the Spatial Manifestation

Shi'i communities observe the Karbala tragedy through an endless number of rites and rituals that they have invented throughout history. Nakash

(1993), like many other scholars,[6] categorizes Shi'i rituals mainly according to actions that are performed. In his seminal paper, Nakash argues that the Shi'i Muslims developed five major rituals over the last twelve centuries: (1) the mourning service session, (2) the pilgrimage to the tomb of Hussein on the day of Arba'aein (i.e. the fortieth day after Ashura), (3) the public mourning procession, (4) the representation of the battle of Karbala in the form of plays, and (5) self-flagellation (Nakash, 1993: 163). These rituals are generally aimed at narrating or performing the Shi'i grief over the tragedy of Ashura. For example, *majlis* (the service session) is a ritual in which an orator narrates the passion of Hussein in Karbala for the audience. Some other rituals, such as chest-beating and flagellation, are aimed at performing the Shi'i sorrow. Nevertheless, all of the rituals are orchestrated as a grand ritual to commemorate the tragedy during a period of fifty days, from the first of Muharram to the day of Arba'aein. The commemoration is especially intense during the four days from the 7th to 10th of Muharram.

Although the Muharram rituals are often reduced to a very limited number of rituals, as Nakash does, it is rather problematic to reduce Muharram rituals into a few ritual categories especially when categorization is based on actions performed during the commemoration. Based on my own fieldwork in seven Iranian cities and Mumbai (India), I can easily name a number of rituals that defy the categorization of the aforementioned five major groups suggested by Nakash and others. *Nakhl-bardari* (lifting a symbolic coffin) is mainly practised in central Iranian cities such as Yazd; the ritual of *bill-zani* (playing or hitting the shovel, intimating the soundscape of battlefield) performed in the city of Birjand; and *choo-bozi* (playing wood, a kind of dancing that imitates the battle of Karbala) is performed in the city of Dezful – these are but a few that do not fit into the five-category scheme.[7]

It would be problematic to make of a list of performances/rituals that I have either heard of or personally encountered. For one, every community has its own rites and rituals, therefore having a comprehensive list of countless rituals is impractical and probably impossible. Secondly, such a list is not useful since the rituals practised by each community are not fixed; the rituals are constantly reinvented, changed, suppressed or die out over time.[8] For example, the rite of playing wood (*choo-bozi*) was a kind of dance performance practised in the Iranian city of Dezful until the early 1980s. In this ritual, participants gather in a circle, each holding two short logs of wood about 10–15 cm long. They beat the logs rhythmically while walking and bouncing to the beat. The ritual died out due to the cultural and political changes after the revolution of 1979, when the joyfulness of this ritual was seen as inappropriate for observing the tragedy of Karbala. Therefore, considering that the ritual landscape is so dynamic, having a fixed list of performances is pointless. Moreover, as I will show through more examples, diverse rituals around similar symbolic actions may be recognized as similar rituals even though they are not the same. For example, both the Shi'i street play and the Iranian passion play dramatically represent the Karbala tragedy but it would be erroneous to treat them as the same ritual.

There is a need for an analytical/conceptual categorization when a grand ritual such as Muharram is constituted by numerous rites and rituals. To provide this categorization, ritual studies has taken different approaches such as symbolism, functionalism or structuralism.[9] My specific contribution is to use a spatial approach as the conceptual framework for investigating the historical patterns by which rituals have been invented, developed or appropriated for the commemoration of Ashura. In this chapter I focus on the spatial manifestation of rituals and categorize all rituals into two major categories: (1) rituals that are spatially manifested in a concentrated form, such as the mourning service session; and (2) performances that are dispersed throughout cities, such as processions.

## The *Majlis*: An Initial Form of Ashura Commemoration

The mourning service session, generally known as *majlis*, is the earliest form of Ashura commemoration and today it remains one of the principle ways of observing the tragedy of Ashura. The service session is based on an Islamic tradition (also practised today) that calls for the holding of a remembrance gathering after an individual's death (Baktash, 1979: 96). The Arabic term *majlis* means congress, assembly or session; the term is commonly used in Urdu and Farsi with a similar meaning. However, the mourning service session has different names in different linguistic contexts. In Iraq it is called *majlis al-ta'zyeh* or simply *ta'zyeh*,[10] and also *majlis al-niyahah*. The service session is called *majlis-i rowzah-i khani* or simply *rowzah* in Iran, and *majlis* in India. Nevertheless, *majlis* is a general term that can be used to refer to all of these contexts.

After the tragedy of Karbala during the late seventh century and then under Umayyad rule, Shi'i communities were suppressed and under scrutiny. Although there were Shi'i rebellions during a century of Umayyad rule, the Shi'i community lived 'for the most part in hiding and followed their religious life secretly without external manifestations' (Tabatabaei, 1975: 60). Therefore, the commemoration of Ashura was limited to secret sessions held at the house of Prophet families and their closest allies. The initial service sessions were simply aimed at commemorating the martyrdom of Hussein; then they became a way of keeping the memory of the tragedy alive by narrating the battle of Karbala. The combination of political contexts with Arab oral culture, in which oral media was more important than written documents, contributed to circumstances in which the tragedy was mainly narrated in the form of poems and dirges. These oral literary narratives created a foundation upon which the Shi'i myth of Ashura is constituted; later on, these narratives were documented in textual format during the Abbasid dynasty (established in the mid-eighth century) when Arab/Muslim culture experienced a shift from oral to textual media.[11]

A century of Umayyad rule (662–750) was overturned by the Abbasid revolt; early Abbasid Caliphs encouraged the commemoration of Ashura in order to legitimize their revolution.[12] Therefore, the Shi'i service sessions were no longer held in secret. In this new political landscape, the service sessions were held in mosques (Nakash 1993). As Hussain (2005) has explained, while the service session was mainly a commemorative gathering, it was also a literary occasion to recite poems and dirges. The developed form of the service session has even been called *rowzah-khani*, meaning 'reciting *rowzah*', since the orators' sermons were dominated by the recitation of the book of *Rowdat al-Shuhada* (Waeiz Kashifi, 1979; orig. 1501). The title of the book is pronounced *Rowzat al-Shohada* in Iran, which means 'the paradise of the martyrs'. Vaeiz Kashifi (d. 1504), a prominent Iranian orator, scholar, and poet, wrote *Rowdat al-Shuhada* during the Safavid era and it is based on all the major narratives of the Karbala tragedy. The book was, and has remained for centuries, the most significant text that narrates the tragedy of Ashura as the Shi'i myth. The orators predominantly recited the Persian text of *Rowzat al-Shuhada*, even in India, until the mid-nineteenth century, when the text was translated into Urdu as women could not understand the Persian idioms of the original text (Howarth, 2005: 14; Rizvi, 1986: 355). The given narratives by Vaeiz Kashifi would be considered far from factual, but obviously the book is significant in establishing the myth of Ashura and not its history. Although the ritual has developed over time, it principally remains a gathering in which orators narrate the Shi'i narrative of the battle of Karbala.

During fieldwork in Iranian cities and Mumbai, I have observed diverse ways of holding the service sessions in private and public spaces; the ritual can be accommodated at a home, Shi'i community places (e.g. *husseini-yeh, imambara*), a mosque, a local square, a bazaar lane, a street, and even between residential blocks. These places obviously have different forms: they are open, semi-open or enclosed spaces. They also have different shapes, with linear, centralized, clustered or irregular forms. However, no matter where the service session takes place, the ritual is simply a gathering, manifested in a concentrated form that functions as an event for community solidarity.

I participated in the service sessions during Muharram in Mumbai which were held in religious community places (e.g. mosque and *imambara*) or in

FIGURE 2.1 A *majlis* at Khuja Jaame Masjid in Bandra during Muharram. Mumbai, India, December 2009. Photo by the author.

open public spaces such as between residential blocks, as the community does not have a community/religious place (Figures 2.1 and 2.2). Although the physical reality of host places was totally different, the events created a similar experience as both were spatially alike and manifested a concentrated form. In other words, the ritual space supersedes the effects of built environments. I have also experienced this in a large and impressive Dawodi Bohras' service session, in which the community members gathered from all over the world. I participated in the service session held at Saifee Masjid in the south of Mumbai in 2010. The crowd not only spilled out of the mosque and the shrine next to the mosque, *Rowdat at-Tahera*, but also occupied all surrounding streets (Figure 2.3). The sense of ritual space was not defined by the built environment, the mosque or the shrine, but by the crowd. This ritual was an exclusive space for the community, by which they practised and maintained not only the memory of Ashura, but also social bonds among the community.

The Muharram service sessions are the most important of the Bohras' annual events that both distinguish them from other Shi'i communities while also practising their social solidarity (Blank, 2001: 84; see Masoudi Nejad, 2012: 108–11). In fact, the community principally focuses on maintaining their solidarity and has historically avoided tension with other groups. Therefore, they do not organize processions in Mumbai and only

FIGURE 2.2 A *majlis* in an open space between BIT Residential Blocks, off
Mohammad Ali Road, during Muharram. Mumbai, India, December 2009.
Photo by the author.

commemorate Ashura through the service session that is exclusively for
community members. The spatially concentrated rituals that are exclusive
events also create solidarity among the community while simultaneous
erecting a symbolic boundary between them and others.[13]

The mourning service session is considered to be the initial way to commemorate the Karbala tragedy; today it remains one of the principle rituals
of observing the tragedy. Although the service sessions have expanded from
their most private forms (taking place in individual homes) to public Shi'i
community centres and urban public spaces, the mourning service has never
left private residences. In contemporary Iran, the public mourning service
sessions are mainly held during the ten days of the mourning period, from
the first to the 10th of Muharram. However, the private service sessions are
held based on different schedule routines. For example, the service sessions
are held according to two different procedures in the city of Dezful (Iran).[14]
Based on the first and most common procedure, the service session is held
for forty days, starting on Ashura day and ending on the day of Arba'ein.[15]
The second procedure is based on holding the service session once a week
throughout the year, excluding the time of the first routine. In other words,
the public and private service sessions are dispersed throughout the entire
year. This means that a sincerely religious Shi'i person is engaged with the

FIGURE 2.3 A Muharram *majlis* of Dawodi Bohras, who are Isma'ili Shi'a, in the south of Mumbai, December 2010. Bohras congregated for a *majlis* during which their spiritual leader, Sayyedna Mohammed Burhanuddin, delivered his sermon. The photograph shows the mass in Bhendi Bazaar. Photo by the author.

commemoration of Ashura tragedy throughout the entire year. Therefore, while the service session is spatially concentrated, its temporal dimension is dispersed.

## The Public Procession: Dispersing the Ashura Commemoration

The first spatial evolution of Muharram observation was initiated under the Buyids in the tenth century, when they established the Shi'i public procession for the first time in Bagdad. Nozari (2006) explains that Iranians continually attempted to end Arab political domination after the introduction of Islam to Iran (see also Haqiqat, 1968: 162–97; Ravandi, 1979: 505–32). They commonly associated their movements with the Shi'i school to religiously legitimize their revolt against the Caliphs. The Iranians finally succeeded when a movement led by the Buyids defeated the Abbasid ruler and invaded Baghdad, the capital of the Abbasids (Faqihi, 1978: 482; Jafariyan, 2001: 1186). While the Ashura tragedy was mainly observed by the service session, the Buyids initiated a public procession in Baghdad as a new way of commemorating Ashura. Ibn Kathir, in *Albadayeh va Alnahaye* and Ibn-Athir in *Al-kamil fi al-Tarikh*, among others,[16] reports that the first public procession was carried out on the day of Ashura in 963 in Baghdad. Ibn Kathir reports:

> On the tenth of Muharram of this year [A.H. 352], Mu'izz al-Dawlah Ibn Buwayeh, may God disgrace him, ordered that the markets be closed, and that the women should wear coarse woollen hair cloth, and that they should go into the markets with their faces uncovered/unveiled and their hair dishevelled, beating their faces and wailing over Husayn ibn 'Ali ibn Abi Talib. The people of the Sunna could not prevent this spectacle because of the Shi'a's large numbers and their increasing power (zuhur), and because the Sultan was on their side. (Mazzaoui, 1979: 231)[17]

This short order reveals a clear attempt to establish a ritual by set repertoires, including symbolic performances, bodily expressions and dress codes throughout the procession. What makes the Buyid's initiative important is that the procession was fundamentally a new way of practising the Shi'i myth of Ashura. While the service session is a congregation to narrate the Shi'i myth of Ashura tragedy, the procession expresses the Shi'i grief over the tragedy by performing a symbolic funeral. Recalling Parkin's idea (1992), although the procession can be associated with verbal performances like the singing of dirges, it is essentially based on performing rather than narrating the Shi'i myth.[18] The procession was not simply the result of re-accommodating a commemoration previously held in a private space or public place in urban spaces, it was a new way of manifesting and performing

FIGURE 2.4  A public procession on Ashura day, in the old city of Dezful in Iran, 2006. The recent form of the Shi'i procession is a symbolic funeral procession towards a cemetery. Photo by the author.

the Shi'i myth. The sharp differentiation between the service session, even when held in public space, and the procession is that the service session is spatially concentrated whereas the procession is a dispersed performance.

The first Shi'i procession in Baghdad and the dispersed Shi'i presence in the city soon led to Shi'i–Sunni conflicts. As processions are spatially dispersed, they can be a performance/mechanism to cross socio-spatial borders and boundaries in the city. This can lead to an association between processions and social tension or violence.[19] There are numerous historical testimonies, e.g. by Ibn Juzi, Ibn-Athir and al-Mugharizi, about conflicts between the Shi'i quarter of Karkh[20] and the Sunni quarters whenever the Muharram procession was carried out in Buyid Baghdad (see Faqihi, 1978: 267–68; Haqani, 2002: 499–500).[21] In order to conceive the significance of the Muharram procession in Baghdad, it is necessary to note that the population of Bagdad exceeded one million in the Buyid era (see Modelski, 2003).

As Ibn Kathir's testimony[22] indicates, the Sunni community of Baghdad responded to the Shi'i procession with a counter procession/carnival in Baghdad, challenging the Shi'i community of Baghdad. Therefore, violence had been reported throughout the processions and counter-processions for years in Baghdad. The Shi'i procession commemorated the tragedy of

Karbala, and the Sunni processions in Baghdad addressed the battle of Camel (in the year of 656) and discredited Ali, the first Shi'i *imam* and the father of Hussein.[23] On the reaction to Sunni communities, Ibn Khathir reported that around the year 973:

> In this year on Ashura, the despicable innovation was celebrated according to the custom of the Shi'is. A great riot broke out between the Sunnis and the Shi'is, both parties being of little intelligence. A group of Sunnis laced a woman on a camel and called her 'A'ishah and someone took the name Talhah, and someone took the name Zubayr, and they said: 'We are going out to fight the followers of 'Ali'. Many people on both sides were killed. (Ibn Kathir, Al-bidayah va al-nihiyah, XI, p. 253) (Hussain 2005: 84)

These processions and counter-processions dramatized historical events; however, these processions facilitated the communities in dispersing their authority beyond the territory of their localities and negotiated their power in the city. This is partly what makes the procession a particularly urban practice, as urbanization processes are essentially about creating and negotiating social, cultural and political boundaries.

Following the Buyid dynasty's initiative, the Fatimids, a Shi'i dynasty that ruled in Egypt, tried to do what the Buyid dynasty did in Baghdad. However, they were not successful; Hussain (2005)[24] reviews the first ever Shi'i procession carried out under the Fatimids in 1005. He explains that the first procession in Cairo was followed by serious violence between Shi'as and Sunnis. The commemoration was forced back to the service sessions in mosques, and even some Sunni people attended. However, the Sunni community never again tolerated dispersed Shi'i rituals through Cairo's urban spaces.

The Shi'i service session and procession are aimed at commemorating the tragedy of Ashura. However, the two rituals create different kinds of social engagement since their spatial manifestations are distinctive. While the service session facilitates communities in generating and maintaining social solidarity and identity, the procession is a dispersed spatial practice that not only creates social bonds but also engages the community with others. Therefore, although the Shi'i service sessions did not lead to serious violence in Baghdad and Cairo, even when they occurred in public spaces, disputes and violence arose when the processions were dispersed throughout cities. In other words, the dispersal rituals and collective performances create a platform for much more engaging social interactions when compared with ceremonies that are spatially concentrated.

## The Safavid Era and Development of Muharram Rituals

The Ashura commemoration was popular in many Iranian cities during the Buyid era (923–1055). Faqihi (1978) explains that the population of the repressed Shi'a communities grew enough that they could claim their right to public rituals in cities like Isfehan, Hamedan and Saveh. Nevertheless, apart from very few cities like Qom, the Shi'i community remained the minority in Iran until the time of Safavid (Madelung, 1988). When the orthodox Sunni Saljuqids (r. 1037–1157) came to power, Shi'i rituals were aggressively suppressed and banned in Iran, and were only conducted in private and secret ceremonies (Jafariyan, 2001).[25] The Saljuqid rule was replaced by Moghuls (r. 1217–1335), then the Timurid rule (1370–1507); these two dynasties did not claim a religious legitimacy for their rule and gave relative freedom to all sects, including Shi'as, to practise their rituals (Mazaheri, 2006: 41). Throughout these periods there were exceptional periods when the Shi'i community had more freedom or even support in Iran. For example, during the reign of Sultan Muhammad Khoda-bandeh (r. 1304–1316), the eighth Moghul sultan, who converted to Shi'i Islam. However, it was during the Safavid era that Shi'i rituals were greatly developed in Iran.

Shah Ismail took power in 1501 and established the Safavid dynasty (r. 1501–1772) and made Shi'i Islam the official state religion in Iran.[26] The Safavids succeeded in establishing a kind of national state based on the Shi'i faith, reinforcing the Safavid dynasty against the Sunni Ottoman Empire. The Safavid era is commonly known as the most stable and flourishing post-Islamic era in Iran. This was not only the most prosperous time for the advancement of Shi'i theology and philosophy, but also the period of 'the greatest impetus for the development of the Ashura celebration as a popular religious and artistic phenomenon' (Ayoub, 1987: 875). Calmard (1996) notes that by the time of Shah Abbas the First (r. 1587–1629), ceremonies in the month of Muharram became the core of socio-religious life

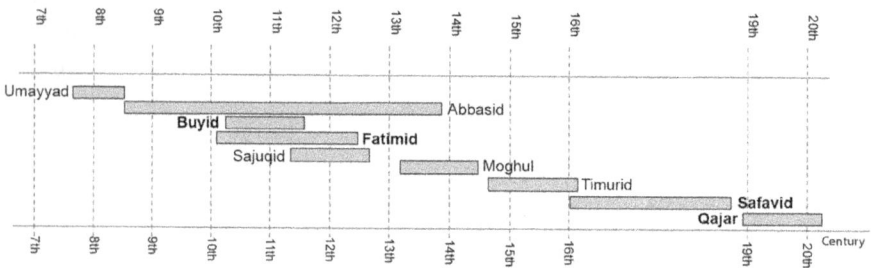

FIGURE 2.5 The timeline of the major dynasties in Shi'i history. Figure by the author.

**FIGURE 2.6** The street play in the city of Dezful on Ashura day, Iran, 2006. Photo by the author.

and a civic-religious festival in Iran. Rahimi (2004, 2011) argues that during the Safavid era the Muharram commemoration developed and was reinvented into an extraordinarily rich repertoire of rites and rituals that created a public sphere. The commemoration was ultimately transformed into a carnivalesque celebration of misrule and transgression. In other words, this was the time when Muharram rituals were considered a social event as well as a religious ritual.

Tavernier visited Isfahan, the capital of Safavid, in the seventeenth century and called the Muharram commemoration 'the Grand Festival of the Persians' (Tavernier, 1684: 161).[27] Tavernier wrote about the service session in the royal court, which was predominantly a religious mourning event. However, his testimony has generally shown that the public processions were at the core of these events. The account of Tavernier and other travellers such as Chardin (1671; 1993) show that the public processions not only expressed the Shi'i grief but were also a socially charged practice. Each urban community ran their procession throughout the city, ready for altercations with rival processions, during the first ten days of Muharram. The public processions were highly developed and associated with many symbolic performances such as the Shi'i street play, the carrying of new symbols like the *'alam*, and the fighting performance between urban communities in front of the king (see Figure 2.6).[28]

The Shi'i street play was one of the rituals developed in association with the procession and is a replication of the Karbala tragedy. Rahimi (2004) states that the Shi'i street play, as a new ritual, was established under the support of Shah Tahmasb the First in the mid-sixteenth century. The earliest testimony about the Shi'i street play dates back to 1602 from the Portuguese traveller, Antonio de Gouvea (1646: 75–76),[29] who described a public procession associated with a street play in the city of Shiraz (Iran). Della Valle,[30] Kotov[31] and Tavernier also described the public procession associated with the street play in Isfahan during the seventeenth century. According to these testimonies, an empty coffin is carried through the procession and numbers of children and women sit on camels to represent the aftermath of the battle of Karbala, when members of Hussein's families were captured and moved to Damascus, the capital of the Umayyad Caliphs.

By and large, the historical testimonies depict a landscape of commemoration during the Safavid era that sounds very familiar to what we observe today. On one hand the service sessions are predominantly mourning events, where the Shi'i grief is narrated and expressed in modest ways. On the other hand the very diverse rituals in urban public spaces are predominantly theatrical performances that display the Shi'i sorrow and are particularly charged with social agendas.

## The Spatial Suppression of Shi'i Rituals and the Passion Play Initiation

The flourishing period of Shi'i culture in Iran ended when the Sunni Afghans suddenly toppled the Safavids in the second half of the eighteenth century. Under these new political circumstances, the Shi'i rituals were suppressed again and banned from public urban spaces for more than three decades. Therefore, rituals such as the street play that were dispersed throughout cities were severely affected. The suppression of the street play transfigured it into the early form of *ta'zyeh* play, i.e. the Iranian passion play. As Mottahedeh (1986) argues, the passion play was a way for Iranian Shi'i society to culturally survive under the Sunni Afghan invaders by developing a folk tradition.[32] The Muharram street play is dispersed through urban spaces and does not have a verbal spoken dimension. However, the passion play, like a theatre play, manifests itself in a concentrated form and engages vocal performance. What I do want to emphasize here is that the early form of the passion play was the result of spatial (de)evolution of the street play, a spatially dispersed performance evolved into a spatially concentrated ritual.

After the Afghan interval, the Qajars gained power in Iran and they were enthusiastic patrons of the Muharram rituals. The Qajar dynasty (1796–1925) was a Shi'i state whose establishment marked another significant period for Shi'i rituals in Iran. Under the Qajars, the service session and public procession were supported; importantly, the early form of the Shi'i passion play was encouraged and reached its most developed form and highest popularity. As Aghaie (2005) states, the developed form of the passion play became the core of the Muharram rituals during the Qajar era. The passion play became an operatic play performed by professional actors narrating the tragedy of Karbala.

Schechner (1988, 1994) distinguishes between ritual and theatre in stating that the difference between the two lies in the fact that the ritual emphasizes 'efficacy' and the theatre emphasizes 'entertainment'. He explains that efficacy and entertainment converged in some historical periods in the Western theatre, such as in Elizabethan England in the sixteenth century.[33] He has argued that these convergent periods signify flourishing periods of Western theatre. This argument can be applied to the history of theatre in Iran as well, since the most flourished period for Iranian theatre is considered to be the Qajar era, when entertainment and religious devotion converged in the form of the Muharram passion play. While the service sessions were led by clergies and orators who narrated the tragedy of Karbala, the talented actors of the passion plays became celebrity figures during the Qajar era. The passion play dominated urban religious and cultural life during this era, undermining the role of the service session during Muharram. Therefore, some members of the clergy challenged the performance of passion plays during Muharram as they had an entertainment dimension and were not solely devoted to grieving.

In the Qajar era, when the passion play was highly developed and became the core of Muharram events, the play took place at *husseinyeh*, *tekyeh* or a city square. The play was also held in open fields in the countryside and villages. Nonetheless, this ritual manifests itself in a concentrated form, regardless of the place where it is performed. The most famous Qajarid *tekyeh* was Tekyeh-i Dowlat, or the state's *tekyeh*, that Naser al-Din Shah (r. 1848–1896) built solely for the purpose of holding the passion play (Figure 2.7). Interestingly, the architectural idea of this famous building allegedly came out of a visitation of the shah to the Royal Albert Hall in London. This *tekyeh* was differentiated from the usual *tekyeh*, which is a place where all kind of Shi'i rituals can be hosted, as it was dedicated and designed to host the passion play.[34] The founding of Tekyeh-i Dowlat indicates the significance of the passion play ritual in this period. Moreover, it can be seen as an attempt to introduce a new building type, a religious opera house, to create an appropriate place to house the passion play. However, this process in the history of Iranian architecture was interrupted by the establishment of the Iranian modern state (the Pahlavi dynasty) that destroyed the Tekyeh-i Dowlat.

**FIGURE 2.7** Tekyeh-i Dowlat, Tehran, in the Qajar era. This is Kamal al-Molk's famous canvas. Public domain image.

The new Pahlavi dynasty demolished the *tekyeh* and many other Qajarid buildings; this was justified as being part of the Tehran urban development scheme, but many of the demolished buildings had nothing to do with the scheme. This was part of the policy of eliminating symbols of the previous dynasty (e.g. see Makki, 1982: 449 and 453).

Looking back throughout the history of Shi'i rituals, it is clear that the passion play is the result of a long historical process. The passion play has its roots in the initial procession in Baghdad that had a performative dimension and in the street play of the Safavid era. However, it was the political suppression of Shi'i rituals from urban spaces that essentially transformed the street play into the passion play. In other words, the passion play can be seen

**FIGURE 2.8** A *ta'zyeh* scene at an open space in the Qajar era, Dieulafoy, 1887. Public domain image.

as the result of successive spatial expansions and reductions of Shi'i rituals, a process that I call 'the spatial evolution of ritual'.

## The Development of Shi'i Places

Throughout history Shi'i communities have developed their own religious/community places. The specific building types were developed as a result of the formation of Shi'i colonies – residential quarters and localities. There is no historical evidence showing that the emergence of Shi'i-specific buildings contributed to the initiation or evolution of the Muharram rituals. As explained in the case of Tekyeh-i Dowlat, the building was designed or appropriated according to the nature of rituals. Nonetheless, the dynamics of Shi'i pilgrimages may have a more direct relationship with the building of Shi'i shrines. The architectural elaboration of shrines is often the consequence of a popular pilgrimage site, which in turn contributes to the emotional experience and perception of the pilgrimage. This is due to the fact that pilgrimages are bound to a particular sacred location, while this is not the case for other Shi'i rituals.

Some consequences of the early Abbasid era and then the Shi'i dynasties of Fatimid (909–1171) and Buyid (923–1055) were that Shi'i residential

**FIGURE 2.9** The *husseiniyeh* of Fahadan in the city of Yazd, Iran, 2007. Photo by the author.

quarters gradually took shape in large cities across the Middle East, in Egypt, Syria, Iraq and Iran. Faqihi (1978) has reviewed historical accounts about the Shi'i localities in Baghdad and in the cities of Ray and Qazvin in Iran during the tenth and eleventh centuries. According to al-Hadarat al-islamiyah (Cairo, 1366, Vol. 1, p. 97), there was a notable group of Shi'a Muslims in Tripoli, Nablus, Aleppo and Herat (in Afghanistan); and the city of Ahwaz in southwestern Iran was known as a predominantly Shi'i city during the tenth century (Tabatabaei, 1975: 64). Moreover, according to *Tarikho-i Qom*[35] and *Mujam al-Boldaan*,[36] the cities of Qom and Kashan[37] were known as Shi'i cities even prior to the Buyid era, when Iran was predominantly a Sunni country. In this socio-political context, the service sessions were transformed from (secret) ceremonies in private places into events held at public and community buildings such as mosques. Moreover, a new building type called *husseiniyeh*[38] emerged in predominantly Shi'i quarters. Ayoub has mentioned that numerous *husseiniyeh* had been built in Baghdad, Aleppo and Cairo by the tenth century (1978: 154).

A *husseiniyeh* is simply a community place that is dedicated to Muharram commemoration and where other Shi'i ceremonies and community events can also be held. In Iran, a *husseiniyeh* is alternatively called *zaynabiyeh*, *abbasyeh* and *qasemyieh*, named after Zaynab, Abbas and Qasem, members of Hussein's family who accompanied him in Karbala. However, all these sister buildings are identical. In Iran, *tekyeh* is another name for places dedicated to Shi'i rituals; as Tavasoli (1987) and Bozorgnia (2004, 2006) discussed, historical *tekyeh* and *husseiniyeh* buildings are identical and it is not clear what differentiates the two. Nonetheless, the term *tekyeh* refers to different types of buildings throughout history; most commonly it referred to medieval era Sufi places across the Middle East and Iran. Chardin, who visited Iran during the seventeenth century, noted that Iranians called Sufi monasteries the *takyeh* (1993: 473; orig. 1671). Moreover, Kampfer (1981: 136) described a *tekyeh* during his visit in the seventeenth century as a place like an inn where dervish/Sufis were temporarily settling. It seems that during the Safavid era, either *tekyeh* buildings gradually began to be used for the purposes of Muharram commemoration or the term semantically evolved and referred to places dedicated to Shi'i rituals. These dynamics also reflect the shift of Safavid state policy from Sufism towards an orthodox Shi'ism. However, as Monfared noted, it was in the Iranian Qajar era that the term *tekyeh* came to commonly refer to the places dedicated to the Muharram rituals and the term was no longer used in reference to Sufi monasteries (Monfared, n.d.: 3812). More recently *tekyeh* usually refers to stalls that are temporarily set up in open/public places during Muharram. In India, a *husseiniyeh* is commonly called an *imambara* (also *imamwada*) or *ashur-Khaneh* (the house of Ashura). Although all kinds of community events are permitted in these places, the endowment registration document of these places (*waqf* document) often requires that any usage of the place should include mentioning the martyrdom of Hussein during the event (see Masoudi Nejad, 2017a).

It is rather difficult to give a building or architectural definition for a *husseiniyeh*, as they are built in a myriad of forms and shapes. The layout of a *husseiniyeh* could be considered very similar to that of a mosque (see Figure 2.9); it can simply be an ordinary house that is dedicated to Muharram commemorations. It is also referred to as an open public space or a small square in a bazaar that is temporarily converted into a place to host Muharram rituals. Therefore, instead of using an architectural definition, it is reasonable to describe it as a public building/place that is associated with Shi'a rituals, facilitating solidarity among the community. A *husseiniyeh/imambara* is differentiated from a mosque as follows: (1) while mosques are built facing to the direction of Mecca, *husseiniyeh* buildings can face any direction; (2) menstruating women are not barred from entering; and (3) since the mosque is a place of sanctity, there are some activities for which it cannot be used. In contrast the *husseiniyeh* can be used for any kind of activity as long as the activity does not breach the terms and conditions set forth in its endowment document. For example, as I have discussed elsewhere (Masoudi Nejad, 2017b), the ritual of flagellation cannot be practised at mosques since shedding blood is forbidden there, but this ritual can be practised at *husseiniyeh* buildings. In short, although the *husseiniyeh* is considered a religious place where community members experience emotional religious moments, it is not a sacred place such as a mosque. While *husseiniyeh* and other sister buildings play a major role in the socio-religious life of Shi'i communities, there is no historical evidence that the construction of these places has played a role in the evolution of the Shi'i rituals.

## Distinguishing Shi'i Rituals Based on Their Spatiality

As discussed, it is necessary to have a conceptual framework that can categorize a large number of rites and rituals that come together as the Muharram ritual. In this section I will use examples to discuss how similar symbolic actions can be performed in different rituals. These rituals are distinguishable by their spatial manifestations, which point to different social implications of the ritual. Although this subject is partly discussed in the case of the Shi'i street play and the passion play, this point will be further articulated by first comparing the rituals of *nakhl-gardani* (carrying the *nakhl*) and *nakhl-bardari* (lifting the *nakhl*) which are practised in Iran.

The two rituals are focused around the *nakhl*, a symbolic coffin, and presumably have a genealogical relationship similar to that of the Shi'i street play and the passion play. The Shi'i procession has always resembled a symbolic funeral, and Shi'a communities invented different symbolic coffins to be carried during the procession.[39] One of these symbolic coffins developed in Iran is the *nakhl*, meaning palm. It is a wooden structure, constructed in different sizes and forms. Although the *nakhl* is commonly known as a symbol associated with cities in the central region of Iran such as Yazd,[40] this symbolic coffin was also very common in other cities, such as Dezful in southwestern Iran (Figure 2.10).

In his study about the city of Maybod, Jenab bol-lahi (2000) notes that *nakhls* are the vital symbol of localities and are mostly kept in the squares of these localites throughout the year. These *nakhls* are adorned during the month of Muharram and carried through the procession of Ashura. Generally, the idea of carrying the *nakhl* is similar in all cities. Interviewees in Dezful have explained that a respected person would sit on the *nakhl* while reading the holy book, and dozens of emotional youth carried it throughout the city alleys and thoroughfares.[41]

The ritual of lifting the *nakhl*, however, feature the raising up and lifting of a gigantic *nakhl* by hundreds of participants. This ritual is mainly practised in cities like Yazd and Taft in central Iran. The *nakhl* of Amir-chakhmaq in the city of Yazd (Figure 2.12), and the *nakhl* of Husseiniyeh of Shah Nemat-olah-i vali in the city of Taft (Figure 2.13), are among the best known

FIGURE 2.10 The *nakhl* of Kalb-Ali Khan (left) on Ashura day in Dezful, photograph dated 1350, i.e. 1931. From the collection of the Saba Photo Studio (Dezful); copyright unknown.

FIGURE 2.11 A *nakhl* located in a local square, Yazd, Iran, 2006. Photo by the author.

FIGURE 2.12 The *nakhl* of Mir-chakhmaq at the corner of the square in the city of Yazd, Iran, 2006. Photo by the author.

FIGURE 2.13 The ritual of lifting the *nakhl*, at *husseiniyeh* Shah Nematolah-i Vali, in the city of Taft, Iran, 2011. By courtesy of Mohammad Hassan Assareh.

*nakhls* in Iran. This ritual is currently limited to a few places. Mr Malek-sabet (interviewed in 2006 in Yazd) mentioned that the *husseiniyeh* of Shah abul-Qasem is one of the very few places where the ritual is practised in Yazd. In recent years, the lifting at the *husseiniyeh* of Shah Nematolah-i Vali in the city of Taft has also proved very popular and attracts the attention of the media in Iran for being one of the most authentic examples of the ritual. The symbolic coffins in the ritual of carrying the *nakhl* are of modest size and can be carried by tens of people throughout the city roads. However, the ritual of lifting the *nakhl* is associated with gigantic *nakhls*, therefore the ritual involves lifting and turning around the *nakhl* within the place where it is kept. Hundreds of men participate in lifting the *nakhl* of their community, a practice that clearly exhibits the solidarity of the community. While the size of the symbolic coffin has been exaggerated into its current enormous structure, the spatial manifestation of this ritual is limited to within a demar-cated place.

Although both rituals of carrying and lifting the *nakhl* resemble a symbolic funeral, they are two distinct rituals that are manifested in different spatial forms. One is spatially dispersed throughout the city and the other is spatially concentrated. The ritual of carrying the *nakhl* is like a procession that engages the community with others as they are passing through the territory of other city localities, crossing socio-spatial borders. This can be a means of showing intimacy and friendship with other localities that they visit throughout the ritual; however, it can also trigger tension between communities.[42] As the ritual of lifting the *nakhl* is manifested in a concentrated form, its central purpose is to bring the community together in solidarity around a structure that symbolizes their community. These two rituals are aimed at performing symbolic funerals of Karbala martyrs; this symbolic performance is dramatized and spatially manifested in different forms and thus mediates different social interactions.

There are many other Shi'i rituals that are based on similar actions but spatially manifested in different ways. I turn now to *sineh-zani* (chest-beating) as the most basic action to express grief over the tragedy of Ashura. Chest-beating is the main action performed throughout the Shi'i procession. However, this basic action is manifested in a different way in a ritual called *ha'ya-mola*, in which participants rhythmically beat their chests while walking in concentric circles. This ritual is known as a traditional practice in the city of Bushehr, a port city in the south of Iran. It is commonly claimed that this ritual is practised exclusively in Bushehr. Interestingly, Firoz Shakir (interviewed in November and December 2009) has also talked about a similar ritual practised in Bandra in Mumbai. The ritual was obviously brought by immigrants from Bushehr to Mumbai, as it is called Bushehr-i matam.[43] However, during my fieldwork in the northeastern Iranian city of Birjand,[44]

**FIGURE 2.14** The ritual of *ha'ya-mola* in Bushehr, Iran. © Mostafa Gholami-Nejad, ISNA News Agency. Published with permission.

interviewees also described a similar ritual but they called it *Saf-i Heydar Ali* (the line/queue of Heydar Ali).[45]

In the ritual of *ha'ya-mola*, participants gather in their local mosque, *husseiniyeh* or local square, and rhythmically beat their chests while walking in concentric circles. Each participant takes the belt of the person next to him in one hand, and beats his chest with the other hand. The participants encircle a singer who sings an emotional dirge about the Karbala tragedy. Interviewees[46] who discussed the details of this ritual in Bushehr explained that senior and more respected members of the community join the ritual at the inner circles. The ritual of *ha'ya-mola* can be recognized by any observer as a kind of dance aimed at expressing grief. Moreover, this ritual can be seen as a procession that is spatially reformulated in a concentrated and abstract form. The community practises its solidarity and social hierarchy through this ritual; however, as the ritual is spatially concentrated, any engagement with other communities is naturally minimized.

As mentioned, considering the spatiality of rituals instead of the actions helps to characterize the ways in which rituals function. Spatially concentrated rituals such as *majlis*, *nakhl-bardari* and *ha'ya-mola* are based on congregation so they mostly facilitate the practice of solidarity among members of a community. In contrast, the procession, the street play and *nakkl-gardani* (carrying the *nakhl*) maximize the degree of social engagement with other communities as they are spatially dispersed in the city across social borders.

## Conclusion

This chapter does not contribute to finding new historical materials (data) about the Muharram rituals; rather, it offers a spatial reading of the rituals' history by shifting the focus from 'actions' and 'places' to 'spatial manifestations' of rituals. This chapter reveals that the spatial manifestation of ritual can be conceived as being more important than the action and the place of ritual, and that this conception aids in understanding how the rituals evolved and how they perform social functions. Moreover, this chapter shows there is not a cause and effect relationship between 'the spatial evolution of rituals' and 'the development of Shi'i buildings'.

The spatial manifestation of rituals particularly helps to capture the genealogy of the Shi'i rituals based on the spatial expansion and reduction of previous rituals. The development of some of rituals, e.g. the passion play, was the result of a series of spatial expansions and reductions over a long period of time, a process that I call the spatial evolution of ritual manifestation. The discussions here have shown that the spatial evolution of rituals is politically driven although social and cultural conditions have also affected the process.

For the purposes of this research, it is particularly important to pay attention to the spatial manifestation of ritual, since the Muharram rituals are explored here as a part of the urban process. As discussed, the spatial manifestation of rituals plays an acute role in their social function. However, the next chapters will demonstrate how the ritual manifestation is not the sole determinant for how urban communities engage with each other.

### NOTES

1. Hayden White (1975) argues that histories combine a certain amount of 'data', theoretical concepts to 'explain' this data, and a 'narrative structure' to represent events that happened in the past.
2. In fact it was only in the eight century that a distinctive Shi'i discourse began to emerge (Haider, 2011; Newman, 2012).
3. There was a previous revolt against the rule of Mu'awiyah in the city of Kufa around the year 671 (Watt, 1960: 158).
4. The date has been converted using www.fourmilab.ch. However, it can be converted differently; for example, Crow (1986: 72; 2008: 53) notes the date as 10 October 680.
5. For example, see Good and Good (1988) who reduced the Muharram commemoration to a depressive event.
6. See also Bosworth et al. (1983), Calmard (1996), and Hussain (2005).

7. These rituals will be described later in this chapter.
8. See chapter one and the conclusion.
9. This is discussed in chapter one.
10. As the Shi'i rituals were developed in different linguistic territories, some terms or names may have different meanings across Shi'i communities in the world. *Ta'zyeh* literally means mourning in Arabic so it generally refers to the mourning ceremonies among Arab-speaking communities. In Iran, *ta'zyeh* refers to the passion play of Ashura. However, the Indian *ta'zyeh* is the recreation of Hussein's tomb carried throughout the Muharram processions.
11. This cultural revolution was partly due to mass paper manufacturing and book production in parallel with drastic scientific developments and the translation movements in the Muslim world during the Abbasid era, which is signified by large libraries in Baghdad and Cairo (see Green, 1988).
12. Nevertheless, later Abbasid Caliphs gradually lost such affinity with the Shi'i community and even suppressed them.
13. Van der Veer argued that religious rituals construct a self that 'not only integrates the believers but also places a symbolic boundary between them and outsiders' (1994: 11).
14. This can be seen in other cities, but as this is based on my observations in the city of Dezful, I keep it in the context of that city.
15. The fortieth day after the death of individuals is also commemorated by Muslims.
16. Faqihi has noted and cited accounts of the first procession in *al-Montazam fi Tarikh al-molok va al-omam* (by ibn Juzi, d. 1182), Vol. 7, p. 15; *Takmalet al-Tarikh-i al-Tabari* (by M.A. Hamedani, d. 1127), p. 183; and *Merat al-Janan* (by A.A. Yafeei, d. 1367), Vol. 3, p. 147.
17. Ibn Kathir, Al-Bidayah wa al-Nihiyah (Cairo: Matba'a al Sa'ada, 1358 AH), Vol. XI, p. 243.
18. This is discussed extensively in chapter one.
19. This is not always the case. As I will discuss in chapters four and six, processions can be a medium to initiate social reconciliation and intimacy. I have also elaborated (Masoudi Nejad, 2014) on the role of processions in social reconciliation in the context of Mumbai.
20. Karkh, on the east bank of the Tigris, is still known as a Shi'i quarter in Baghdad.
21. Haqani and Faqihi review the conflict between the Sunni and Shi'a communities in Baghdad, based on testimonies made by Ibn-Athir, Ibn Juzi and al-Mugharizi.
22. See Ibn Kathir, Al-Bidayah wa al-Nihiyah (Cairo: Matba'a al Sa'ada, 1358 AH), Vol. XI, p. 275, or see Mazzaoui (1979: 232).
23. This is known as the first Muslim civil war, when one of the Prophet's wives, A'isha, mobilized some troops against the authority of Ali, who was appointed as the fourth Caliph. For more, see *The Community Divided* (Tabari, 1997: 26–122).
24. Hussain (2005) has cited Taqi al-Din's *Kitab mawa'iz al-i'tibar*, Vol. 1, p. 429–31; he has also referred to Sanders (1994).
25. The anti-Shi'i policy of Saljuqid rule was seriously aggressive, especially under Sultan Mahmmud Qaznavi. For more, see Jafarian (2001: 956).
26. On the process of establishing Shi'i as the state religion by Shah Ismail, see Parsadust (1996: 692–97).

27. Tavernier's travelogue was published in Persian in 1957. The oldest English copy of his travelogue that I have reviewed was published during 1684–1688 in London by Moses Pitt. The copy is held at the library of SOAS, University of London.

28. These historical testimonies depicting the ritual in the Safavid era will be reviewed in greater detail in chapter three.

29. For an English translation, see Nakash (1993: 169–70) and Rahimi (2004: 177–80); for a Persian translation of Gouvea's account, see Falsafi (1985: 584–87), Vol. 3; the book was originally published in 1954.

30. Della Valle described the ceremonies in 1618–1619. For his full testimony in English, see Rahimi (2004: 181). For a Persian translation, see Falsafi (1985: 848–54).

31. Kotov described the ceremonies in 1624–1625. For his full testimony in English, see Rahimi (2004: 185).

32. She has also mentioned that Iranians developed Sufism as another cultural reaction to Sunni Afghans. For more, see Mottahedeh (1986: 176).

33. Schechner refers to Elizabethan England as being the 17th century; however, the reign of Elizabeth is 1558-1603, occurring mostly in the 16th century.

34. In the following section, I will review several Shi'i religious buildings.

35. *Tarkh-i Qom* was written in the late tenth century by Hassan ibn Muhammad al-Qomi.

36. This was written by the Arab geographer, Yaqut al-Hamavi, in the thirteenth century.

37. Motamedi (1999: 57–79) has also reviewed historical accounts about the Shi'a community of Kashan.

38. *Husseiniyeh* is the transliteration of its Iranian pronunciation, but based on Arabic pronunciation it would be transliterated as *husseiniyyat*.

39. Bolokbashi (2001) has reviewed different symbolic coffins that have been developed for the Muharram ritual in Iran.

40. Chelkowski (2005: 157) and Pooya (2000), among others, have stated that *nakhl* is used in towns in the central desert of Iran.

41. The narrations given by interviewees refer to the ritual as it was carried out before the 1950s; the rite of *nakhl-gardani* is no longer practised in the city of Dezful. However, there are still a few *nakhls* in the city, kept in some quarters. These interviews are mainly addressed in chapter three.

42. This will be extensively discussed in chapters three, four and five. See also Masoudi Nejad (2014, 2015a).

43. *Busheri Matam* literally means 'to mourn in the way of the people of Bushehr'.

44. This is mainly referred to in interviews with Mr Mohammad-Ebrahim Dayyani (interviewed in Birjand, April 2006), and Mr S.A. Barabadi (interviewed in Birjand, April 2006).

45. The ritual is named after Ali-ibn Abi Taleb, the first Shi'a *imam*. For more about the ritual in Birjand, see also Barabadi et al. (2002).

46. This is mainly based on an interview with Mr Mohammadali-Pour (interviewed in Tehran, April 2006), Mr M. Gerashi (interviewed in Bushehr, April 2006) and Dr Hamidi (interviewed in Tehran, April 2006).

# PART II

═══════════

# THE SPATIAL ORGANIZATION
# OF RITUAL

The second part of this book principally deals with the idea of 'the spatial organization of ritual', which is one of the two theoretical components of this book. The first part of this book explained 'the spatial manifestation' of Muharram rituals. First, the ritual is described as an intrinsically spatial performance. Then, it is explained that rituals are spatially manifested in either concentrated or dispersed forms. This idea provides a platform to spatially read the history of Muharram rituals. This spatial reading narrates the genealogy of Muharram rituals based on the evolution of spatially concentrated rituals into dispersed rituals and vice versa. The second part of this book, however, focuses on 'the spatial organization' of Muharram processions as they are dispersed across the city. Throughout the next three chapters I explain how the arrangement of procession routes creates complex social interactions. The idea is to investigate the social and spatial logic of procession routes before and after the transformation of Iranian urban society. However, chapter four particularly pays attention to the period of modern transformation, a process that led to the re-arrangement of Muharram procession routes in the early 1950s in Dezful. In other words, the second part of this book looks at the transformation of Iranian cities from traditional to contemporary urban settings by investigating the spatial dynamics of Muharram processions. This passage reflects the ideas of Van Gennep (1960), who formulated the role of rituals in the transitional passage from one to another stage of life. While Van Gennep and later Victor Turner (1969) mainly formulated the passage of individuals throughout their social states, this book articulates the transitional process of city and urban society.

These discussions provide evidence that Muharram processions are some of the most significant social practices through which the constitution of urban societies and power relations were constantly negotiated. Chapter three investigates the social logic of procession routes in traditional urban settings on the eve of the Iranian modernization. However, the discussion contextualizes the subject in a broader historical landscape. Chapter four deals with the transitional process of urban transformation, leading to the re-arrangement of procession routes, an event that I describe as a 'rite' in its own right, signifying the passage of the traditional Iranian city to a contemporary one. This discussion reveals a complex relationship between rituals, urban violence and conciliation. Then chapter five exhibits how the re-arranged processions create a performed space in which the past and present of urban society are simultaneously manifested, revealing a sophisticated way of performing urban history through collective performances. These chapters evidently demonstrate the fact that Muharram rituals are by no means limited to the observance of the Ashura tragedy; rather, urban negotiations predominate the landscape of these rituals.

CHAPTER 3

# THE TRADITIONAL MUHARRAM PROCESSIONS

This chapter principally investigates the social logic of Muharram procession routes before the transformation of Iranian cities in the early twentieth century. The discussion is not focused on the symbolic and performative aspects of Muharram rituals but on the spatial organization of processions within their socio-political landscape. The investigation begins with an explanation of the idea of urban locality (residential quarter), and the traditional division of urban society based on the Heydari and Nemati[1] parts. The discussion reviews the historical background of the Heydari–Nemati division and explains how the division reflected urban realities and how Muharram processions were organized. This subject leads to another important discussion: the traditional local ruling system and its relationship to urban landlordism. These discussions clarify the landscape of local power relations in which Muharram rituals were performed. This comprehensive socio-political contextualization is relevant not only to the discussion of this chapter, but also the following two chapters. The discussions throughout this chapter are ultimately aimed at explaining the social logic of procession routes. Although this chapter mainly focuses on the city of Dezful, the discussions are contextualized in a broader geographical landscape.

## The Traditional Urban Society and Muharram Rituals

Muharram processions are run by a group of socially bound men, organized as a *dasteh* (group), representing a *mahalleh* (locality). The processions, like any other ritual, are a socially charged collective performance; as Nakash (1993) notes, the processions reflect a concrete social reality and the tensions within each society. Therefore, the spatial organization of processions addresses three social aspects of Iranian cities: (1) the locality is the principle component of urban society; while (2) the localities were traditionally divided into Heydari and Nemati factions, (3) there was a social intimacy amongst the localities that bound them to each part of the city.

*Mahalleh* means locality or residential quarter. The traditional locality can be simply defined as the settlement of a community that is socially and spatially bound. While a locality in modern Iranian cities would be associated with a social class, the traditional localities encompass different social classes. In other words, a locality was a micro urban society formed by a range of social classes bound as a community. In Dezful, the social classes of people would be generally described as poor, middle class and wealthy. However, more elaborate language was also used to describe social status. For example, Mirza-Ali Karami talked about diverse social classes in their locality, Foolaadioun,[2] which was one of the smallest localities in Dezful. He explains:

> There were four or five social groups in our locality. The labourers or working class who were mainly involved with building construction [in our locality]. Another group was *Khosh-neshin* which includes those who had seasonal jobs, such as reaping at the end of the agricultural year. Generally, *Khosh-neshin* means someone who does not have a permanent job and does not own land. *Pisheh-varon* (artisans) were another social group that mostly had a fabric mill in our locality. *Kaasob-karon* (tradesmen) who were shopkeepers that were considered as a middle class. Finally, families like our family, who have owned agriculture, we also had sheep flock, kept by nomads. Our family was considered as *dolamand*[3] (wealthy), but not landlord. Although we had some agricultural lands, mostly leased lands from landlords, and hired peasants and other labourers to manage our agriculture. (Interviewed in September 2005, Dezful)

The locality described by Karami is very small, but it still includes very diverse social groups. More interestingly, the terminologies indicate more than social class, addressing whether the family had land, the security of their job, and how they were paid for their labour and services. For example, *Khosh-neshin* means someone who is neither landowner, nor received a share from harvest, but is paid for his labour.[4]

The traditional locality is often idealized as an independent residential area that has its own community places, such as a local mosque, local market, public bath and school. However, this idealistic description is based on built entities and does not reflect the reality. Throughout my fieldwork in seven Iranian cities, I came across many old localities that do not have many of the aforementioned public places. For example, the locality that Karami described historically had neither market place, public bath, nor even a local mosque. Interestingly, the Muharram processions appear as collective performances by which localities can be identified. The procession defines the locality, since every single locality organizes its processions, representing its own social identity. To find out what locality a neighbourhood is associated with, it is enough to see which procession the inhabitants of the neighbourhood are participating in. For instance, during my interview with Mr Haj Mohammad Amir-Gholami, we had a conversation about traditional localities in Dezful before the modern transformation. I asked him whether his neighbourhood was a part of the locality of Seeyah-poushan.[5] While our conversation was not about Muharram rituals, Mr Amir-Gholami (b. 1921) said: 'We did not run our procession with Seeyah-poushan locality; we had our own union and procession in Kornassioun' (February 2006, Dezful).[6] This statement simply explains that he was in a neighbourhood affiliated with a locality, which has a separate social identity from Seeyah-poushan.

Muharram rituals were, and still are, organized by the union of localities known as *heyat* [hey-at]. The union is a local committee or council that can be seen as a kind of socio-religious NGO that is in charge of religious rituals in each locality. The union represents the local community and organizes diverse religious rituals, the most important of which are the Muharram processions. Therefore, the union is often referred to as the Muharram union. The union includes individuals from different social backgrounds that are socially respected by the community. The union members should be able to keep solidarity among the community, mobilize the local community for rituals and processions, and collect financial support from residents and local elites. Although the term *heyat* principally refers to the union or the local committee of Muharram, the term could also refer the group of processionists who represent their locality; that is known as *dasteh* (the group). The *heyat* is often used as a synonym of *dasteh* since both words refer to representatives of the local community. The term *juloos*, in Turkish and Urdu, means procession. However, there is no corresponding term for procession in Farsi. The procession is called *heyat-gardani* or *dasteh-gardani*.[7]

The territory of each locality has never been defined by a fixed border, as the solidarity of neighbourhoods as a locality is not a static status. It was common to see that two neighbourhoods socially unite as a locality or divide as independent localities for socio-political reasons. This means that sometimes a neighbourhood became a locality in its own right, or it would sway its social affiliation from one locality to another. Therefore, the borders of localities were rather flexible. Muharram unions and processions would seamlessly manifest such social changes, since Muharram was an acute time to define, manifest and practise the social constitution of urban communities.

Social events were traditionally entwined with religious ceremonies. In fact, there was no division between religious and social (or, if you like, profane) events. Muharram was the most important annual event where

people ritually manifested their social identity and affiliation. People often
have a clear affiliation to a specific Muharram union. However, some people
may have a kind of hybrid affiliation. This was often the case for those who
live in buffer zones between two localities. These individuals join the final
procession of a locality with which they have ultimate solidarity. However,
they might participate in the Muharram service sessions of other localities to
which they have social intimacy through marriage or financial relationships.
Depending on their economic status, they may financially support the unions
of both localities. For example, Mr Ahmadzade (b. 1940) narrates that:

> Our home was between the two localities of Katkatoun[8] and Sardarah,[9] in the north
> of Dezful. My father was keen to keep his relations to the union of both localities, [so]
> financially supported both unions. Later, the two localities united and the unions were
> integrated as one union ... This integration made a convenience for our family that had
> a relationship with the two localities. (Interviewed in September 2005, Tehran)

This description shows that although each locality is illustrated on a map
with a clear and distinct border, we should always be aware that such borders are arbitrary and subject to change. It is better to imagine the border
of localities not as a sharp line, but as a blurry one that denotes a buffer
zone between localities. The mapping style that we often employ is indeed
appropriate for the arbitrary divisions that modern bureaucrats use to define
administrative territories. The modern boundaries are clear-cut borders
throughout streets and roads. However, the borders of traditional localities
should be imagined as a line through urban blocks, not through alleys. If
houses have access to the same allay, they are probably socially associated
to the same locality. Therefore, although even here I have mapped the traditional localities in a modern manner, it is only to give readers an idea about
the position of localities in Dezful. We should be aware that these kinds of
maps are arbitrary and do not reflect the dynamic realities of traditional
cities.

The Farsi term *mahalleh* generally means the locality or the residential
quarter, which as described, refers to a community that is socially and spatiality bound. However, the content of interviews shows that people in Dezful
use the term *mahalleh* to signify different urban territories. Interestingly, Haj
Muhammad Saifi (b. 1935; interviewed in February 2006, Dezful) directly
addressed four meanings of *mahalleh*. The most common meaning of the
term is 'the locality', but he also explained that the term could refer to 'the
place', addressing the centre of a locality which is specifically called *sar-ma-
halleh*. This can be the equivalent of the 'high street' in English cities. The
term *mahalleh* also means 'neighbourhood', which refers to houses that are
in a close proximity, such as in an alley. A locality could be made of one
neighbourhood or more. For example, there are a couple of old localities

in Dezful that were made of a single neighbourhood, such as the localities of Sakioun[10] and Foolaadioun. These localities insist on their own distinct social identity, and ran their own Muharram processions. Additionally, *mahalleh* refers to a larger area in the city, comprised of one or more localities, translated as a 'borough' in English. A borough, here, refers to an area of the city that was under an elite landlord family. In short, a locality was often made of socially bound neighbourhoods that can be considered the smallest social component of urban society. A borough would be made of one or more localities that were governed by a local governor. In other words, the borough can be considered the smallest polity in the traditional Iranian city. This would be the equivalent of the parish, the smallest unit of local government in traditional English cities.

The social affiliations and bounds between neighbourhoods and localities have never been static, but rather constantly negotiated and changed. For example, the entire northern part of Dezful was one borough, known as Heydar-khoneh. However, following a riot in the late nineteenth century, the locality of Seeyah-poushan became an independent borough.[11] This borough consists of only one locality. Therefore, the idea of the *mahalleh* of Seeyah-poushan refers to both notions of locality and borough.

During the late Qajar era (the early twentieth century), Dezful was governed based on six main boroughs: Seeyah-poushan, Heydar-khuneh, Mahalleh Masjed, Qaleh,[12] Eastern Sahrabedar[13] and Western Sahrabedar (Map 3.1). Some of the boroughs included only one locality; however, a borough like Masjed comprised several localities. As already mentioned, the local landlord families, who ruled localities, teamed up in two socio-political groups that competed for greater power in the city. In this political landscape, the first two boroughs were bonded as Heydari and local governors of other boroughs were allied as Nemati. The Heydari–Nemati division was one of the most important socio-political characteristics of Iranian cites until even the mid-twentieth century. Muharram processions were collective performances that manifested the social bond among local communities. The procession routes also clearly address the traditional urban division, as the processions of localities was organized in two separate territories of Heydari and Nemati. This implies that Iranian urban society was not traditionally integrated, but rather constituted on the basis of two rival factions.

## The Idea of Social Moieties: Heydari and Nemati

There are numerous historical accounts reporting that Iranian cities have been socially divided into Heydari and Nemati factions since the late sixteenth century. Social historians, such as Mirjafari (1979), Floor (1987),

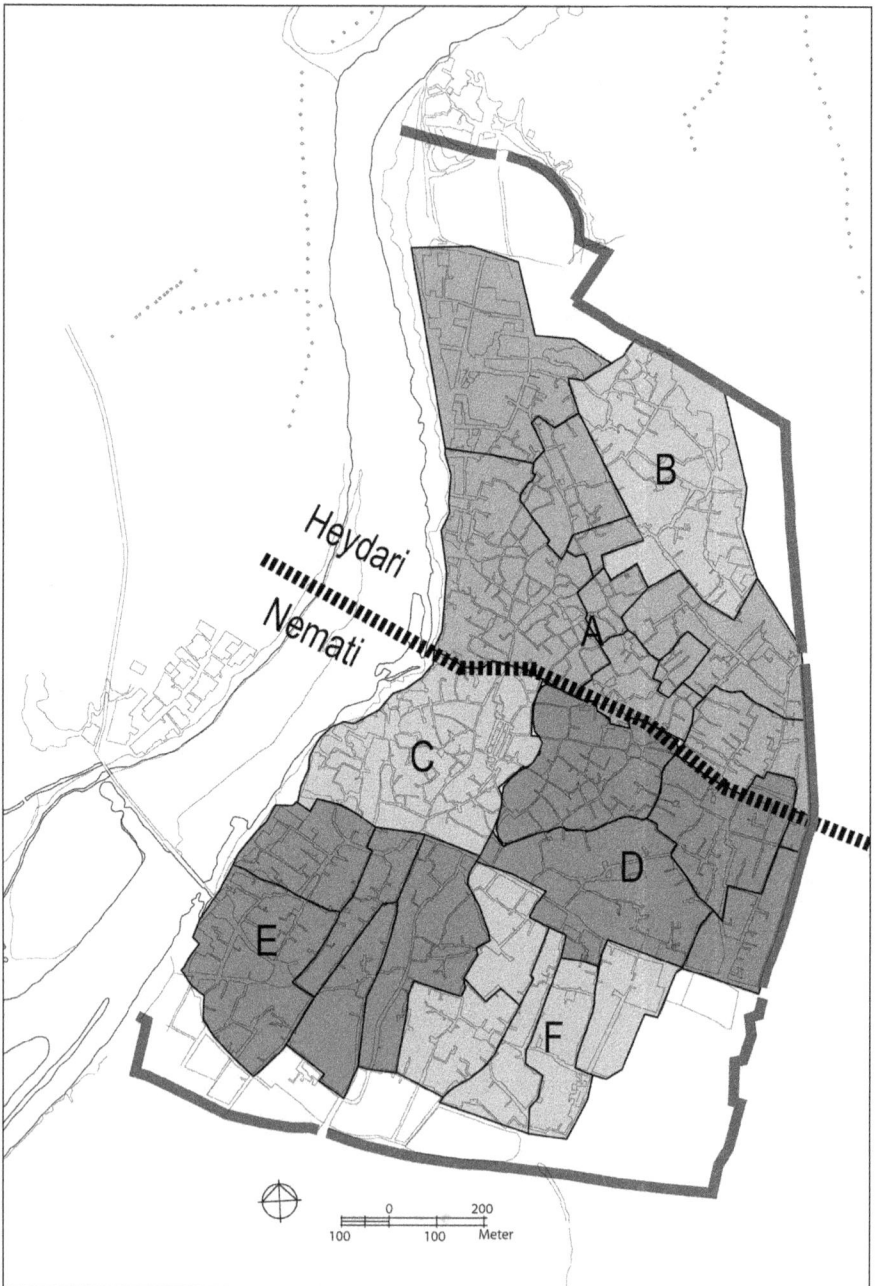

**MAP 3.1** The localities and boroughs in the city of Dezful, early twentieth century. (A) Heydar-khuneh, (B) Seeyah-poushan, (C) Qaleh, (D) Mahalleh Masjed, (E) Western Sahrabedar and (F) Eastern Sahrabedar. Map by the author.

Calmard (1996) and Perry (1999), have related the Heydari–Nemati division to an older division of two Sufi schools in the fourteenth century. One school was led by Mir Heydar Tuni (d. 1427), who was a Shi'a, and the other school was headed by Shah Nematollah Vali (d. 1431), who was a Sunni. Mirjafari (1979) explains that the dispute between the two schools gained a social dimension in Tabriz, where both Sufi orders had gained large numbers of followers. During the second half of the fifteenth century, the division led to a political dispute when the Aq-Qoyunlu dynasty took power in some parts of Iran and supported the Nemati order. Then the Safavids rose up in the early sixteenth century and proclaimed Shi'a as the state religion. Under the Safavids, Iranians mostly converted to Shi'a Islam; the successors of Shah Nematollah Vali, who had a good relationship with the Safavids, also converted to Shi'a Islam.

By the second half of the sixteenth century, Heydari-Nemati no longer implied the Sufi division, rather it referred to the social division among urban communities. The Italian traveller Vincentio d'Alessandri visited Tabriz and observed the Heydari–Nemati division as a prime factor in the constitution of urban society during the Safavid era as early as 1571 (Barbaro et al., 2010: 244). Chardin (1671, 1993), who visited the capital city of Isfahan in the 1670s, described the city as divided into Jubareh-Nematollahi in the west and Dardasht-Heydari in the east. He explained that the tension between the two parts of the city was pronounced during Muharram. Further accounts were reported by Tavernier (1684, 1957)[14] who described the Muharram commemoration as 'the Grand Festival of the Persians, which is the famous Feast of Hocen and Hussein' (Tavernier, 1684: 161). He reported the conflict between the Heydari and Nemati parties during Muharram in Isfahan under Shah Sulayman in 1667. Tavernier's account shows that there were Muharram service sessions in many places, including at the royal court. There were also all kinds of performances and processions across the city. However, the final public processions in the Royal square, Naqsh-i Jahan, played the central role in the Muharram commemoration. He noted that although the public procession was controlled by royal security, there was some fighting and conflict between the different groups of participants because they wanted to show their braveness and ability in front of the king. He explained that Iranians believe that if they die in this fighting they will directly enter into heaven. Tavernier recorded that when the king left the square, the group of processionists left the square and paraded through thoroughfares and alleys. If two groups found themselves face to face at a junction, a fight would break out, because each group wanted priority over the other.[15]

The historical records clearly show that the urban division was a sociopolitical issue during the late Safavid era. For example, Calmard (1996) has referred to a statement by Father Krusinski (1675–1756) who argued that the Heydari–Nemati division was based on Shah Abbas Safavid's policy to create artificially opposed parties in all cities, called Pelenk and Felenk. Calmard has explained that not only Shah Abbas the First, but also other Safavid rulers after him, encouraged the feud between two social groups in cities. This policy served the Safavids in keeping political power within safe margins. Calmard, like other historians, explained that the tension and contests between the two factions annually reached its climax during Muharram (Calmard, 1996: 147).

The Heydari–Nemati division was a well-established social constitution in Iranian cities during the Qajar era (r. 1781–1925), and it seems that the idea of Sufi division had already elapsed. There are extensive historical accounts that described urban division in different parts of the country, from Shiraz, Shushtar and Meybod, to Kerman, Qazvin, Ardabil and Tabriz[16] (e.g. see Mirjafari, 1979). The Heydari–Nemati division as a social constitution is reported by Seyyed Abdullah Da'ei Dezfuli (r. 1745–1840), a local scholar who frequently discussed the Heydari and Nemati localities of Dezful in his book (Da'ei Dezfuli, 1826). Sir John Malcolm explained that the Qajar dynasty made no effort to stop the conflict between the two factions but used the conflict to its own advantage to impose its authority on the Iranian population. He noted that the tension and fighting between the two urban factions was ritualized, thus taking on a symbolic nature, and would reach a violent peak during Muharram. Describing the landscape of Muharram during the Qajar era, he wrote:

> The division of the chief cities into wards, with the names of Hyderee and Neamutee, which one author has ascribed to the policy of Shah Abbas the Great, still exists, and continues to excite equal animosity to what it did at former periods. There is at all times a jealousy between these parties; but during the three last days of the Mohurrum they attack each other with violence. The object for which they contend appears to be merely the honour of triumph. If a mosque is decorated by one party, the other, if they can, drive them from it, and destroy the flags or ornaments which have been put up. (Malcolm, 1829: 593)

There are extensive historical accounts about the violence between the Heydari and Nemati factions during Muharram. However, the alleged Safavid and Qajarid policy to maintain the two factions is not often contextualized appropriately in relation to the local ruling system and the power struggles among urban elites. Dezful, like many other cities, was governed based on several boroughs and by elite landlord families who teamed up as Heydari and Nemati. The local ruling system was often referred to as 'khankhani' and characterized based on constant competition and struggle among local governor families or khans. The famous landlord families in Dezful during the late Qajar era were the Sohrabi, Zahir, Rashidian and Emad in the Heydari ward, and Moezi, Mostowfi, Asef, Qotb and Tahmasebi in the Nemati ward. On the one hand, these landlord families tried to maintain their authority over boroughs, as their authority could be challenged by local communities. On the other hand, they ultimately competed with other families to gain more political power and to be recognized by the shah and his court. This recognition not only established their political position in cities, but more importantly granted and secured their control over country estates that were the source of power and wealth.

Here, I am purposely looking at landlord families rather than individual khans. The head of a landlord family represents the authority of his family, who indeed played a crucial role in establishing the socio-political and financial status of the family. The heads of most influential families were either appointed or recognized as the governor of the city. However, all male members of elite families were honoured with the title of khan, which con-tributed to maintaining the authority of their family over boroughs, localities and their country estates. This contribution was particularly important for those elite families that ruled large boroughs comprised of several localities. For example, Haj Gholam-Reza Gholami (b. 1932) noted how the borough of Masjed, that included several localities, was governed by several khans who were members of an extended family. He explained:

> In the borough of Masjed there were several Khans: Haj Abbass Khan Asef, and Majid Khan Asef, from the Sartip family. Agha Nezam Mostowfi was in the other side of the borough;[17] each of them had an area under their rule. Moreover, Haj Khosrow Khan [Asef] was in Chouleeioun[18] that was also a part of the Masjid. (Interviewed in Febraury 2006, Dezful)

The authority of landlord families, at borough and city levels, was con-stantly negotiated and challenged. For example, the locality of Seeyah-poushan rioted against the authority of the local governor Heydar-Khuneh during the late nineteenth century, and became an independent borough in Dezful.[19] At the city level, the Asef family were the most influential landlord family in the late nineteenth century. Asad Khan, a member of this family, was appointed as the city governor (*kalantar*) by Nezam al-Saltaneh[20] in 1890, and received the title of 'Sartip'. Ahmad Shah Qajar honoured Haj Abbass Khan, Asad Khan's son, with the royal title of Asef al-Mamalek[21] in 1923.[22] However, soon after, the Mostowfi family and then the Qotb family established their supremacy in Dezful as the most influential landlord family. Interestingly, the landlord families were politically networking even for the recognition of their authority over boroughs by the shah's court. For exam-ple, it seems that while the Asef family were gradually losing their authority over the city, they tried to keep their authority over their stronghold, the

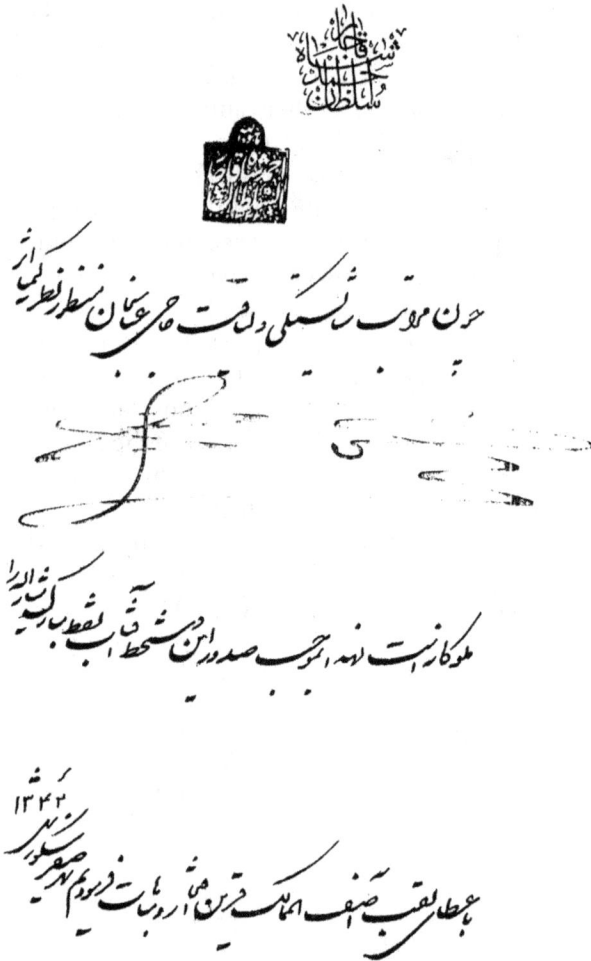

**FIGURE 3.1** Ahmad Shah Qajar honoured Haj Abbass Khan with the royal title of Asef al-Mamalek, letter dated 1923. By courtesy of Ezat-ullah Asef-pour.

borough of Masjid in Dezful. One of the documents that Ezat-ullah Asef-pour kindly gave me from their family collection was a letter stamped by the minister of war,[23] dated 1914. In this document the minister announced Haji Abbass Khan as the head and seigneur of the borough of Masjid, and asked local people to recognize him as such.

The power struggle among landlord families was mostly over agricultural estates that were historically the source of political power and wealth in Iran. The framework of land ownership is often studied in relation to Iranian rural studies. However, this subject is critically relevant to understanding

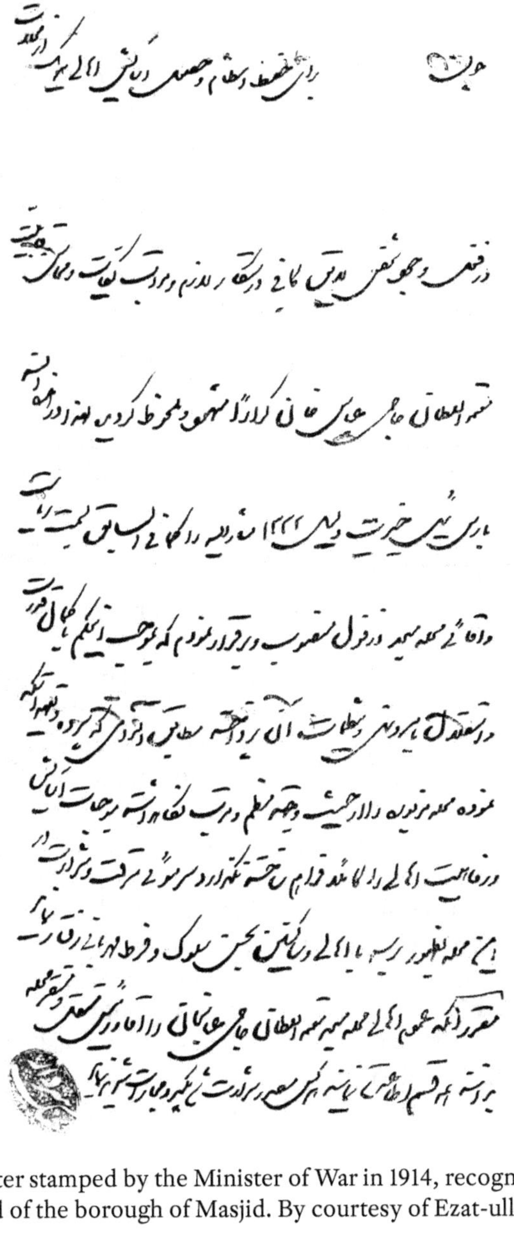

*[Handwritten Persian letter]*

**FIGURE 3.2** Letter stamped by the Minister of War in 1914, recognizing Haji Abbass Khan as the head of the borough of Masjid. By courtesy of Ezat-ullah Asef-pour.

the dynamics of Iranian cities as the local governing system and urban landlordism were entwined. The following discussion not only addresses this subject, but also explains why landlord families historically played a more important role in Dezful than in many other Iranian cities.

## Urban Landlordism and the Struggle for Power

Country lands were classified in five categories: (1) *khaleseh* or state land, also known as *mamalek*; (2) *khasseh* or crown land; (3) *vaqfi* (endowment) land; (3) private land, known as *molk* or *arbabi*; and finally (5) dead land which is known as *mavat* in Farsi (Floor, 1998; Lambton, 1953, 1969).[24] For example, according to Salmanzadeh and Jones (1979: 155) during the 1960s, out of 169 villages, studied in Dezful, 159 villages[25] were privately owned. There were two *khaleseh* villages and eight endowment villages. Private properties were managed by owners, legally known as landlords, and the other lands were managed by someone who was not the owner but was in charge of managing them. The managers of 'endowment lands' was called *motavali*, or overseer, who were from the elite clergy class. State lands were usually given in *tuyul* (fiefs) and held by *tuyuldar* (holders). Crown lands and death lands were managed by the state; however, they were given in fiefs as well. A large part of the country was alienated and managed in the form of fiefs during the Qajar dynasty (Lambton, 1953), which shows the significance of fiefs in the country. Estates were given in fiefs to elite individuals or families to hold, as payment for services to the state or in order to collect tax and share it with the state (e.g. see Najmabadi, 1987: 43). Generally, as Lambton (1953) explains, the landowning class included both landlords and landholders. Sometimes landholders became landowners when the shah became weak or the holder became powerful. Lambton (1969: 21–22) even argued that the conversion of a landholder to landowner happened in the case of endowment lands.

The framework of landowning was under despotic rule, therefore holding and owning land was not a right, rather it was a privilege granted by the shah: 'Although lands could be sold, inherited and bestowed upon others, the security of property only came from the shah's recognition of somebody's claim to a piece of land' (Floor, 1998). As Moghadam (1996) notes, when landlords lost their political power they would lose their ownership of private lands as well. The rise of a new dynasty was usually accompanied by the redistribution of land in favour of the new ruling elites[26] (see Lambton, 1953: 77–104, 129–50; 1969: 224–52), because land was the key source of power.

The interrelationship between land ownership and political power is well illustrated in the oral history of Seeyah-poushan, narrated by Morteza Khan Sohrabi and H. Mohammad Amir-Gholami (both interviewed in February 2006, Dezful). The Seeyah-poushan locality became an independent borough in Dezful after a riot in the late nineteenth century. The riot was led by a very brave young man, Sohrab. When the riot succeeded, the seniors of the locality asked Sohrab to become the khan (governor) of the locality.

But he replied: 'I do not own any land; how can I be a khan without land?' The seniors of the locality bought the huge estate of Sabili, registered it in his name and appointed him as the khan. This land symbolized his social support and political authority; the land ownership politically established and financially maintained Sohrab's authority as the local governor. Moreover, he could not compete with other local governors without social, financial and political resources.

Floor (1998) has explained that all owners, holders and overseers of land were generally referred to as landlords, constituting the most powerful social class in the country.[27] In the case of Dezful, although landlord families had owned estates, to a greater degree they were land holders. For example, Haj Mirza-Ali Hanoosh (b. 1921) explained this point when he talked about his family's agricultural activities:

> Our lands were in Zovaa that is in the vicinities of Shush. We leased the lands and ran our family agriculture. These lands were really good and fertile and belonged to Nezam al-Saltaneh[28] who was in Tehran. Aga Nezam Mostowfi, Anayat-ullah Khan Tahmasebi and Shaikh khalaf [of Shush region] were Nezam al-Saltaneh's agents (*kargozar*). They were holding and letting lands on his behalf. ... we paid landlord share which was 1/8 or 1/10 of crop depending on the type of plantation. (Interviewed in September 2005, Dezful)[29]

In the case that Hantoosh described, the local landlord families, who held the land, collected the income and shared it with Nezam al-Saltaneh Mafi, who was the prime minister during the late Qajar era. The overseers of large endowment estates were also very influential. For example, the Moezi family, an elite clergy family, was the overseer of several endowment estates (village) and ruled the borough of Qaleh, one of the biggest boroughs of the city. As Lambton also emphasized (1969: 20), the landlord class, as the most affluent social class, was to a large extent an urban class. The landlord families acted as local governors in the city, while they had full authority over their peasants and even wielded extensive judicial powers.

As discussed, landlord status was not secure and even private lands were cruelly converted to crown or state land (e.g. see Lambton, 1953: 154). In this landscape landlords practiced complex socio-economic and political gymnastics. The landlord families were in constant competition with other local elites to have a good relationship with the royal court in order to receive and secure the privilege of owning or holding lands. Having the upper hand in this competition was also inter-related with the acceptance of the landlords' political authority by local communities. In other words, the local communities were a social resource of a landlord family in competition with rival local elites. In this complex power struggle, the landlord families teamed up into Heydari and Nemati parties. Therefore, Perry (1999) describes Heydari and

Nemati as two 'moieties' (halves) that were like two parties in a democratic system that competed with each other for greater power.

The Heydari–Nemati division was not limited to cities; this socio-political division was extended into the countryside by urban landlord families. Therefore, each village was considered as a Heydari or Nemati village. In other words, each ward of the city has a strong social bound with the countryside. When tension escalated between Heydari and Nemati boroughs in cities, it was common that villagers were mobilize to support their urban allies in fighting against the opposition boroughs. Unlike medieval Europe where the city comprised an integrated society that competed with feudal rule, traditional Iranian urban society was not an integrated social organization – it was divided into two competitive moieties.

The significance of urban landlordism in Dezful to the discussion at hand is even more important than in other Iranian cities. While merchants and traders were part of the elites in many Iranian cities, elite merchants as an affluent social class did not exist in Dezful. This made the supremacy of the landlord families in Dezful even stronger. Ashraf (1969) explains that merchants were part of the urban elite class that included clergies and local governors. He explains that the elite merchants held a unique position. On the one hand, they were at the top of the bazaar's financial hierarchy. On the other hand, their social status distinguished them from bazaar shopkeepers and craftsmen who bonded together in unions. In the broader social landscape, the merchants were socio-politically inferior to members of the clergy and local governors, even though they sometimes had a superior financial status. Elsewhere, Ashraf explained that merchants closely allied themselves with religious elites, which bonded the bazaar and the mosque together (Ashraf, 1988). The merchants established their social power through sponsoring the construction of religious places and financially backing religious rituals. This historical socio-financial setting can be seen in the organization of the typical Iranian bazaar that includes not only commercial but also religious and other public places (e.g. see Bonine, 1989: 21). This made the bazaar the heart of financial and socio-religious life in most Iranian traditional cities.

The urban economy of Dezful was based on agriculture and the bazaar did not contribute to the urban economy as was the case in many other Iranian cities. Several historical accounts during the nineteenth century indicate that the city had an 'insignificant' bazaar. Haj Abul al-Ghaffar Najm mol-Molk visited Dezful in 1882 and noted that 'Dezful does not have a credible Bazaar' (Najm mol-Molk, 1962: 23). The same thing was reported to be true of Shushtar, Dezful's sister city. Curzon, who visited Shushtar in 1889, wrote: 'There are no khans, or caravanserais in bazaar, for merchants such as are usually found in Oriental cities' (Curzon, 1892: 368). The bazaar in Dezful can be described as solely a retail bazaar, while the typical Iranian bazaars were socio-commercial complexes that contained retail and commercial spaces, as well as all religious and public places. The bazaar in Dezful was a kind of petty bazaar, partly since the city was not connected to the historical network of trade routes. The trade routes included the Royal Road (Shahi Road), which had national importance, and the Spice and Silk Roads, which were the most important trans-regional networks connecting India and China to Europe.

Najm mol-Molk and Dieulafoy (1887) reported that local industries in Dezful, such as indigo production, suffered from limited access to the network of trade routes. As a result, the local industries and trades remained underdeveloped. Consequently, neither craftsmen nor local traders obtained enough financial status to be considered as an affluent urban class with a major financial impact in shaping socio-religious urban life. This was not a unique condition, as it could be observed in many other cities, like Birjand in northeastern Iran. The bazaar in Dezful was mainly a cluster of retail shops and small workshops and did not encompass major religious, cultural and public places. The typical Iranian bazaars, such as the bazaar in Kashan or Ardabil, were always the most significant places for Muharram rituals and were even one of the destinations for processions. In contrast, the bazaar in Dezful has never played a role in organizing the rituals.

In this context, the landlord families hold a unique social and political position in the city of Dezful. This position was enhanced as many of the families possessed the religious status of being *sayyed*, meaning they were decedents of the Prophet Mohammad, an important status in orthodox traditional society. For example, the Qotb family, one of the most influential landlord families, was *sayyed*. As mentioned, the borough of Qaleh was even ruled by an elite clergy family, the Moezi family. Therefore, the religious status of some elite families added a religious dimension to the tensions between boroughs and localities. For example, Najm mol-Molk (1962) reported in the late nineteenth century that the city elite were surrounded by fanatic subjects and gangs who were not afraid of killing people from rival boroughs.

## The Socio-spatial Logic of Muharram Processions in Dezful

Muharram rituals begin from the 1st of Muharram and intensify between the 7th and the 10th days. The last two days, Taso'a (the 9th) and Ashura (the 10th), are particularly important for the commemoration. The local mosques or *husseinyeh-s* host the Muharram service sessions during this period. The centre of the localities, which is either a local square or an open space adjacent to the local religious places, are where all kinds of performative rituals take place.

The performative rituals in Dezful included all kinds of symbolic performances that imitate the battle of Karbala, such as *choo-zani*, sword-fighting and the dancing of the symbolic flag, known locally as *alam-yaraq* or *alam-bozi* (playing flag). As explained in chapter two, *choo-zani* is a performance in which participants flock in a circle, each holding two short logs of wood about 10–15 cm long. They beat the logs rhythmically while walking and bouncing to the beat of music, often played by drums. The sound of beating logs in this abstract dancing performance imitates the sounds of battle. The sword-fighting, locally called *shemshiel-sopar* (sword-shield), is also a dance-like performance using either swords or wooden sticks, imitating the battle of Karbala. The most common performance was, however, *alam-yaraq*. The *alam* of the localities is a symbolic flag of 3–9 metres in height (or sometimes even taller), ornamented by hundreds of shawls. The flag symbolizes the union of localities and is carried throughout the procession. *Alam-yaraq* is a performance that symbolizes the struggle to keep the flag of Imam Hussein flying in the battle of Karbala. The person who has the best skill in lifting and keeping the flag balanced is known as the locality's *alam-dar* (flag-holder). *Alam-yaraq* is performed every evening during Muharram, when local youths gather to show off their skill in lifting and dancing around the flag. This performance is orchestrated with drumming and playing the *sorna* (a kind of traditional oboe). These performances at local squares often attract a local crowd of spectators, a kind of introduction for the procession.

The Muharram processions can be categorized into minor processions which take place during the first days of commemoration, and the main procession on Ashura day. The processions mainly attract crowds around the 7th of Muharram when the commemoration intensifies. The processions begin at local squares where other performances also take place and attract a crowd. But generally, the call for the procession is traditionally announced by drumming at a local square. Traditionally, the minor processions were carried towards the community places of neighbouring localities with whom they have social intimacy. These minor processions also visited or passed by the house of wealthy families, where Muharram service sessions were held. These affluent families were those who financially supported the union, and the visits were to pay respect and express loyalty to those families.

Interviewees across different localities in Dezful explained that the union visited the houses of a few landlord families within their borough. But the processions on the 9th of Muharram traditionally visited the house of the borough's most influential landlord/khan who is considered the local ruler. The visitation symbolically registers the authority of landlord families; it was also a ritualized way to collect money from landlord families. On those occasions, the head of the family had attached some cash to the symbolic flag of the unions. Habib-ullah Qotb recalled the time when the local processions visited his family's house. He was born in 1930 and graduated from MIT. His father was the most influential landlord in the 1940s in Dezful. The Qotb family resided in the borough of Eastern Sahrabedar in Nemati part. He recalled that

> Each locality had an *alam*, ... the *alam* of Sahrabedar was *Alam-i Abbas* which was the most famous and sacred flag in the city ... it was a rule that they carried and located the flag in front of our house. Then my mother and other members of family went on the roof top and attached some money to the flag. [I was not so keen about this ceremonial but] My family forced me to do this too ... If the flag holder would realize that we did not attach enough money, he would say that the flag is really heavy as you did not attach enough money; so the flag is not going to leave. Then we attached some more money to the flag. (Interviewed in Dezful, February 2006)

Very similar scenes were described by interviewees about different parts of Dezful. For example, Haj Eidi-Mohammad Masoudi (b. 1925), who was raised in a locality in the Heydari part of the city, recalled that

> The procession usually went to landlords' house during the first 10 days. For example, our union used to take the *alam* [flag] to Sayfullah khan Rashidian and located it in his courtyard. Then he and his wife attached some cash to the flag. However, the main procession was toward Roodband Shrine [on Ashura day]. (Interviewed in Dezful, September 2005)

Muharram was a typical liminal period when otherwise uninfluential members of the community had the opportunity to play an important role in their community. During my fieldwork, I interviewed individuals from very diverse social backgrounds, from the traditional elite to poor and even marginalized members of a community. What uninfluential individuals' interviews shared was that they often enjoyed social recognition during Muharram. Uninfluential individuals enjoyed a temporal social status garnered by, for example, being in charge of the locality's symbolic flag (aka flag-holder or *alam-dar*), being known as a skilled drummer or *sorna* player, or being a skilled player in performative rituals. One interviewee (b. 1930) from a very poor family background recalled that he had a very tough life during his late teens as he had to financially support his family. However, his narrative about Muharram demonstrates that it was the most stimulating period of the year. He explained with great excitement that he was very skilled in the sword-fighting performance, therefore he was invited to all localities to join their performances (interviewed in February 2006, Dezful).

The locality's union members gain important social status during Muharram. They decide where the minor processions shall visit. For example,

Yousef-Ali Karami (interviewed in September 2005) explained that their minor processions often visited neighbouring localities with whom they had social intimacy. He explained that the social network of influential union members played a role here. He illustrated his point by mentioning that they always visited the locality of Qaleh as the head of their union was a friend of the person in charge of Qaleh's union.

Although the locality's union arranged the destination of the minor processions, ultimately the landlord/local ruler of a borough could ask the union to visit or not visit the other localities. The landlord families were constantly competing with other elite families and Muharram was a critical occasion for negotiating the power relations and for practicing their superiority over the other landlord families. This competition was among landlord families within and across boroughs, as well as over establishing the supremacy of a landlord family in the city. The socio-political negotiations intensified during Muharram, as it was practically much easier to mobilize the people of localities. Therefore, the tension between and disputes among landlords would reach their climax, inflamed by strong religious feelings that are already elevated during Muharram. Habib-ullah Qotb and Ezat-ullah Asef-pour, both from very influential landlord families, explained that while they had family relationships with other landlord families, there was often tension between them over their estates. For example, Habib-ullah Qotb explained:

> Disagreements and clashes between khans had economic reasons and were based on expansionism in the region. For example, my father had bought 1/3 of the Kootioun estate and the rest of it was rented by Bakhtiari Khans. My uncle, who was from the Asef family, bought two *nokhod*-s [a traditional share unit] of this estate and became shareowner of the estate. This caused a conflict between Qotb and Asef families ... it had been said that it was offense to our ownership. The purchase of two *nokhod*-s of Kootioun easte made 10-12 years struggle between these two families. (H. Qotb, interviewed in Dezful, February 2006)

In another interview H.E. Masoudi explained:

> Each Khan had his own gang and when he had a problem with other Khans, the gangs made a conflict between people by some simple excuses during Muharram rituals. It was the way that each khan was applying his power upon the society and controlled localities. In these conflicts and violence in Muharram rituals, people were breaking the flag of other localities or tearing their drums apart. (Interviewed in September 2005, Dezful)

H.E. Masoudi (b. 1925) also explained that the violence and tension were far more serious during his father's generation in the late nineteenth and the very early twentieth centuries than in his generation. Apart from tension between different localities, violence could also occur if a landlord wanted to exercise his authority over the locality he governed. The khan could refuse permits to the unions that wanted to carry the locality's symbols in the processions. The unions were usually symbolized by an *alam* (symbolic flag), *shaydouneh* (symbolic shrine) or *nakhl* (a symbolic coffin). Ahmad Masoudi (b. 1944) mentioned that his older brother (b. 1918) narrated a story about carrying the symbolic coffin (*nakhl*) of their locality, which was part of a Heydari faction. The coffin was carried through the procession on Ashura day to Roodband shrine in the north of the city. He narrated:

> The khan said that without our permission you should not carry the *nakhl* to Roodband. Youth who were vain, took the *nakhl* by force from the local square. They emotionally carried it while running through narrow alleys, and a poor nomadic man, who carried bushes, [was] stuck between the *nakhl* and a wall and died. Further down the road, the landlord assigned an ambushed gunman to one of the covered alleys and he shot [to] death the man who was reading the holy Quran on the *nakhl*. It means that the tension over carrying the *nakhl* killed two innocent men for nothing.

This landscape shows a liminal time when complex social negotiations were practised. Uninfluential and ordinary individuals were empowered and enjoyed temporary social authority. However, the elites did not lose their social position, rather they fulfilled and performed their authority in more symbolic ways. They negotiated their superiority over other elite families by mobilizing people through the local unions and processions. The elite families could not compete without the social support of the local community. Therefore, while the tension was because of power struggles among urban elites, most people perceived the social tension during Muharram as a competition between local communities. Even the socially informed interviewees, who blamed landlord families for social conflict in Dezful, talked extensively about the role of urban violence as a way of practising their social superiority over other localities and boroughs during Muharram.

The minor processions did not have defined destinations and had much more flexible schedules and routes. However, the final processions on Ashura day were much more defined event. Ashura day was when socio-religious emotion reached its climax, enhancing social solidarity among members of each community. The procession routes on Ashura day particularly demonstrated that urban society was constituted based on two moieties. In Dezful the final processions of localities were organized within the two separate territories of Heydari and Nemati. The procession on Ashura day is a symbolic funeral thus the final processions of localities went towards two separate cemeteries in Dezful. The final processions of Heydari localities went towards Roodband cemetery, named after the shrine of Sultan Ali Roodbandi. This cemetery was outside the city wall, at the northern margin of the city. The destination of Nemati processions, however, was the

Abu-a'la shrine and cemetery, locally pronounced as Bul-a'la, at the eastern margin of the city. I discussed the route of final processions with every single interviewee who could recall the traditional procession routes in Dezful. The aggregation of all the data is illustrated in Map 3.2, which depicts the social division in Dezful very well.

The Heydari–Nemati division was physically invisible in the city, but it could be traced through many social indicators. Social life was predominantly localized within each part of the city. Marriages were often arranged within a family or borough; many interviewees explained that people rarely married someone from another borough. The predominantly localized urban life and the lack of interaction between different parts of cities resulted in diverse local dialects in each city. My interviewees in all case studies talk about the fact that one's affiliation to a certain part of the city could be quickly identified by their distinct accent. Such linguistic diversities is conceivable in large/mega cities; however, it is interesting to have such phenomena occur in medium or small cities. Nonetheless, the organization of final Muharram processions (Map 3.4) in particular highlights the urban divisions[30] and illustrates the hidden Heydari–Nemati border. This border is hidden in the city map, and even complex mathematical modelling and analyses of the city structure would not directly detect it (e.g. see Masoudi Nejad, 2013), while the division of the city was extensively addressed by interviewees. Interestingly, the map of the final procession routes clearly captures the division and illustrates that Dezful, like other Iranian cities, was not a socially integrated system but was instead constituted on the basis of two rival moieties.

The strong social bond among people of each locality and the division of urban communities into two parts were two significant characteristics that manifested in the Ashura day processions. However, the organization of the final procession routes was related to a much more complex social reality. The spectrum of social relationships includes degrees of intimacy among localities within each part of the city which can be described as greyscales between solidarity and division. Van der Veer (1994: 11) argues that religious rituals create boundaries by defining a *self* and bond the members of a community together. Simultaneously, the created boundaries separate them from *others*, weakening the social relations with *others*. I agree with Van der Veer since the solidarity among members of a community obviously energized and highlighted the urban division during Muharram. However, social intimacy with others is also emphasized during the ritual time. The social intimacy among the localities cannot be described as social solidarity, as each local community emphasized their own distinct identity and distinguished themselves from others through the rituals. However, while they refused to be dissolved into other neighbouring localities, the ritual mediated the maintenance of intimacy with others. The relationship between localities

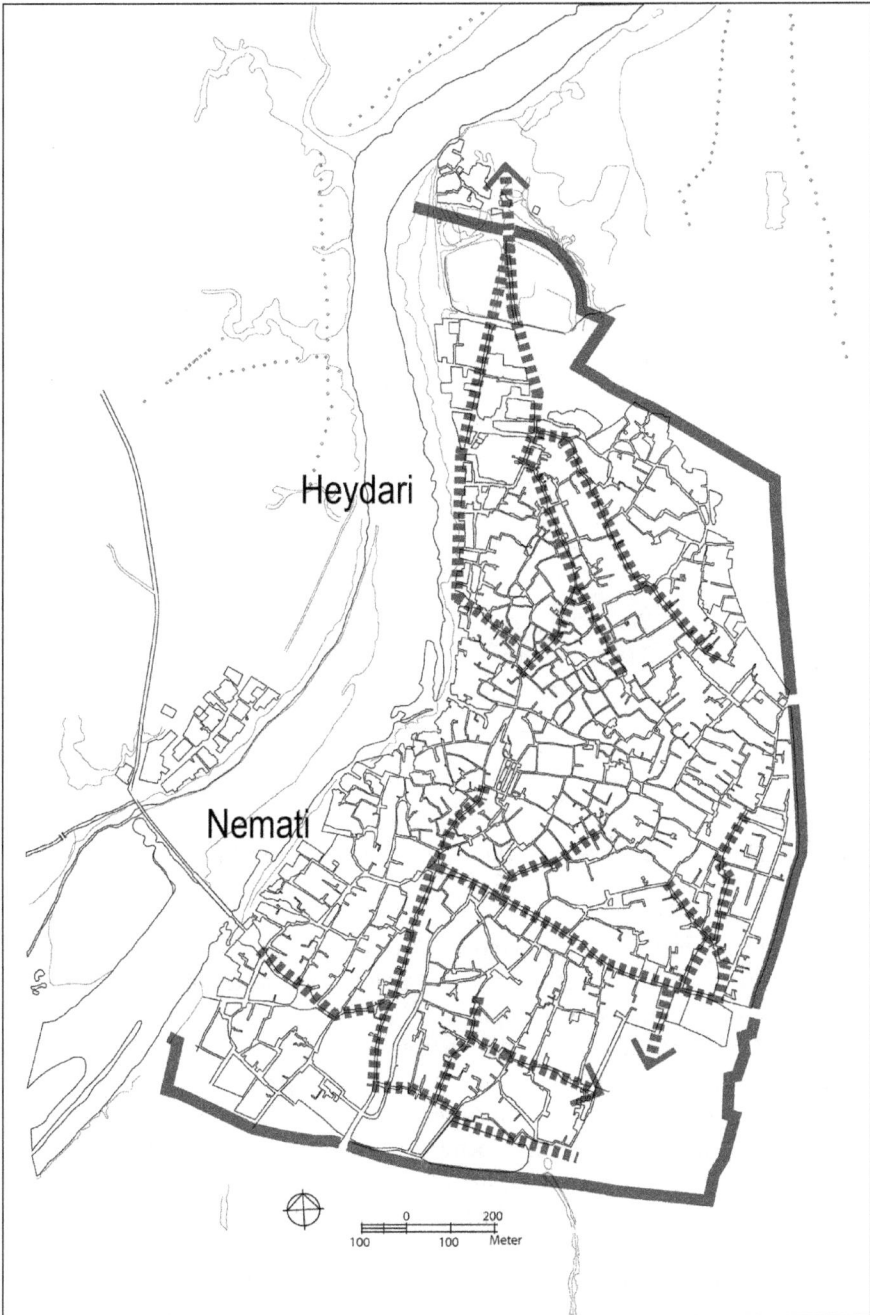

**MAP 3.2** The aggregation of procession routes on Ashura day, depicting the social division in Dezful. Map by the author.

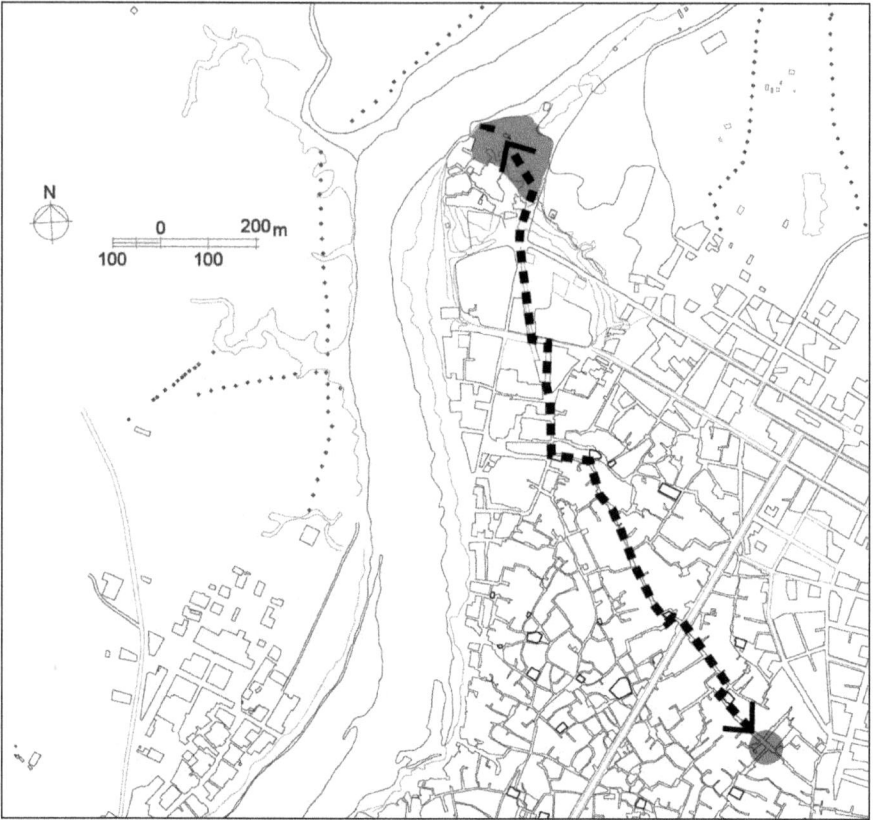

**MAP 3.3** The procession route of Qopi-Agha Husseini on Ashura day. Map by the author.

within the Heydari or Nemati parts was not free from tension. Therefore, the intimacy among the localities was also negotiated, and tension could arise between two localities or boroughs.

The social division shapes the spatial organization of the final procession. However, social intimacy among localities plays a significant role in selecting the final procession route on Ashura day. The localities plan their procession route to pass certain other localities with whom they have relationships, rather than simply taking the shortest way to the final procession destination. For example, according to M. Montazeri (b. 1950, interviewed in April 2006, Dezful),[31] the final procession of the locality of Qopi-Agha Husseini neither takes the shortest route toward Roodband Shrine nor passes the Seeyah-poushan (locality). They run their procession throughout Kornassioun, Kheymeh-gah[32] and Doo'eioun,[33] demonstrating their social intimacy with those localities (Map 3.3). In this case the procession went

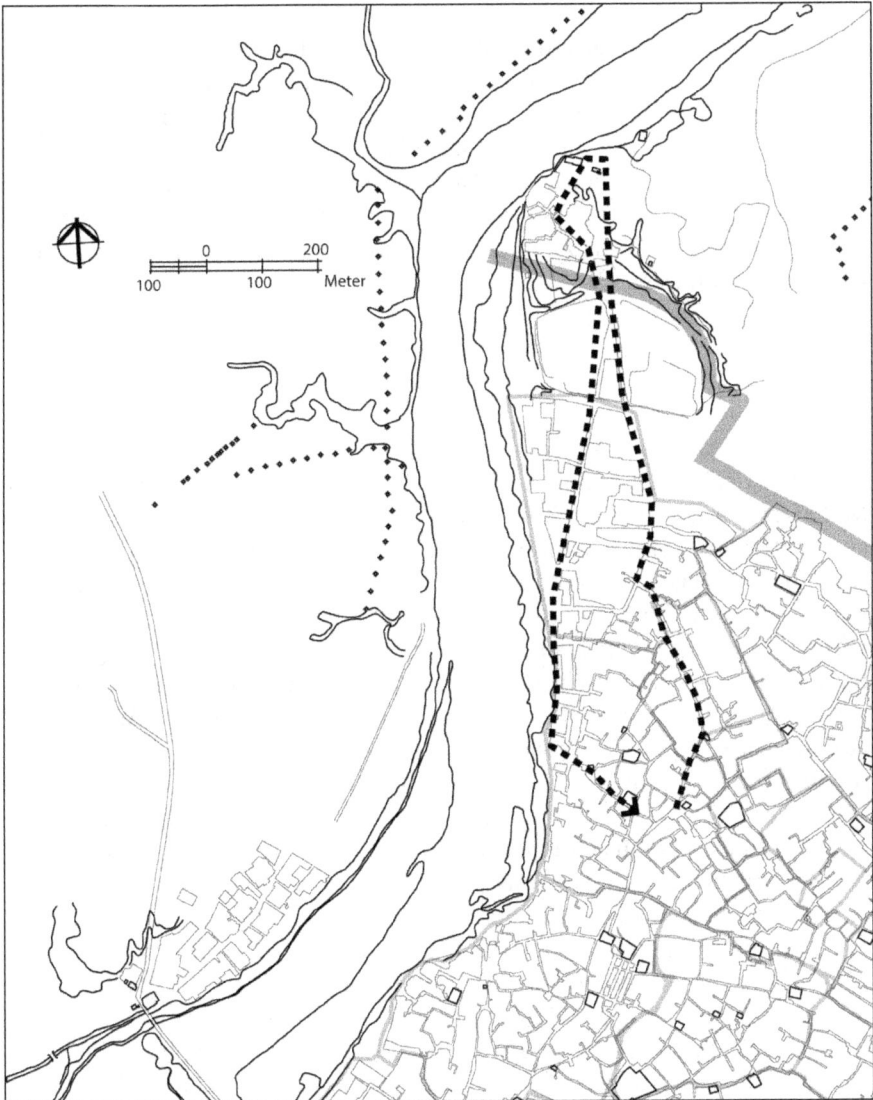

**MAP 3.4** The procession route of Lourioun on Ashura day. Map by the author.

to the shrine and returned via the same route. In many other localities the procession of Ashura is carried out throughout looped routes. For example, Map 3.4 shows the procession of the Lourioun locality. As mentioned, social intimacy was also subject to the negotiation among elites and common people, which was reflected in the route of their procession towards the cemetery that they visited.

This leads to the concluding point that the organization of Muharram processions was a spatial system shaped by complex social negotiations. The Muharram processions created a space in which social solidarity, intimacy and division were preformed, maintained and negotiated. The spatial organization of processions was a performed space that mediated social negotiation. It cannot be conceptualized as the passive result of social negotiation or an inactive mirror/representation of urban society. It was an active part of urban negotiation to shape, maintain or change social relationships among urban communities.

## Conclusion

The very nature of discussions throughout this chapter shows how the socio-political constitution of the city and the spatial organization of Muharram rituals were traditionally entwined. The articulation of the social and spatial logic of processions intrinsically calls for a very detailed understanding of social constitution, urban economy, and urban governing. In return, all these dimensions of traditional Iranian cities cannot be captured without exploring Muharram rituals. The discussions throughout this chapter make it clear that Muharram rituals were discursively aimed at addressing the Ashura tragedy as well as social and political agendas. The Ashura tragedy is narrated in service sessions by orators, the battel of Karbala is imitated by diverse performances, and the final processions on Ashura day are the symbolic funeral of Karbala martyrdoms. Muharram rituals can naturally be considered as religious ceremonies since they are developed around a religious myth. Nonetheless, these rituals were undoubtedly socio-politically charged and the ritual dynamics were driven by socio-political agendas.

The Muharram processions of localities, as a collective performance, created solidarity among community members and were a spatial mediator for the practice of social intimacy between neighbouring localities. The landlord families practised and imposed their local authority through the rituals, and the negotiations of power with other local elites intensified during Muharram. The final processions on Ashura day are a symbolic funeral, but the spatial arrangement of procession routes was aimed at performing social solidarity, intimacy and division. It is not hard to see how the story behind the ritual, aka the Shi'i myth of Ashura, is pushed into the background and social agendas predominate in the logic of procession routes. This does not mean that the Ashura tragedy loses its significance, rather it addresses the fact that the spatial arrangement of procession routes has a socio-political logic rather than a religious backbone. Therefore, instead of being a solely religious ritual, Muharram processions can convincingly be considered as 'urban rituals'. This means that Muharram rituals were heavily involved in the process of socio-political negotiations that shaped social relations by which urban society was constituted.

The discussions throughout this chapter show how urban society was constituted on the basis of the social cohesion of local communities, social intimacy among urban localities, and the division of localities into Heydari and Nemati wards. By exploring the Muharram processions, we can reveal the social constitution and complexity of socio-political negotiations. These discussions also show that the dynamic of Muharram rituals was by no means driven by the class struggle. Each community, aka locality, is composed of very diverse social classes and each traditional locality appears as a micro-society. In the traditional urban landscape, the power struggle was among urban communities, not social classes. I would argue that the struggle for power was driven by community struggle. This form of power struggle was the social consequence of the traditional local governing system that manifested itself as the Heydari–Nemati division. This is not to ignore the role of social classes in the traditional Muharram rituals, but rather to highlight the fact that historically, the social dynamics were not driven by class struggle. The following chapter will show how this landscape of power struggles was gradually changed by the establishment of the modern Iranian state in the 1920s, the abolition of the local ruling system and the rise of the middle class.

## NOTES

1. This name should technically be transliterated as Neᶜmati. However, as the pronunciation of 'Nemati' is very close to the Persian pronunciation of the name, I prefer to use simplified transliteration.
2. Pronounced as Foo-laa-di-ioun.
3. This is the local pronunciation of *doulatmand*.
4. Traditionally the payment of services and labours related to agriculture, e.g. from landlords to peasants, were paid based on a share of the crops.
5. Pronounced as See-yah-poo-shan.
6. Pronounced as Kor-na-see-ioun.
7. *Gardani* means taking out or moving along.
8. Pronounced as kat-ka-toon.
9. Pronounced as sar-darah.
10. Pronounced as Sa-ki-ioun.
11. This is based on an interview with Haj M. Amir-Gholami (b. 1921) and Morteza Khan Sohrabi (b. 1923), both interviewed in February 2016.
12. Qaleh means castle, pronounced as Qa-leh.
13. Pronounced as sah-ra-be-dar.
14. Jean Baptiste Tavernier, Baron d'Aubonne (1605–1689). His travelogue was translated and published in Persian in 1957. However, the oldest English copy of his

travelogue that I have reviewed was published during 1684–1688 in London by Moses Pitt. The copy is held at the library of SOAS, University of London.

15. For a full description, see Tavernier (1684: 160–163), and for a Farsi translation, see Tavernier (1957: 412–416).

16. The social division was predominantly described as a Heydari–Nemati division. However, it could refer to divisions between various religious schools of thought, such as Sheikhi vs Motashraeh, Akhbari vs Osuli or Sheikhi vs Sufi (Azkaei, 1985; Kagaya, 1990; Mirjafari, 1979), which are different schools of Shi'i jurisprudence. For example, according to Kagaya the division in the city of Qazvin was based on Sheikhi vs Motashraeh.

17. As explained in the next paragraph, Sartip and Asef were surnames of the same family. Moreover, in another interview Ezat-ullah Asef-pour (February 2006 in Dezfuli) explained that the Asef and Mostowfi families were part of an extended family. Nonetheless, a dispute arose between these families over their estates as well.

18. Pronounced as [choo-lee-ioun].

19. This is based on an interview with Morteza Khan Sohrabi and H. Mohammad Amir-Gholami who narrated the oral history of the event (both interviewed in February 2006, Dezful).

20. Mirza Hussein-quli Khan Nezam al-Saltaneh Mafi (previously known as Saad al-Mulk). Nezam al-Saltaneh himself owned very large agricultural estates around Dezful in the north of Khuzestan.

21. *Asef* literally means 'minister' and *mamlek* means 'the state's lands' or 'the government's estates'.

22. This is based on the copy of two royal documents that Ezatullah Asef-pour kindly gave me when I interviewed him in February 2006 in Dezful.

23. The minister of war would go on to abolish the Qajar dynasty and establish the Pahlavi dynasty.

24. Lands were classified in different ways; for example, Salmanzadeh (1976) and Salmanzadeh and Jones (1979: 114) have categorized rural lands into four types: public domain (Khaliseh land), crown land, endowment land and private land. See also Najmabadi (1987: 43).

25. The unite of agricultural land traditionally was the 'village' rather than a metric size. For more, see Salmanzadeh & Jones (1979: 113).

26. This can be seen as an arbitrary description and would be inconceivable in modern times. However, the forceful abolishing of land ownership was experienced when the Pahlavi dynasty was established in the 1920s and after the 1979 revolution in Iran.

27. For more details on each landlord class, see Floor (1998: 107–25) and Moghadam (1996: 31) see also Lambton (1953: 153–55).

28. This refers to Nezam al-Saltaneh Mafi, who was the prime minister during the late Qajar era.

29. Later in his interview, he explained that these families later bought the estates.

30. Nonetheless, in some cases, such as Isfahan, due to the presence of an absolute authority, the king, Heydari and Nemati processions shared some common spaces such as the Royal Square. In these circumstances, as described by Tavernier, the competition between the two parties was demonstrated by symbolically fighting in front of the king at the Royal Square.

31.  Mr Montazeri was raised in the Qopi-Agha Husseini locality. He is passionate about the oral history and culture of Dezful. He was hosting a show on the local radio station about local history and culture during my fieldwork in 2005–2006.
32.  Pronounced as Khey-me-gah.
33.  Pronounced as Doo-ei-ioun.

CHAPTER 4

# THE RITE OF URBAN PASSAGE

The transformation of Iranian cities was part of the modernization project initiated by the modern Pahlavi state (founded in the 1920s). The modern Iranian state wished to engineer Iranian society and restructure the shape of cities as the way to create a new society. The modern state cartelized political power, abolished local ruling systems, established the civil bureaucracy and achieved a state monopoly in industrial and commerce sectors. Furthermore, it secularized and centralized the judicial system. The modern state also introduced secular national education and a national dress code. The most visible manifestation of the new era was the drastic change in the shape of Iranian cities. The organic and irregular structures of historical Iranian cities were engineered and transfigured over a very short period during the early 1930s. However, the transformation of urban society advanced in an unpredicted process throughout a longer period. The Iranian moderniza-tion project triggered social transformation but it was an indeterminate and complex process.

Iranian urban transformation cannot be reduced into only a few aspects. However, it is encapsulated by the end of local ruling systems and the Heydari–Nemati division in Iranian cities. As has been extensively discussed in the previous chapter, the Heydari–Nemati division and the traditional local ruling system were intimately entwined, a particular characteristic of traditional Iranian cities. The transformation of traditional cities was not a smooth process, but a tense and violent transition. In fact, the social and physical transformation of Iranian cities came about through a process asso-ciated with two-fold tension: state and social violence. The new state used military force to harshly suppress autonomous local powers and abolish the local ruling system that relied on landlord families. The physical trans-formation of Iranian cities was also executed in a harsh way. As social and political historians such as Anasari (2003) and Banani (1961) explain, Reza Shah's modernization project was a set of reform programmes that were imposed on an unwilling and conservative religious society in an authoritarian manner. Chehabi (2004) argues that the 'dress codes' in Iran are a great example of a modernization reform that was imposed from above. He argues that Reza Shah wanted to transform Iranian society from a traditional one to a 'civilized' one by creating 'new men'. There was no time to gradually create 'new men' so he urged drastic changes by force.

The new political landscape, in which the traditional local ruling system was abolished, stimulated the grassroots social demand for a new social order and the abolishment of the 'social authority' of landlord families. In Dezful, the transition from traditional social order to a new urban reality was not a smooth, but a rather violent process during the early 1950s. This violent process left a bitter taste in the oral history of Dezful. However, it is also celebrated since it is associated with the abolishment of the authority of landlord families, the ending of the Heydari–Nemati division, and social conciliation among urban localities. As in many other cities, the end of urban violence and the integration of Heydari and Nemati localities were ritualized by establishing new Muharram procession routes. In this chapter, I describe the spatial re-arrangement of processions as *the rite of urban passage*. This rite mediated the passage from the traditional divided urban society into a new social make-up in which the historical Heydari and Nemati moieties are united.

The idea of Iranian modernization is rooted in the Iranian Constitutional Revolution (1905–1909). Therefore, this chapter begins with a short discussion on the emergence of the Iranian modernization concept during the late nineteenth and early twentieth centuries. The first section that is about the broad landscape of Iranian Modernization, also deals with the specific case of Dezful. The second section is a brief discussion about the morphological transformation of Dezful, then the discussion focuses on the violent process of social transformation in this city.

## The Broad Landscape of the Iranian Modernization

The idea of modernization refers to programmes aimed at modernizing societies known as the Third World or undeveloped countries. Modernization projects across the world emphasized diverse aims; however, they shared the idea that economic development, and cultural and political changes were interrelated. As Inglehart (1997) explained, these projects were commonly deterministic, assuming the process of change has a universal and predictable pattern that can be implemented in all kinds of societies. It was claimed that the behaviour of non-Western society could be predicted and coached into adopting the Western paragon and standard (Pappe, 2005). However, history shows that economic development is not necessarily associated with Western social and political development; and social change is far from a predictable and universal process. As Pappe noticed, the first signs of a fundamental challenge to the conventional idea of modernization appeared in the 1970s. He has stated that the 'political scientist and sociologist seemed to be the first to realize that modernization was not as structured and linear [a] process as hitherto conceived' (Pappe, 2005: 7). Soon, modernization as a predictable process of development, and its universal definition were questioned by the argument that every society has its own definition of development. However, when modernization as a historical subject is studied, the questions are less about how it should be defined but how modernization was understood and carried out. For Middle Eastern elites and intellectuals during the late nineteenth and the early twentieth centuries, modernization was all about achieving European development, which was believed to be the result of powerful and centralized states and industrial societies. Many of those intellectuals argued that by introducing Western technology and bureaucracy to the Middle Eastern countries, they could achieve what the Western world had achieved.

As mentioned above, the story of Iranian modernization, as a project, has its roots in the Iranian Constitutional Revolution (1905–1909) that was materialised by the modern Pahlavi state (established in 1925). The Constitutional Revolution was a movement to establish the rule of law, thereby opposing the traditional arbitrary rule of the Iranian monarch. The idea of modernization was not clear for intellectuals and reformists of the nineteenth century, known as Constitutionalists. However, they were looking for a modern army, industry, roads, modern education and health services, as well as modernized cities and the like (Katouzian, 2000). As Ansari argued: 'while Constitutional Revolution introduced many novel ideas into Iranian political discourse, it was the rise of Reza Khan to power which brought the modern to Iran in the material sense, which affected every section of the population' (Ansari, 2003: 2).

The Constitutional Revolution (*enghelab-e mashrouteh*) succeeded in 1906. However, soon the confrontation between Mohammad Ali Shah (r. 1907–1909) and the newly established Parliament led to the shah's coup against the parliament in 1908, causing chaos in the country. The chaos worsened towards the end of First World War (1914–1918), when Russian, Turkish, British and German forces and agents were active in Iran, and tried to benefit from this situation by escalating the tribal revolts in various parts of the country. This extremely chaotic situation, combined with the inefficient Qajarid state, led the country in the dangerous direction of disintegration (Bahar, 1944: 61–66; also see Katouzian, 2003), leading to yet another coup in 1921. In the days following the coup, Ahmad Shah of Qajar (r. 1909–1925) appointed leaders of the coup to positions of power. Reza Khan, one of the coup leaders, became the commander-in-chief of His Majesty's Army and was appointed as minister of war shortly after. Although Reza Khan was not the main leader of the coup, he became the most significant political player in its aftermath. 'Immediately after becoming War Minister in May 1921, he put forward his plan for building a new army. He intended to create a unified, centralized, national army, free of foreign officers' (Cronin, 2003: 38). Within two years, Reza Khan and his modern army became the most influential power in the country, defeating all revolts across the country. In 1923 the last shah of the Qajar dynasty appointed him as prime minister. Reza Khan, now the PM as well as the minister of war and the commander-in-chief of the army, became the most influential figure in the country. In fact, the last Qajar shah did not hold any power, and Reza Khan was recognized as a national hero who ended the chaos. The coup and its aftermath soon led to the overthrow of the Qajar dynasty. The parliament abolished the Qajar dynasty and appointed Reza Khan as the shah of Iran in 1925.

The Constitutional Revolution destroyed traditional despotism in Iran, but the ensuing chaos denied any opportunity for the country to achieve any of the revolution's wishes. However, when the 1921 coup ended the chaos, Reza Shah materialized all the reformists' wishes within a short time. Reza Shah established the Iranian modern state and carried out the drastic changes in a military manner that entirely transformed traditional Iran into modern Iran. Social and political historians, such as Anasari (2003) and Banani (1961), explain that nationalism and secularism (de-Islamization) were the core ideologies of Reza Shah's reforms that ignored and suppressed the socio-cultural and ethnic diversities of the country in order to invent a national state, and rejected the religious values of traditional society.

The military manner in implementation of the modern reforms was linked to Reza Shah's military background, and reformists of the time favoured it. However, the ideology of Iranian modernization, e.g. de-Islamization, was not necessarily his own personal idea: this was associated with a group of intellectual elites who believed modernization and Western secular values were intermingled. Reza Shah used Muharram rituals to establish his social popularity when he was the chief commander of the Royal Qajarid Army, since religious rituals played an important role in legitimizing socio-political authority in religious Iranian society. Bahar reported that

On the 10th of Muharram, the day of murder, the group of Cossacks came to the Bazaar as a [Muharram] union in a special order and format; some military marching bands also came to the Bazaar while were playing grief melody ... and Sardar Sepah,[1] himself, was seen in front of the union while he was bare-head and pouring straw on his head. Behind him, other Cossacks officers were doing mourning performances. A group of Cossacks had mud and silt on their face and head, [to express their] grief. It is obvious that observing this emotion was not ineffective on people and the minister of war was then known by common people as a religious person who is dedicated to the mourning ceremonies that Iranians are very much interested on. Also, he individually attended in the Muharram service session of [bazaar] unions. Some of orators on pulpit were praising him and praying for him then people would realize that the minister of war had come to the service session.

...

The [Muharram] union of Cossacks also came to the Bazaar and held the ceremony of *Shaam-e Ghariban* on the night of 11th. And Sardar Sepah, himself, [while was] bare head and bare foot, held a candle and came to the Great Tehran Mosque and Sheikh Abdul-Hussein's Mosque, where the biggest Muharram service sessions of the time were held ... These demos show that Sardar Sepah tremendously care about religious sainthoods; for two-three years these demos were repeated every year until he became the Prime Minister. Then step by step he banned Muharram rituals all together. (Bahar, 1944: 183–84)

The policy of banning the Muharram rituals in public spaces could not last for long, and after a few years, the public rituals resumed. Aghaie (2005) has argued that Reza Shah was not against religion and that he banned the Muharram processions in the same way that he introduced the dress code. Nonetheless, this indicates that the Pahlavi dynasty and its policy-makers failed to understand the significance and effectiveness of Muharram rituals in controlling and shaping Iranian society.

The Allied powers removed Reza Shah from power in 1941, and Mohammad-Reza Shah succeeded his father. Politically, the young shah was not as strong as his father, at least in the first decade of his reign. Although Iranian modernization was still an imposed reform based on secularist and nationalist ideologies, its authoritarianism was moderated. Naturally, Iranian modernization during the second Pahlavi dynasty was affected by the consequences of the Second World War and the oil industry, which became the major source of state revenue. Another milestone in the history of Iranian modernization was the nationalization of the oil industry that led to the Anglo-American backed coup (1953) against Prime Minster Mosaddegh which has had a long-lasting effect on Iranian political history.

This brief historical review leads us to the landscape of Iranian modernization as it took place in Dezful. The Constitutional Revolution (1905–1909) energized political debates across the country, leading to the birth of political unions and parties for the first time in the history of Iran. Dezful, a provincial city, was no exception. Archived materials published by Saeidi (1999) report the establishment of several unions in Dezful during the chaos following the coup in 1908. The manifesto of these unions is often saturated with the jargons, common to universal liberal values; however, these manifestos ultimately show that these unions were mainly established to deal with the devastating chaos and the lack of security in Dezful during the post-coup era. Imam (2003: 186–87) reports that old tensions between rival landlords and boroughs were inflamed during the Constitutional Revolution in Dezful. Seyyed Abdul-Hussein Qotb, one of the most influential landlords, supported the constitutional rule, and the rival Khan[2] supported the monarch. After the 1908 coup, the lack of security in the region reached such levels that all villages between Dezful and Shushtar were evacuated and the villagers took refuge in the two cities. Imam (2003: 187) also explains that this chaotic situation only abated when British troops controlled the south of Iran during the First World War. He has argued that the British consulate in Dezful not only stopped heavy fighting between city boroughs but also temporary diminished the rule of landlord families in the city. However, he has argued that the local ruling of landlords, known as *Khan-Khani*, was effectively abolished when the modern Pahlavi state was established.

The Pahlavi state replaced the traditional local ruling system with modern institutions and organizations such as city municipality and governor. Some members of landlord families remained influential as they held new administrative positions such as city mayor, but their power was granted by the modern state, not their family. In other words, the modern state did not abolish the influence of landlord families as such, but changed the constitution of their power. The land was still the source of economic wealth, but was 'not necessary' to their source of political power.[3] This was an important shift as the middle class was about to emerge and play an important role in the process of urban transformation.

Echoing the common narrative, Shiravi (b. 1925, interviewed in February 2006) explained that 'the landlord families dominated the city both financially and politically; effectively they could do whatever they wanted. The landlords were the source of finance as they were the main employer in the city and hamlets, at the same time they ruled the city boroughs'. Shiravi argued that the modern state changed this completely. He explained that 'the Pahlavi state carried [out] enormous number of development projects, such as the building of road, national rail, silos, and military bases, across the region. This made the modern state the major employer and source of finance for middle class and working class alike'. In this new landscape, the relationship between people and landlord families gradually changed. He explained that 'the landlords were still influential in the city, but the city gradually experienced the diminishing of landlords' authority'.

The Reza Shah reign was a time of drastic changes; however, the second – and arguably more important – phase of urban transformation in Dezful was during the second Pahlavi era. The beginning of this period was heralded by the entrance of Allied troops into Iran, removing Reza Shah from power, and by the presence of Allied troops in Dezful. Among the Allies, the Americans founded a major military base in Dezful. The presence of the Allies further weakened the role of landlord families. Interviewees noted that the establishment of the base in Dezful was a financial opportunity for the city. Young workers were hungry for work and the Americans needed manpower to build the base and run its services.

The socio-political changes in Dezful that had been occurring since the late nineteenth century reached a tipping point after the war and during the nationalization of the oil industry. Political parties boomed in Iran. In Dezful, a political party mobilized people against the traditional authority of landlords (Khans), leading to a violent confrontation between localities. This social movement eventually abolished the landlord families' domination in the early 1950s, a turning point in the social history of Dezful. As mentioned, the establishment of the modern state and the modernization project deterministically transformed the physical shape of Dezful in the early 1930s. However, there was some lag as the social transformation unfolded in a non-deterministic way.

## The Morphological Transformation of Dezful

The most visible aspect of urban modernization was the drastic transfiguration of urban structures by the street development scheme. This involved superimposing a regular shape upon the irregular and organic structure of Iranian cities. The street development scheme had its legal basis in the ratification of the Municipality Act in 1930. The act was based on an earlier act of the Constitutional parliament, signed in 1907. However, the new act gave executive power to city mayors for physical intervention, commonly associated with the demolition of public and private buildings in order to construct the new streets. The Act (1930) was followed by an 'Act of Building and Widening of Roads and Streets' which was signed in 1933 (Habibi, 1996; Zandi, 1969). The Street Widening Act (1933) introduced a simple and uniform regulation for the whole country. As Ehlers and Floor (1993) have explained, the instructions for modernizing cities were a set of simple codes for the size and width of roads and pavements, with an emphasis on uniform urban façades. The new organization of cities was usually based on two streets running perpendicular to each other, and a central circus.[4] During the early 1930s, this scheme uniformly transfigured the country's cities forever.

**FIGURE 4.1** The first modern streets of Dezful, early 1930s. The circus can be seen in the middle of the photograph. Public domain image. After Lockhart (1960, 152), originally obtained from Iran Oil Participants Ltd.

The transformation of Iranian cities was very much like the dress code; the idea was to quickly transform cities into Western-style cities, as it was imagined. The nature of this change was like other changes: drastic and based on authoritarian intervention. Kiani (2005: 182, 190–91) has noticed that many city councils were chaired by military officers, leading to a martial manner in physical interventions in cities. For example, Makki (1982) has reported that the mayor of Tehran was Sergeant Karim Agha Buzarjumehri, who carried out the street development scheme in a military manner. He ordered houses and shops to be demolished at night; the demolition often began before the occupants could evacuate the buildings, causing great distress in the city. The modernization of cities was clearly a political statement, demonstrating that an authoritarian modern state was in charge.

The spatial transformation of Dezful began in the early 1930s with the construction of three streets and the central circus. The streets were initially named Street Nos. 1, 2 and 3. As Figure 4.1 shows, Street No. 1 ran from the Sasanid Bridge toward the west. This street was partly constructed upon an old thoroughfare at the southern margin of the old city. Street No. 2, also

FIGURE 4.2 The Circus with roofed pavement at the junction of two of the first streets of Dezful (the late 1950s or very early 1960s). Public domain image, obtained from Saba Photo Studio, Dezful.

known as Pahlavi Street, connects the first street to the circus, located closed to the Friday mosque. Finally, Street No. 3 connects the circus to Shushtar Gate in the eastern part of the city; this street was laid out on one of the old city thoroughfares. These three streets had roofed pavements with simple and uniform façades. These streets were mostly at the southern part of the city but extended across the entire city by the 1940s. Street No. 2 extended to the northern edge of the city and became the major city street; Street No. 3 extended to the west and terminated at the river cliff. These three streets shaped a new spatial pattern around which the modern city grew (Figure 4.2 and Figure 4.3).

The authoritarian method of demolishing houses and buildings for the sake of new streets was taken up by the municipal authorities; Eidi-Mohammad Masoudi narrated that the municipality forced shopkeepers to move their businesses from the old bazaar and use shops in the new streets. By the 1940s, the shops in the old bazaar were locked by authorities in order to force shopkeepers to move their business to the new streets (interviewed in September 2005). Similarly, Mr Gholami narrated that 'when the street[5] was built, the mayor whose name was Sharifi shut the shops in the bazaar by force and moved them [shopkeepers] to the street. It happened in around 1940-1941... it was Reza Shah's era' (interviewed in Dezful, February 2006).

The urban modernization under Reza Shah has been criticized by scholars because it paid too much attention to the visual aspects of cities, such

**FIGURE 4.3** The city of Dezful and the new streets. Courtesy of National Cartography Organization, Iran (Ref: 631/60-619).

as the façades of streets, and remained ignorant about fundamental aspects of urban development such as infrastructure. Moreover, as the fieldwork interviews have also shown, the changes were imposed on an unwilling society. Interviewees extensively narrated people's total resistance to the changes. They explained that people were neither ready for nor keen on the changes that were imposed. Authoritarianism was not only behind the spatial transformation and re-arrangement of shops and urban land use;

interviewees noted the force used to install public medical services, upgrade toilet sanitation, close the traditional schools and establish modern schools. For example, Mr Shiravi (interviewed in February 2006) explained that although some free medical services, like vaccinations, were given door to door, people tried to avoid using the services by hiding their children. Consequently, the authorities forced people to vaccinate their children. In the case of education, he explained that the police closed the traditional school which he was attending. His father was told to register him in the new school that provided free education. However, he only did so after being officially warned several times by the authorities. The unwillingness of society to accept the imposed reforms was demonstrated when Reza Shah was removed from power by the Allies during the Second World War. For example, Mr Gholami (interviewed in February 2006) explained that when the arbitrary state was removed, shopkeepers, including his father, went back to the old bazaar and reopened the previously closed shops.

Generally, there was an interesting paradox in the narrative of those inter- viewees who experienced the Reza Shah era. While they often recalled and expressed their anxiety due to the brutal manner of the modern state that imposed reforms, at the same time they described the social resistance to changes as a sign of cultural backwardness. Their lived experience recalls a painful transition that runs counter to their current judgements about Reza Shah's reforms.

While urban modernization was initially dominated by the building of new streets, it was later characterized by the introduction of urban sanita- tion and infrastructure/utilities, i.e. piped water and electricity. Ehlers and Floor (1993) have stated that none of the cities had proper plumbing without danger of infection by 1941, except for Abadan and part of Ahwaz, where piped water was provided by the Anglo-Iranian Oil Company. However, in comparison with the Qajar period, the basic elements of modern infrastruc- ture, such as electricity and very basic piped water (not drinking water), changed urban life in many Iranian cities. For example, Dezful had two pri- vate companies that supplied limited electricity to the city by 1935. These companies provided electricity for street lighting and to the houses of those who could afford it. Moreover, Mr Shahrokni and Mr Fatehi (interviewed in February 2006) explained that Dezful Water Co., also a private company, had been founded in 1945 and was supplying piped water to the city by 1948.

The urban modernization during the first half of the twentieth century has been widely criticized for the lack of urban design vision, misunder- standing of urban modernity, and ignoring the value of traditional built environments that were profoundly damaged by the modern physical inter- ventions. However, as mentioned, the discussion here is about the process of Iranian modernization as a historical episode. We could challenge the transfiguration of Iranian cities and accuse the modern state of reducing urban modernization to 'street building'. The Iranian modern state even called the development plan of Tehran 'The Map of Streets' and assigned similar plans to all other cities. The street maps reflect the idea that the modern state had to engineer Iranian cities, a plan that was fully executed, changing the cities forever. In other words, Iranian cities were transformed by and large as the modern state intended and wished. However, social transformation was a very different story. The modern state interventions certainly triggered the process of social changes, but by no means did it determine those changes.

## The Social Transformation in Dezful

The urban society in Dezful was traditionally constituted on the basis of Heydari and Nemati moieties, a social organization that had the traditional ruling system as its political backbone. Traditionally, each borough was ruled by an elite family, therefore the city was governed by a polarized system. The local elite families, aka landlord families, teamed up in two socio-political groups that competed for greater power in the city. In this political landscape, the urban boroughs divided into two rival groups, Heydaris and Nematis. The division deeply affected social and everyday life in the city and could be plainly seen in the organization of religious processions.[6] The social interaction between people across the Heydari–Nemati border was minimal, but the modern institutions gradually changed this. In the new political order, not only the local ruling system was abolished, but local traditional institutions, such as traditional schools, were gradually replaced by their modern alternatives.

As mentioned above, the removal of Reza Shah in 1941 by the Allied troops had a direct effect on Dezful, as the Allies founded military bases in the city. The Americans, who established a major military base in Dezful, became a new employer in the city. Engaging with the Americans, Indian soldiers and the Russian troops was a unique cultural experience for people in the city. Considering that Iran had never been colonized, these were not typical encounters for people in a provincial city like Dezful. Mr Ahmadzadeh (interviewed in September 2005) argued that:

> The [presence of] Allied troops in 1941 were one of the first things that changed the traditional city; people were working for them and used their facilities to make better conditions for the city. People became familiar with other cultures because of the Allied troops. Moreover, the Allies became an employer in the city, which diminished the [financial] domination of landlords.

The changes since the Reza Shah era resulted in greater independence from local landlord families. This was due to the elimination of any political authority the landlords had, the improvement in the financial situation of urban families, and an emerging petty middle class. In this context, people sought to transform the traditional social order in Dezful. In contrast with imposition of the Modernization project, this was a bottom-up reform. Unsurprisingly, people started challenging the power of landlords during Muharram. For example, H.E. Masoudi (b. 1926) narrated an incident during the 1940s that happened over carrying the *nakhl* of their locality:

> The *nakhl* of Sheykh-Reza belonged to [the union of] Sarmidon. When I was young and about 17-18 years old, we [him and some of his friends] were opposed to carrying the *nakhl* while the landlord's son was sitting on it, because he was humiliating people when they were carrying the *nakhl*. So, we pulled him down and abolished this custom. Then after, a young clergyman sat on the *nakhl* and read the holy book while people were carrying the *nakhl*. (September 2005, Dezful)

As noted in the previous chapter, Muharram rituals were a medium by which the landlord families practised their authority over localities and boroughs. The *nakhl* of localities would not be taken into procession without the permission of the local landlord. Then the rituals became events in which landlord authority was challenged. The narrated event indicates the independence of local communities and their new ability to finance the Muharram rituals themselves. The improvement in the families' financial status was minor by today's standards, but at the time it constituted a major shift in the lifestyle of urban families. Esfahani and Pesaran explain that even though Reza Shah's state takes much of the blame for the lack of a comprehensive economic programme, nonetheless the country managed to grow relatively fast during the late 1930s and by the eve of the Second World War (Esfahani and Pesaran, 2009).

The movement against landlords in Dezful began in the late 1940s and grew when political activities energized it during the struggle for the nationalization of the oil industry, led by Dr Mosaddegh. Iran experienced a brief semi-democratic era, after Reza Shah, who acted more like a dictator towards the end of his reign.[8] The second Pahlavi shah was young and not confident enough to follow his father's policy. The result was a boom in political parties throughout the country. A wide range of political parties allied as the National Front to put political pressure on the young shah to promise a fair and free election for the sixteenth parliament. Dr Muhammad Mosaddegh, who initiated this political campaign, was appointed as the leader of the Front. They gained a strong position in the following parliament and Dr Mosaddegh was soon appointed as prime minister.

Mr Arab (interviewed in September 2005, Dezful) and Ahmad-zadeh (interviewed in September 2005, Tehran) explained that during the late 1940s many political parties were established in Dezful. The new political parties were mostly based on local agendas, and the members of each party were often concentrated in the locality of the party's founder. In other words, the new political parties were the reproduction of the traditional social organization, constituted on the basis of localities. However, Hezb-i Zahmatkeshan (the Toilers' Party) soon gained popularity across the city by connecting to grassroots urban society and mobilized people against the landlords' authority. Mr Ahmad-zadeh, from a Heydari locality, stated that 'people were looking for someone to lead them against landlords, ending the feudal system in the city. People did not care about the actual policy of the [Toilers'] party. Their favour was to challenge landlords in the localities' (September 2005, Tehran). Mr Arab, who was from the locality of Eastern Sahrabedar in the Nemati part, also made an interesting statement about the political landscape of Dezful in this period:

> Political parties were established in Dezful like other cities, but they followed local issues and did not care about real political aims of parties. Dr Gosheh-Gir led the Toilers' Party in [the locality of] Western Sahrabedar. And our locality established the National Front. These two parties were in the same political side, however in the city they opposed each other. People just followed landlords or the local leaders [of Toilers' Party]. (September 2005, Dezful)[9]

What Mr Arab notes about the National Front in Eastern Sahrabedr is that Seyyed Kazem Qotb, the most influential landlord in the city, established the local branch of the National Front. The leader of the Toilers' Party was Dr Mozaffar Baghaei, who was one of the founders of the National Front (Azimi, 2004: 63). He was also in the circle of Dr Mosaddegh during the struggle for the nationalization of the oil industry. When the Iranian government legally defeated the British Government and eventually nationalized the Anglo-Iranian Oil Company in 1951, Baghaei even claimed credit for this victory. However, he soon distanced himself from Dr Mosaddegh and opposed his government. He even supported the Anglo-American backed coup in 1953 against Dr Mosaddegh (e.g. see Katouzian, 2004: 11). In Dezful, however, politics played out differently: the two local parties opposed each other right from the beginning.

The interviewees' narratives mostly show no awareness of the National Front in Dezful. The common narrative describes the movement as a struggle between the Landlords' Party and the Toilers' Party. The interviewees often simply talked about the landlords and the Party. Even today, in any conversation about the local history, 'the Party' implies the Toilers' Party. In fact, it is difficult for local people to associate the landlords with the National Front that was led by Dr Mosaddegh, who initiated the first land reform in the Middle East in 1952. The act forced landlords to turn over twenty per cent of their land revenue to their tenants (Pappe, 2005: 76). The dominant narrative describes the landlords' political position as supporters of Muhammad-Reza Shah and opposed to Dr Mosaddegh. Therefore, the social movement against landlords in Dezful cannot be articulated solely based on the official position of these two parties in the larger political history of Iran; it should be contextualized on the basis of national and local politics.

The Toilers' Party was a social-democratic party established in 1951 as an alternative to the Tudeh Party, a communist pro-Soviet Union party. The Toilers' Party was founded by Dr Mozaffar Baghaei, a democrat, and Khalil Maleki, a Marxist intellectual and former member of the Tudeh Party. The Toilers' Party was formed by a group of democrats and a circle of left-leaning intellectuals who separated from the Tudeh Party. The separation happened when the Tudeh Party campaigned for the Soviet Union's concession for the oil resources in northern Iran. 'The main clauses in the program of the Toiler's party called for the establishment of a genuine constitutional monarchy, elimination of upper-class privileges, encouragement of small industries, national independence from all forms of imperialism, including Russian imperialism and alleviation of class tensions between employers and employees' (Abrahamian, 1982: 256). The party attracted large numbers of students from the University of Tehran. Apart from Tehran, the party had strongholds in Kerman (Baghaei's home town), Karaj, Ahwaz and Dezful (see Abrahamian, 1982: 256; Makki, 1989: 595). *Shahed Newspaper*, which Baghaei had been publishing before 1951, created the political platform on which the Toilers' Party was founded. This newspaper remained the official voice of the party. Historical accounts often refer to the Toilers' Party prior to 1951, as it is usually considered as a part of the National Front that formed in 1949.[10]

The branch of the Toilers' Party in Dezful was established by Dr Sayyed Mosa Gosheh-Gir in 1951 (Mahmoodzade, 2002: 99). Dr Gosheh-Gir was a GP (doctor), a graduate of the University of Tehran, and a strong orator who quickly gained popularity across localities in Dezful. He embodied the stereotype of the new generation raised during the Reza Shah era. He came from a non-elite family,[11] was educated in modern schools, and after studying at the University of Tehran, he became a political figure, fighting for liberal values. The deputy of the Toilers' Party in Dezful was Shah-Bazaz, a salesman who had a shop in the old bazaar. In his essay (an interesting personal political memoir), Radfar (2002) described Shah-Bazaz as a young bazaari who was a well-respected local figure who gained popularity in the city. Radfar narrates: 'I observed that during the month of Muharram and Safar he [Shah-Bazaz] attended in many *Rowzeh-Khani* [Muharram service sessions] that became political gatherings; his fans and the party supporters followed him from one to another service session' (Radfar, 2002: 49).

The leader of the Toilers' Party, Dr Baghaei, was part of the National Front joint venture that formed on the eve of elections for the sixteenth Parliament in 1949. Dr Mosaddegh was appointed prime minister after the election. Then the Front, which was an initiative in order to campaign for a fair and free election, became a political platform to campaign for nationalization of the oil industry, and pressured the shah to accept the constitutional framework of power. The National Front was not a party, but a coalition led by Dr Mosaddegh who believed that 'Iran was suited more for a loose coalition of organizations with a general goal than for a structured political party with disciplined members and elaborate programs' (Abrahamian, 1982: 253). The Toilers' Party in Dezful was established in this landscape to support the nationalization of the oil industry – a symbol of the fight against colonial/imperial powers – and challenge the privilege of the upper classes. However, the Toilers' Party was soon preoccupied with challenging the socio-political authority of landlords in Dezful. The party's official newspaper, *Shahed* (Witness) was widely distributed in Dezful. The party also published its own local paper called *Farid-i Dezful*, named after Dr Gosheh-Gir's son (Mr Arab, interviewed in September 2005). Dezful became an important stronghold for the party and made Dr Gosheh-Gir a well-known figure within the party network across the country. Mr Arab explained that 'Dr' was the nickname of Dr Gosheh-Gir in *Shahed Newspaper* articles, showing that he became a well-celebrated figure in the Toilers' Party.

In reaction to the Toilers' Party, Sayyed Kazem Qotb founded the local branch of the National Front. The narrative given by Mr Arab (interviewed in September 2005) and Ghaffari's memoir (Ghaffari, 2005: 141–62) show that Qotb was acting like the godfather of the National Front in Dezful, not as its public face or local leader. Instead, a circle of activists around him, such as Seyyed Ali Kamali, Mr Hudjati and Abdul-Muhammad Rokni, were publicly leading the campaign. This political circle had its own local paper, *Roken Iran*, named after its editor Mr Rokni. Like the Toilers' Party, the National Front in Dezful focused on local agendas. Seyyed Kazem Qotb was the most influential landlord in Dezful and his initiative was aimed at defusing the mobilization of people against landlords. Therefore, people were either not aware of the local branch of the National Front, or they saw it as a cover up to support landlords' authority in the city. By no means was this political initiative perceived as a campaign for supporting the National Front agendas of implementing the constitutional framework of power and nationalizing the oil industry. The members of Dezful's Toilers' Party accused Mr Qotb of establishing the National Front in Dezful only when a dispute arose among national figures of the Front. For example, in an interview Haj Rajb Zahari-Far argued that: 'Against the Toilers' Party, the landlords initially established *Havadaran Vatan* [the devotees of motherland], that supported the monarch and were actively against the people. When the dispute raised amongst the leaders of the National Front, then the landlords founded the Society of Pro-National Front in Dezful against the Toilers' Party' (Darkatanian, 2009: 83). This perception dominates not only the narrative of interviewees who were in favour of the Toilers' Party, but also those of interviewees who gravitated towards Qotb's campaign. This point is also reflected in the memoir of Seyyed Ali Kamali. He argued that the Toiler's Party in Dezful was behind a vicious and brutal campaign against landlords who made positive contributions to the society. He blamed the Toilers' Party for insincere populist rhetoric that claimed the party was aimed at supporting the poor against the landlords who exploited society. Regretfully he explained that the old enmity among localities and urban elites was one reason that the Toilers' campaign triumphed in the public of Dezful (Kamali Dezfuli, 2005: 203–209).

The Qotb family supported the Constitutional Revolution (Imam, 2003: 186), which points to this family's celebration of liberal values. Based upon this political background, Sayyed Kazem Qotb had developed a good relationship with political figures in the close circle of Dr Mosaddegh, such as Dr Fatemi who was the foreign minister in Mosaddegh's cabinet.[12] The circle around Qotb also tried to develop a relationship with other influential figures of the National Front in Tehran when local tensions flared in 1952. Despite that, the National Front of Dezful clearly failed to connect with local people, and the so-called Landlords' Party only gained the support of the borough of Eastern Sahrabedar, where the Qotb family resided. The interviewees described the city of Dezful as being divided into two parts: Eastern Sahrabedar vs. the rest of the city. Interestingly, interviewees also referred to the polarization of the city as the Heydari–Nemati division. The division clearly does not correspond to the Heydari and Nemati territories as Eastern Sahrabedar was only one of four Nemati boroughs.[13] However, it seems that the interviewees used this narrative as a familiar cliché to describe the new social division in the city.

Sayyed Kazem Qotb's initiative to establish the local branch of National Front was regarded as the landlords' party. This narrative reflects the nature of the social movement against the landlords in the city, rather than the actual position of his campaign or even the political unity of landlords. In fact, while the Toilers' Party succeeded in mobilizing people against landlords across city boroughs, the landlords never formed a genuine political coalition. Seyyed Ghaffar Ghaffari's memoir echoes the testimony of Kamali (Kamali Dezfuli, 2005) who argued that old enmity among urban elites was one of the reasons for the successful campaign against the landlords. The enmity was rooted in the nature of the traditional ruling system, in which the borough heads teamed up as Heydari and Nemati, and competed with rival boroughs for greater power. Ghaffari's memoir shows that he had a tendency towards Qotb, though he refused to be a loyal devotee. He writes: 'It was years that the local power and social influence were merely in the hand of Aga Kazem Qotb; affluent figures of Dezful society were bearing all kind of contempt and inattentions, and blamed Mr Qotb as the cause of all these' (Ghaffari, 2005: 155–56). Here Ghaffari narrates the situation after the establishment of the modern state, when the landlords were not in a privileged position in the new political order , while Mr Qotb remained an influential figure. Although Qotb was from a traditional landlord family, he restored his position in the new political landscape. Interviewees often noted that not only was Mr Qotb an important figure himself, but his wife was also very influential and would easily intervene to appoint or dismiss someone from a governmental position. Ghaffari mentioned that the members of elite families were not offered job positions in modern bureaus, upon which Mr Qotb and his wife exerted significant influence. Therefore, Ghaffari argued that while the elites and landlords may have publicly expressed their support for Mr Qotb, they were not actually loyal to him at all (Ghaffari, 2005: 156). In other words, while Qotb's campaign was perceived by people as the symbol of traditional landlord domination, it is rather difficult to articulate it as a platform established to represent landlords. Such was the complexity of the socio-political landscape in which the social movements against the traditional social order unfolded in Dezful.

Mr Seyyed Taj-uldin Ashrafi-Zadeh (interviewed in February 2006, Dezful) explained that the city was divided between the khans' party and the Toilers' Party. Ashrafi-zadeh (b. 1932), from the locality of Eastern Sahrabedar, the Qotb family stronghold, explained that those who supported the landlords were called *Hetoon*, meaning fibbers in the local dialect. In response, those who supported the Toilers' Party were called *Baghoon*, after the name of Dr Baghaei as a means of humiliating them (*Baghoon* means 'frogs' in the local dialect). Ashrafi-Zadeh explained that when Dr Mosaddegh was appointed as prime minister,[14] the tension in the city escalated between the two groups (Ashrafi-Zadeh, February 2006). Although the Toilers' Party had organized rallies in Dezful from early 1952 by late 1952 and early 1953 the movement had gradually turned into an ugly and bloody conflict. This corresponds to the period when tensions escalated between the shah and Dr Mosaddegh. Therefore, the local people commonly compared their movement against the landlords with the position of Dr Mosaddegh against the shah, though the pro-landlord supporters would likely reject this analogy. During this violent period, many people were killed in fights, and the landlords' houses in various boroughs were attacked and looted. In this very hostile situation many landlord families left their homes and took refuge in other cities, except the Qotb family who were supported by the residents of Eastern Sahrabedar. During my interview with Dr Manocher

Sohrabi (b. 1928), he briefly addressed this period. Dr Sohrabi graduated from the University of Tehran Medical College and was a member of the Sohrabi family that ruled the borough of Seeyah-poushan. He states:

> For a period, a conflict broke [out] between the mass and the influentials in the city. The influentials supported Mosaddegh and the mass were pro Toilers' Party … the violence made a critical situation in the city and many of [the] influential families [were] exiled from the city to Ahwaz, Tehran and Borojerd, avoiding further violence. Therefore, the city was ruled by the party. (Interview in February 2006, Dezful)[15]

In their respective newspapers and in correspondence with government officials, each party blamed the other for inciting violence and causing casualties. I reviewed archived materials on the riots in Dezful, including official reports at the *Sazeman Asnad Meli Iran* (Iran National Archive). These reports show how police and military forces in Dezful took different political positions when reacting to the violence in the city. This not only inflamed the tension but also increased the number of casualties. Some of the interviewees, such as Mr Ahmadzadeh, mentioned that the Army Chief, Colonel Shahrouz, supported the people against the landlords. Darkatanian also mentioned that 'Colonel Sharooz, the military governor and the chief of the military base, supported the Toilers' Party and the chief of police and the head of city court were pro landlords' (Darkatanian, 2009: 83).

In his memoir, Ghaffari references an occasion when he met the chief of police, Colonel Navaei, at Mr Qotb's home. Ghaffari narrates that the colonel expressed his inability to control the situation because Colonel Shahrouz was on the side of the Toilers' Party, therefore he left the city after only three months (Ghaffari, 2005: 178–80). Navaei and the head of the city court were appointed after an incident in which a student was killed in a fight in December 1952. For the interviewees, this incident was commonly the turning point upon which tensions in the city turned into violent confrontations. In his memoir, Kamali, who was the most active figure against the Toilers' Party, accused Colonel Shahrouz of encouraging and supporting local gangs against the landlord families. For example, he accused the colonel of plotting to loot the house of Morteza Khan Rashidian (Kamali Dezfuli, 2005: 210–11).[16] Kamali argued that the Toilers' Party succeeded in mobilizing people and cracking down on the landlords because of old enmity among urban elites and the direct support of the military's chief officer, as well as indirect help from other government officials (Kamali Dezfuli, 2005: 206).

I also informally interviewed Behzad Shahrouz, Colonel Shahrouz's son, in London (March 2017). He quoted his father, the colonel, as saying 'I was always on the side of the people whether he was in Dezful or later in Isfahan'. Behzad described his father as a man who was loyal to the monarch and had no loyalty to the Toilers' Party or any other leftist party. It seems that Colonel Shahrouz's stance was more of a personal one, supporting the grassroots social movements in Dezful over any political entrenchments. Behzad Shahrouz was proud that the people of Dezful remained loyal to his father throughout the years, and they did not forget him when he died after the revolution in 1979, mentioning that a large group of people from Dezful attended his funeral and service in Tehran.

The confrontation between the two sides reached its highest pitch on 3 February 1952. On this day the landlords attempted to hold a public demonstration which was crushed by the opposition, resulting in many casualties on both sides. This day, as described by those of the pro-landlord faction, such as Kamali, was a tragic day. The opposition saw it as the day of freedom for the people of Dezful. Overall, the early 1950s are remembered as a shameful and dark period because of the bloody and violent confrontations. However, this period is also perceived as an important transitional period in which the urban society abolished the traditional power structure and established a new social order. According to Mr Ahmad-zadeh,

> Because of the movement between 1950 and 1953, people joined together to challenge landlords; so many local disagreements and conflicts were conciliated. [Traditionally] the conflict between localities was serious, [as such] that some of the localities were walled and people did not pass through other localities. They were just passing through the main city road; if they passed through a local road, they were in trouble.

He added:

> Although the Land Reform [the 1960s] released villages from landlord authority in Iran; in Dezful they had already lost their power between 1950 and 1953 ... they have never recovered their power after 1953, they have not been influential in the city anymore. In other words, the landlords' authority was abolished in Dezful sooner than the other parts of Iran. (September 2005, Tehran)

## The Ritualization of Urban Conciliation and New Social Order

The end of violence in Dezful can be studied by going through the official archival reports or by listening to the oral history of the city's inhabitants. There are some limited official reports in Iranian archives that address the incidents during the early 1950s in Dezful, but they are neither extensive enough nor aimed at articulating the social context of this violent period. Interestingly but not surprisingly, the official reports are silent on those subjects that are narrated by the oral histories. The official reports are preoccupied with reporting numbers, dates and so-called facts, but remain silent on public opinions. On the other hand, the oral history and interviewees' narratives are not focused on verified facts, but on social experiences. This demonstrates how oral history and classic historiography are essentially dealing with different questions (e.g. see Thompson, 1998). The official reports focus on how the tension was controlled and eliminated. The interviewees mostly focus on how social conciliation was achieved and established.

An official document reports[17] that following the incident of February 1953, the authorities arrested many activists on both sides. S. Ali Kamali and Gholam-Hussein Mostowfi[18] were found guilty of inciting the 1953 riot. Darkatnian (2009: 86) reported that Kamali and Mostowfi, as well as seven other members of the Toilers' Party, including Dr Goshe-Gir, initially faced the death penalty, but the penalties were never carried out. Darkatanian also reported that there was a local campaign shortly after the 1953 incident for the release of Dr Gosheh-Gir. Although there are limited archival materials on the incident, it seems that the follow-up of the incident (February 1953) was overshadowed by the coup against Dr Mosaddegh in the summer of that year. The post-coup era was a oppressive time when all political parties were intimidated. Although Dr Baghaei, the leader of Toilers' Party, supported the coup, he was soon politically marginalized. While no one was seriously punished over the 1953 riot in Dezful, many local activists were politically marginalized. The landlords lost their traditional social position, and Dr Gosheh-Gir took refuge in Tehran, where he practised as a GP. Therefore, politically speaking both parties lost. However, from the interviewees' point of view, the spring of 1953 was a milestone in the social history of the city. This was a turning point when the reign of landlords was over, the Heydari–Nemati division was abolished, and all city boroughs were united.

The interviews suggest that the violence of the 1950s ended not because of court cases or by punishing activists. Instead, Muharram ritualized the social conciliation between boroughs. The interviewees narrated diverse stories, instead of a common story, about how the conciliation was achieved. These narratives share a meta-story that the conciliation happened during Muharram, which signifies the importance of the religious ritual in initiating a social appeasement. One of the most repeated stories is that Ayatollah Faregh, a well-respected clergyman, led the union of Qupi Agha-Hoseyni, a locality in the Heydari moiety, to visit an evening service session in the locality of Shahrokn al-Din in the Nemati part of the city. Shahrokn al-Din was part of the borough of Eastern Sahrabedar, the stronghold of the Qotb family. The exchange of visits between localities within each moiety, i.e. Heydari or Nemati, was typical. However, a visit across the border of the moieties was unusual. As discussed in the previous chapter, crossing this border during Muharram would normally trigger major violence in the city. Therefore, this visit was a sensitive move considering the tension between the borough of Easter Sahrabedar and the rest of the city.

Yusef-Ali Karami (interviewed in September 2005, Dezful) and Seyyed Muhammad Montazeri (interviewed in April 2006, Dezful) described Ayatollah Faregh as a popular orator and a well-respected high-ranking clergy member in the city. Faregh, like many other influential figures, wanted reconciliation and an end to the hostility after the February 1953 incident. It seems that he chose to visit the Shahrokn al-Din locality at the heart of Eastern Shrabedar especially because of the hostility to this locality. The people of Shahrokn al-Din were mostly *seyyed*, meaning they are descendants of the Prophet Mohammad; thus, they were seen as having greater intimacy with the Muharram tragedy. The visit initiated by Faregh was based on the tradition that people pay condolences to *seyyeds* for the Karbala tragedy. Karami narrated the story according to Haj Mehdi Hedayat-panah, who attended that visit. Haj Mehdi explained that when the union of Qupi Agha-Hoseyni arrived at the service session in Shahrokn al-Din, nobody confronted them, as they were led by Ayatollah Faregh. When they entered the service session, Faregh cried out 'the *seyyeds* of Shahrokn al-Din receive and welcome the mourners of your ancestor, our lord Hussein!' This greeting smoothed over potential hostilities and the visitors received a warm welcome to the service session. In response, the people of Shahrok al-Din later returned the visit. The exchange of visits signified a conciliation and ended the tension in the city. If this story were true, given that the riot happened in February 1953, the visit would have taken place in September 1953, i.e. Muharram 1373 AH. The following year, the union heads of all localities decided to celebrate the reconciliation and friendship between localities by symbolically exchanging visits through Muharram processions. They established new procession routes and schedules to establish, perform and maintain the social conciliation and friendship among the urban communities.

The new processions were organized according to three episodes or stages: (1) the afternoon of the 9th of Muharram (Tasoa afternoon), (2) the morning of Ashura day, and (3) Ashura afternoon. In the first episode, the Nemati localities carried their processions throughout Heydari territory, to show the friendship and conciliation between the two old rivals. The morning of Ashura day is when the unions of all localities share a procession route, symbolically manifesting the unity of all localities. In the final episode, the Heydari localities carried their procession throughout the Nemati areas of the city. The traditional processions were organized within the territories of Heydari and Nemati, highlighting the traditional urban division. However, the new processions practised unification and friendship between the rivals. This initiative ritually signifies conciliation after the violent period of the early 1950s. Although the tension during the 1950s was not between the Heydari and Nemati factions, the re-arranged procession routes mark the end of traditional social division. The re-arrangement of Muharram processions rightly addresses the fact that the traditional local ruling system and the Heydari--Nemati division were entwined. Therefore, the social consequence of ending the landlords' reign was the social integration of divided localities.

## The Rite of Urban Passage

The transformation of Dezful's urban society can be described as follows: the traditional urban society was exposed to the modernization during the 1930s and 1940s. It was then in a liminal or transitional stage during the late 1940s and early 1950s, when the city entered a tense transitional period. Finally, 1953 was the post-liminal stage when the urban violence ceased and the urban society was reconstituted. The new social order was ritually established via the re-arrangement of Muharram processions to signify the unification of Heydari and Nemati moieties. From Victor Turner's point of view (Turner, 1969), this process can be described as moving from structure to anti-structure and back to (new) structure.

The Turnerian reading of this process formulates the violent period in the city as an anti-structural transitional status, when social norms are ignored and violence is justified. The anti-structural, or *communitas*, status is not described as disorder or chaos by Turner. He argued that the anti-structural period is a brief transitional period which is not a socially destructive status, but rather a acute part of the resilience mechanism to sustain and renew social organization. The significance of the anti-structural period lies in the potential it offers for restructuring social organization and power relations in changing urban societies. As Turner has explained, social behaviours, including violence, are not irrational or rational during liminal times; rather, they are based on the tempo-rationality of liminal time. This explains why interviewees simultaneously condemned and justified the violence during this period.

Victor Turner also explains that there are two types of liminal status. First, there are liminal statuses that are created by cyclical rituals, e.g. Muharram commemoration, which are considered a reversible status. This means that communities experience an anti-structure status during annual rituals; however, the previous social order is restored when the ritual period is over. The second kind of liminal status is experienced during non-cyclical rituals, e.g. marriages or funerals, which mediate an irreversible transition from one state to another. This process is also called 'status elevation', as the ritual mediates the establishment of a new social status for individuals or a new social order. Muharram commemoration is an annual event where urban society experiences a liminal time; individuals or social groups gain temporal status, a reversible social position. However, changing the Muharram procession routes in Dezful was a ritual per se, which mediated an irreversible transition that I call the rite of urban passage. The re-arrangement of Muharram processions is a post-liminal rite that ended urban violence and initiated social conciliation. It also marked the passage of urban society from its traditional state into a new order. In other words, *the rite of urban passage* facilitated the transition of the traditionally divided urban society into an integrated urban social system, a major social transformation that encapsulates the changes in Iranian cities during the first half of the twentieth century.

## Conclusion

The policy-makers of the Iranian modernization failed to comprehend the social capacity of religious rituals to mediate social transformation. Religious commemorations like Muharram were considered a backward aspect of traditional society that the modern state wished to eliminate. Although Reza Shah initially practised Muharram rituals to shape his public image and establish his socio-political position, soon the rituals were banned in public spaces due to the ideology of the Iranian modern state. The removal of Reza Shah from power reversed this situation and public rituals resumed. The last two chapters have shown that Muharram rituals are far more than a sole religious ceremony; the commemoration of the Karbala tragedy appeared as a practice that was heavily charged with social agendas. However, the political elites did not imagine that the Muharram rituals could be a key mediator for establishing social transformation.

The failure of Iranian elites to understand the social significance of religious rituals was partly caused by their belief that religious creeds and rituals were a key reason for the cultural backwardness of Iranian society. The Iranian modernization project was the product of the scientific discourse of the late nineteenth and twentieth centuries. In its essentialist approach, this scientific discourse relied heavily on typology and categorization. It is in this atmosphere that Durkheim established his sacred–profane dichotomy. The Iranian political elites could not comprehend the role of religious rituals in the process of modern transformation when the latter was understood as a secular/profane process. However, this chapter not only blurs the border between religious and secular practice by illustrating the critical role of Muharram processions in social transformation, but also challenges the conventional idea that associates religious rituals with social tension and violence.

The social history of Iranian cities has involved discussions of escalating urban violence during Muharram. As discussed in previous chapters, performing Muharram processions engaged crossing borders and boundaries between localities and boroughs and therefore caused tension and violence among these boroughs. However, while social tension was higher during Muharram, the processions also mediated social solidarity and intimacy among urban communities. The discussion in this chapter has revealed an even more complex relationship between so-called religious rituals and urban violence. On the one hand, the Muharram rituals stimulated tension among different segments of society, but on the other hand the rituals also appeared as a mechanism to control violence and initiate social conciliation. More interestingly, the re-arrangement of procession routes itself became a rite that established and maintained the unification of rival segments of urban society.

The physical transformation of Iranian cities was carried out deterministically during the 1930s, when the face of Iranian cities changed drastically in a short period of time. However, it is more difficult to pinpoint the period when social transformation began and spread across the country. Political developments triggered the social transformation during the early twentieth century, however neither its time nor its procedure were predictable. For example, while the new social order was seen in the re-arrangement of Muharram processions in Dezful in the early 1950s, this happened much earlier in Ardabil, arguably during the 1910s.[19] More importantly, in contrast to how physical transformation came about, the modern state by no means determined social changes. Even the political developments in Dezful unfolded through a complex interaction between local and national politics in a way that was far from predictable.

This chapter has mainly focused on articulating the social and political context of urban transformation and the re-arrangement of Muharram processions. The transformation of urban society and processions have significant territorial and spatial aspects that could not be discussed simultaneously. The following chapter examines the spatial complexity of this historic urban transition.

## NOTES

1.  'Sardar Sepah', which means army chieftain, was the royal title of Reza Khan when he was the commander-in-chief of the Royal Qajarid Army.
2.  For some reason, Imam (2003: 186) has censored the name of the landlord who supported the despotism of the monarch, replacing the name with an ellipsis.
3.  As discussed in the previous chapter, land had traditionally been the source of political power.
4.  The city of Hamedan and Ardabil are exceptional cases, where the new streets were designed in a polar (star) form.

5. He referred to Street No 1.
6. This is extensively discussed in previous chapters.
7. This is a symbolic wooden structure carried through Muharram processions, discussed extensively in chapter two.
8. Katouzian (2003) argues that Reza Shah's authoritarian modern state turned into an arbitrary regime between 1931 and 1941.
9. Mr Arab explained that apart from the Toilers' Party and the National Front, other parties were Javanan-e Demokrat [Youth Democrat], SUMKA and Pan-Iranist. SUMKA in Farsi stands for the Iran National-Socialist Workers Party, an Iranian Nazi group that glorified the so-called Aryan identity of Iranians based on a political understanding of Proto-Indo-European theory that has now been abandoned (e.g. see Motadel, 2013).
10. As mentioned above, Dr Baghaei was one of the founders of the National Front.
11. His father was a traditional medic (Mahmoodzade, 2002: 79).
12. This is based on an interview with his son, Habib-ullah Qotb, who shared how his travel to the United States for study was arranged by Dr Fatemi in the very early 1950s (interviewed in February 2005). Habib-ullah Qotb (b. 1930) is an MIT graduate in hydraulics engineering.
13. This is extensively discussed in chapter three.
14. Dr Mosaddegh was re-appointed as prime minister on 20 July 1952, following a public uprising in his support.
15. Kamali narrated the attack on the house of the Sohrabi family (Kamali Dezfuli, 2005: 209), but neither Dr Sohrabi nor Morteza Khan Sohrabi addressed the incident during semi-structured interviews that I had with them (both interviewed in February 2006).
16. According to an Ahwaz Police report (Doc No 2933978, Iran National Archive), the incident happened on 14 September 1952.
17. This is based on a report from the Ministry of Justice, date 20/06/1336 (i.e. 11 September 1957), which is kept at the Centre of Presidential Archives (Iran), Doc No. 23079. See also Darkatanian (2009).
18. As mentioned in the previous chapter, the Mostowfi family was one of the most influential landlord families in Dezful, ruling the borough of Masjid (see chapter three).
19. For more about the case of Ardabil, see Safari (1974: 200–202) and Kasravi (1974: 195–97).

# CHAPTER 5

# ENTWINING PAST AND PRESENT IN PERFORMED SPACE

The social and spatial aspects of the Iranian urban transformation are often investigated either separately or in parallel. This study, however, focuses on the Muharram processions in which the social and spatial dimensions of the city are entangled. The first and second chapters discuss the ritual as an intrinsically spatial phenomenon. Chapters three and four show how the Muharram processions are not merely a religious ritual, but form a collective performance that is heavily charged with social agendas. The Muharram commemoration appears as the most important annual event by which urban communities practise their social relations. Muharram processions are not a passive reflection of social reality but are an active part of urban negotiations and social changes. The previous chapter discussed how the transformation of urban society was ritually established by re-arranging the Muharram procession routes. This chapter, then, interprets the re-arranged processions and explains how the processions mediate practising the new social order while keeping alive the traditional social constitutions. The Muharram processions constitute a performed space in which the past and present coexist.

I begin with a brief theoretical review on the notion of space to lay groundwork for the concept of performed space. The second section will discuss the new Muharram processions in Dezful and decode their social meanings, thereby contextualizing the processions in the contemporary city a half-century after their re-arrangement. To show that Dezful is not an exceptional case, the Muharram processions in the city of Ardabil are also briefly discussed. This chapter also addresses the question of what social situations or conditions may lead to another re-arrangement, and why the current processional organization in Dezful has not changed substantially over the last seventy years. The last discussion will posit performed space as a topological space, an idea that formulates manifold dimensions of the performed space.

## From Built to Performed Space

One of the key ideas in this chapter is to articulate the idea of performed space: a socially produced space that coexists with the performance of a procession. This idea is based on the philosophical idea in which 'space is merely a system of relations' (Russell, 1961, 87; orig. 1946). Descartes and Leibniz were against the Newtonian idea of absolute space as a pre-existing entity that contains objects. They articulate space as a relational system that emerges out of the pattern of the interrelationship among objects (Alexander et al., 1978). Leibniz describes the relational space as a space that exists only as a relation between objects, a space that has no existence apart from the existence of those objects. In other words, space emerges out of and coexists with other objects. Therefore, as Bertrand Russell explains, space is a system out there in the real world; however, it is not a physical entity (Russell, 1945: 86). Thus, space is articulated as real, without having a body of its own. In this regard, Harvey explains that

> The view of relative space proposes that it be understood as a relationship between objects which exist only because objects exist and relate to each other. There is another sense in which space can be viewed as relative, and I choose to call this relational space – space regarded in the manner of Leibniz, as being contained in objects in the sense that an object can be said to exist only insofar as it contains and represents within itself relationships to other objects. (Harvey, 1973, 13)

The classic theory of relational space implies that although space does not have a body itself, it cannot exist in the absence of matter. For example, urban public spaces are constructed by configuring buildings in a certain arrangement. While urban spaces are independent from those buildings, they only exist due to the existence of the buildings as material objects. However, while modern physics took the side of Leibniz (against Newton) in the twentieth century, the idea of relational space was reformulated as a system in the non-material world of quantum physics. In modern physics, distance is no longer conceived as being between things but events, and involves time as well as space. The new territory of physics imagined and formulated by Einstein is not utilized in the normal human life experience. However, it is still stimulating to see that the space between two things is no longer a certain distance, but depends on the observer's point of view (see Russell, 1945: 87–88). Since the 1970s, social scientists have pushed the boundary of space further, reinventing the notion of space as a social product. Since then a growing body of scholarship in social science has taken a spatial turn, associating space with social theories. New jargons, such as conceived and perceived space, virtual space, and media space, signify that space is no longer considered to be a system that exists merely through material objects in the physical realm. Space can be produced through social interactions in real, virtual and mental realms. This theoretical development was established through the work of scholars from Poulantzas (1973) and Lefebvre (1991; orig. 1974) to Giddens (1979, 1984), Gregory and Urry (1985) and Soja (1989). This ontological development caused a substantial paradigm shift in social science, changing the ways that social practices and experiences are articulated and theorized.

Lefebvre's grand project in *The Production of Space* (1991) was to formulate a holistic spatial theory by bridging mental, physical and social realms. In doing so, he focused on the social mode of producing space throughout history. He has argued that the dynamics of the mode of production space are the result of social interactions across perceived, conceived and lived spaces. Lefebvre coined this triad as spatial practice, representational spaces and representations of space. In other words, the social negotiations for producing space do not unfold in built environments, by building or occupying them. Human societies negotiate with others through their perception of the world and the ways they idealize it. Lefebvre outlined his social theory of history by formulating the dynamics of social modes of production, which is an indeterminist version of the Marxist theory of history. Marx believed that history is a process of evolution by which societies pass through various stages towards the ultimate destiny. In this process, each stage is built upon the previous one and destroyed by the subsequent one (Campbell, 1981: 116, 120). While Lefebvre's dialectical process built upon Marx's idea, the process is not as deterministic.

Lefebvre has argued that the social mode of producing space changes by means of a dialectical process: when the mode evolves, previous space will be reproduced. This process begins with the absolute space, that is the space of nature prior to human intervention. Abstract space evolves when the forces of history smash the previous mode of spatial production. Lefebvre argues that 'representational spaces' such as religious and political symbolism and knowledge have a significant role in changing the social mode of production to reproduce abstract space (e.g. see Lefebvre, 1991: 50). He argues that abstract space is reproduced as 'contradictory space': the space of the modern era with its global outlook. Then contradictory space evolves into 'differential space',: the space of the cybernetic and information age. For Lefebvre, differential space will eventually be reproduced when there is a shift in the social mode of producing space. Lefebvre's contribution is not only to offer an indeterminist version of Marx's theory of history, but to establish the notion of space as the keystone of his social theory of history. This was a significant milestone in what is called the spatial turn in the history of social theories.

Soja (1989: 10) has argued that twentieth-century social theories did not simply ignore the notion of space but they actively ignored the spatial dimensions of society and treated them as an un-dialectical and passive concept. In contrast, time was treated as a rich dialectical concept, a theoretical trend that Einstein made it even more attractive. Giddens (1979) asserts that space has been denied by sociologists because of their anxiety about the environmental determinism of the nineteenth and early twentieth centuries. This environmental determinism was part of the modernization paradigm in the Middle East and Iran in the early twentieth century. It was thought that by engineering the physical shape of a city, society could be deterministically transformed. The notion of space, a neglected concept in social science during the first half of the twentieth century, became the keystone in major social theories such as Lefebvre's, Giddens' and Soja's. The spatial turn of the 1970s redefined the idea of space in the intellectual landscape of postmodernism and post-structuralism, which discarded the universal deterministic understanding of social changes. The spatial turn emerged from shifts in epistemological and ontological understandings of space that differ theoretically from the spatial determinism of the nineteenth century or Modern architects such as Le Corbusier. The new spatial paradigm changed the formulation of city and urban dynamics, and explains the failure of Modernism in urban planning.

Lefebvre argues that space can be produced through socially prevalent processes and rejects the idea that the built environment can influence and change society. This idea was laid out when Lefebvre challenged Le Corbusier, who 'believes in and wants to create human relations by defining them, by creating their environment and décor. Within this well-worn perspective, the architect perceives and imagines himself as architect of the world, human image of God the Creator' (Lefebvre, 1996: 98). Apart from Lefebvre's criticism of the spatial determinism in Modern architecture and urban design, he fundamentally challenges the idea of urban planning. Lefebvre (1996) argues that urban planning is a reductionist ideology embodied in a dogma that claims to understand total truth. However, the urban planning discourse only reduces urban questions and problems to the built environment and transportation matters. Lefebvre's idea implies that first, the notion of space cannot be reduced to the built environment and neither can society be deterministically changed by reshaping and engineering the built environment. Second, the space is (re)produced throughout processes that are driven by society, not by professional practices. Moreover, although there are interactions between the built environment and society, social transformations drive the dynamics of social modes of space production. These ideas explain why the modern Iranian state failed to engineer Iranian society in its arbitrary transfiguration of urban structures. Although the physical shape of the city can be extensively transformed, the performed space of Muharram processions changed only when the constitution of urban society transformed.

Lefebvre arguably influenced the field of urban studies more than any other social scientist during the second half of the twentieth century. He and his theoretical successors, who were predominately Marxist and postmodern scholars, made splendid contributions to this field of study. This circle of scholars, from Harvey (1990) and Soja (1989) to Bayat (2010), have focused heavily on everyday life; however, they neglected the significance of rituals (non-everyday practices) as a key part of urbanization processes, and the processes of producing space (see the introduction, also Masoudi Nejad, 2015b). Lefebvre and other Marxist scholars heavily focused on everyday life and the class struggle as driving urban negotiations. As discussed in previous chapters, the urban negotiations during Muharram are about the struggle between communities in Iranian cities (see chapter four). Moreover, although Lefebvre briefly addressed religious rituals, he neglected the fact that rituals create 'liminal/anti-structure status' (Turner, 1968) where everyday norms and social structures are altered. The social interactions and negotiations are practised in entirely different modes during ritual/anti-structure status, leading to an alternative social mode of producing space when the space is liminally produced. The nature of space produced during the liminal time of rituals is much more complex than our everyday space.

The spatial organization of traditional Muharram processions highlighted the division of Iranian cities into Heydari and Nemati parts (see chapter three and four). In Dezful, like other Iranian cities, the urban localities teamed up in two rival moieties, Heydari and Nemati, which competed for greater power. While the division was a socio-spatial phenomenon, it was not reflected in the morphology of urban structures (see chapter four, and Masoudi Nejad, 2013). In other words, despite an established and commonly accepted idea, the physical structure of this organic city did not reveal the constitution of urban society. However, the aggregation of traditional procession routes shows a spatial pattern that clearly revealed the social divisions (Map 5.1). The Muharram processions created a space in which people practised, perceived and conceived the constitution of traditional urban society. Such a space is not contingent on the built space/environment, but is integrated in the performance of Muharram processions. I call this space performed space.

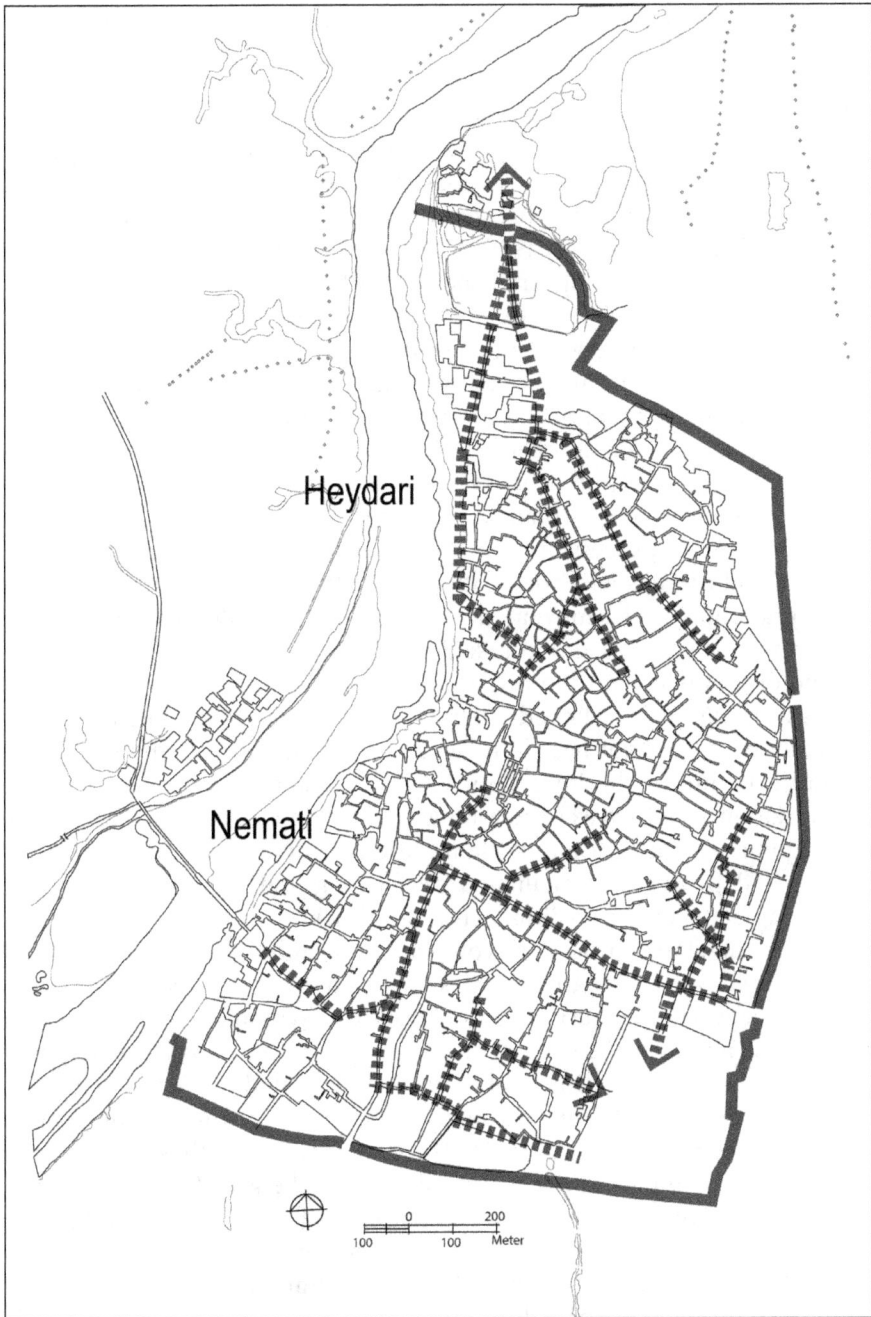

**MAP 5.1** The aggregation of traditional procession routes on Ashura day, depicting the social division in Dezful. Map by the author.

## The Socio-spatial Connotations of the Re-arranged Muharram Processions

Chapter four extensively discussed the transformation process of urban society and the re-arrangement of Muharram processions in Dezful in 1953. The spatial organization of processions changed in 1953 as the consequence of social transformation, not because of the drastic morphological transformation of Dezful in the early 1930s. The discussion revealed that the Iranian modernization project triggered social transformation, but did not determine the result of transformation. The Muharram rituals played a critical role in establishing a new urban constitution. However, the policy-makers of Iranian modernization were so ignorant about the significance of this so-called religious ritual in the process of social transformation that they considered it a secular procedure. The discussions in previous chapters rejected the identification of Muharram rituals as a solely religious practice also rejected the sacred–profane dichotomy.

The Muharram procession routes were re-arranged in 1953 to end urban violence and create social conciliation in Dezful. Urban violence increased when grassroots social movements challenged the traditional power relations, aimed at ending landlords' social domination. The local ruling system of landlord families and the division of the city into Heydari and Nemati wards were tightly interlinked. Therefore, while the urban violence during the early 1950s was not based on Heydari–Nemati division, the end of the landlord era meant the integration of Heydari and Nemati moieties. The Muharram processions were re-arranged based on a three-session schedule that signifies the integration of the traditionally divided urban society. The re-arranged processions facilitated performing and practising unity and friendship between the traditional rival localities.

The first session of processions on Taso'a afternoon (the 9th of Muharram) is associated with Nemati localities that run their processions through Heydari territory. The unity of all city localities is symbolically performed on Ashura morning, when all unions carry their processions toward a cemetery in the north of the city. The final episode is dedicated to Heydari localities that carry their processions through Nemati parts of the city on Ashura afternoon (Maps 5.2, 5.3 and 5.4). The orchestration of these processions was far more complex than you would expect. The grand idea of the new procession routes is to celebrate the unity of all localities and signify the end of social division. While the new arrangement of processions is aimed at practising the new social constitution, it simultaneously enforces the traditional division. Taso'a afternoon is dedicated to Nemati unions while Ashura afternoon is dedicated to Heydari localities, therefore this schedule still references the Heydari–Nemati division. Since 1953 the city has grown

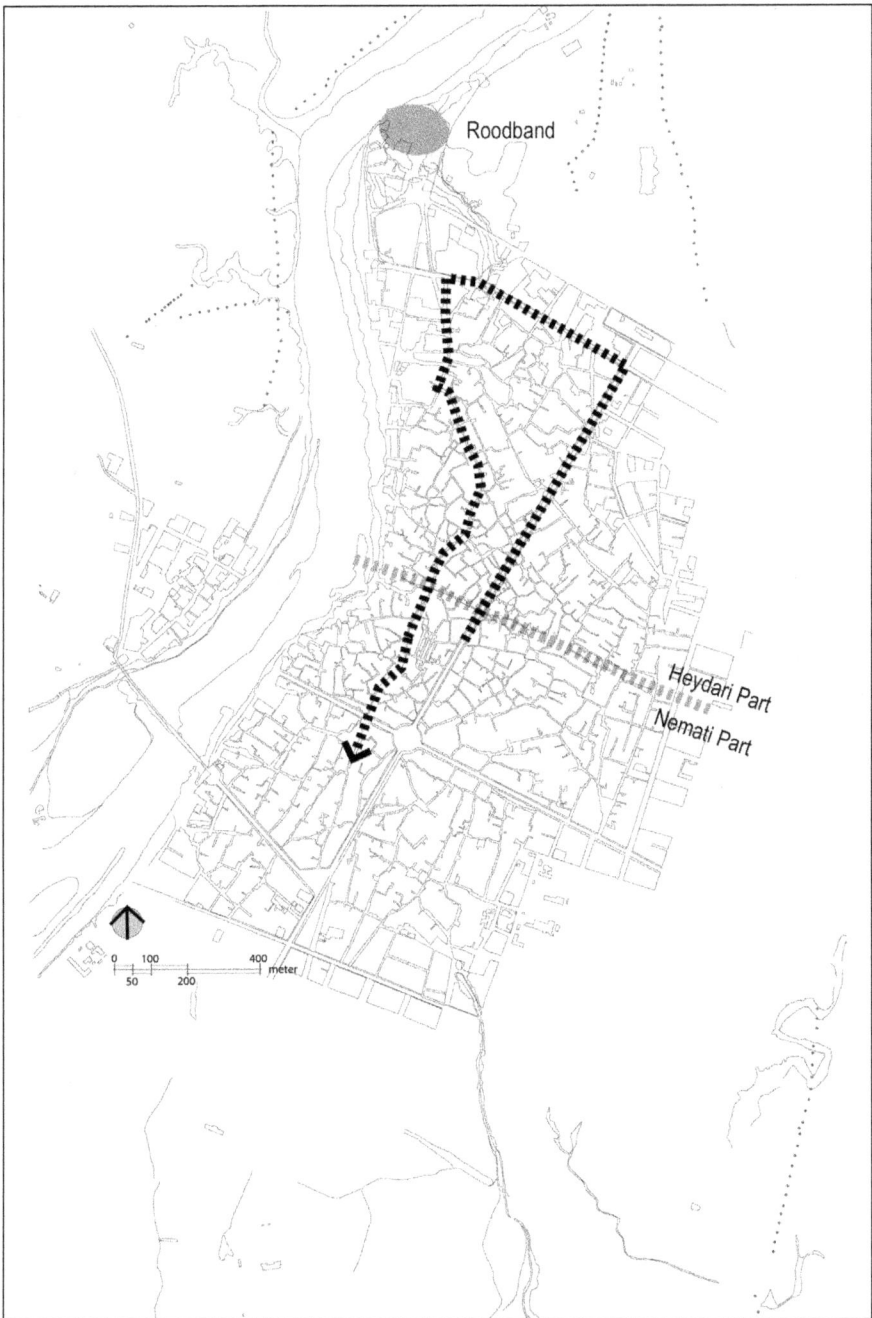

**MAP 5.2** The re-arranged Muharram processions in three sessions, the session of Taso'a afternoon. Map by the author.

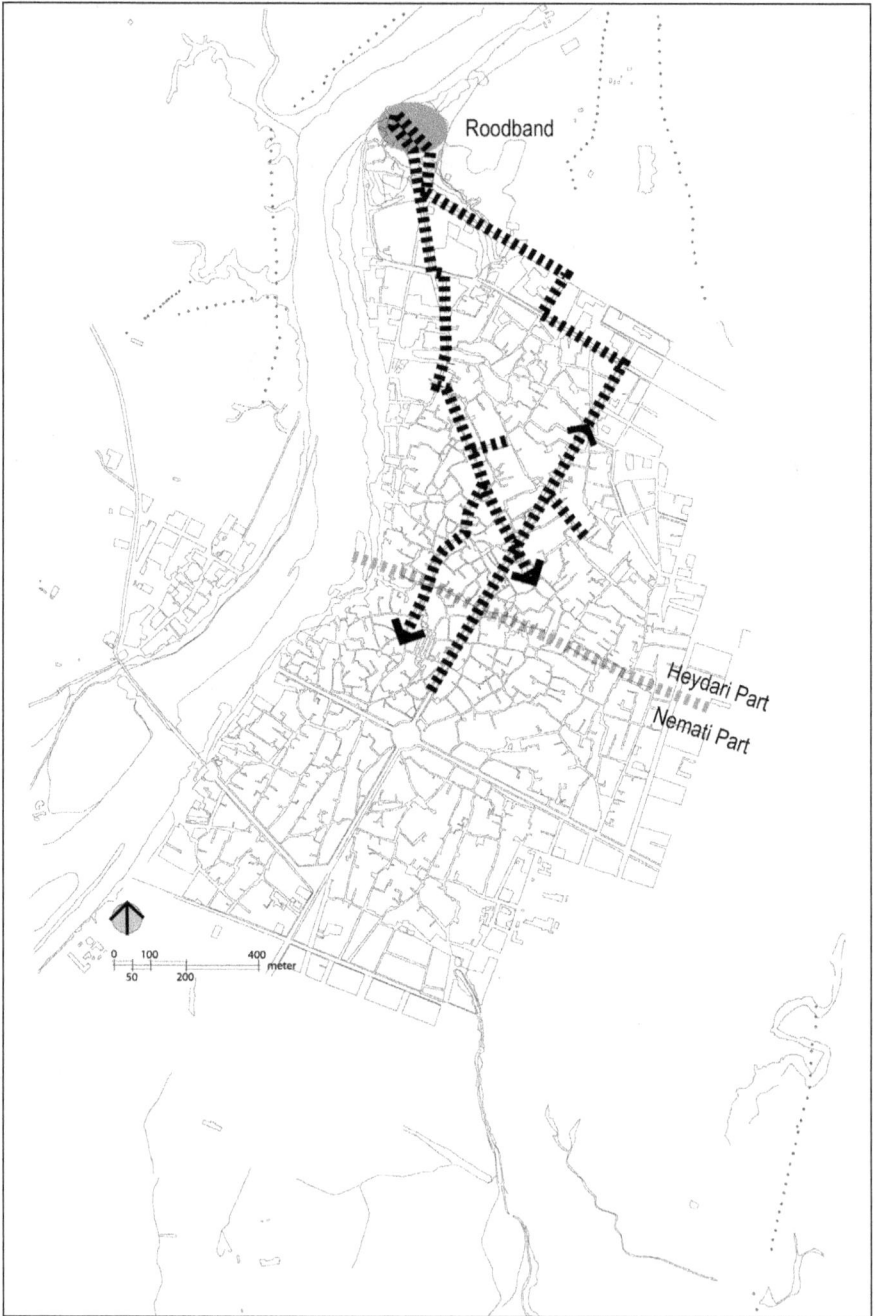

**MAP 5.3** The re-arranged Muharram processions in three sessions, the session of Asura morning. Map by the author.

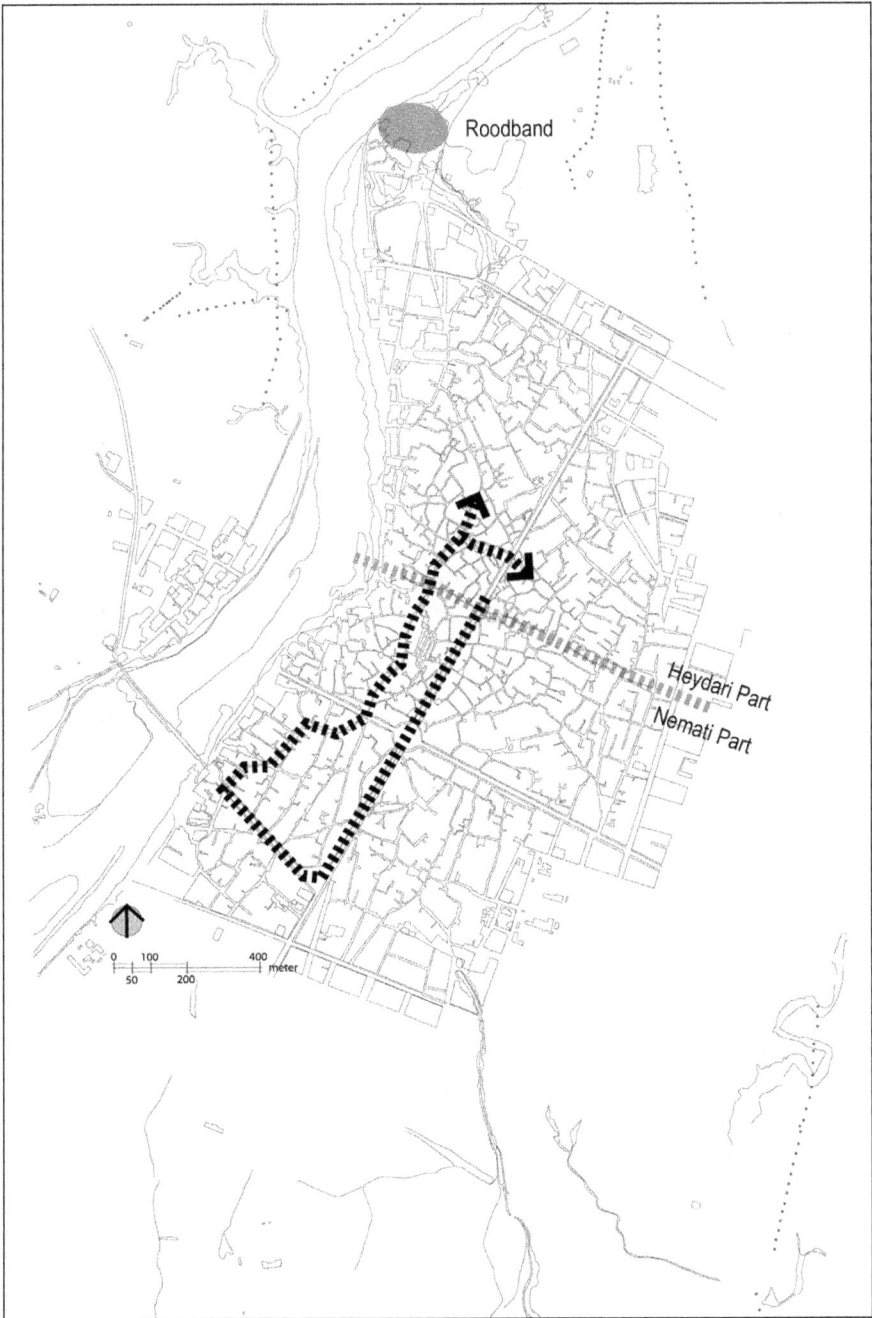

Roodband

Heydari Part

Nemati Part

0   100        400
        meter
   50    200

**MAP 5.4** The re-arranged Muharram processions in three sessions, the session of Asura afternoon. Map by the author.

extensively and many new Muharram unions represent new residential localities. Today, many people have no idea about the traditional social division. Nonetheless, the Muharram unions must still associate their social identity to either Heydari or Nemati moieties to follow the procession schedule. This means that the processions preserve and transmit the traditional social identities into the present time and to the future. This arrangement in Dezful is a very interesting example, but this is not an isolated case.

The re-arranged Muharram processions in other Iranian cities show similarities to the case of Dezful. For example, the processions in Ardabil were re-arranged in a very different way, but they still exhibit a similar socio-spatial logic. Safari (1974) has explain that the six main city boroughs of Ardabil were divided into Heydari and Nemati wards. The boroughs of Towaa, Uchdokaan and Pir-abdolmalek were known as Heydari, and Gazeran, Qonbalan and Aali-qapoo as Nemati.[1] Therefore, as in other cities, the Muharram processions in Ardabil were traditionally organized based on the division of the city into Heydari and Nemati wards. After a violent period in Ardabil during the late Qajar and early Pahlavi eras, the boroughs reached social conciliation.[2] This social conciliation and abolishment of the Heydari–Nemati division was signified by re-arranging the Muharram processions, a re-arrangement which is still followed today. Dr Reza-zadeh (interviewed in March 2006 in Tehran), Asghar-zadeh (interviewed in March 2006 in Ardabil), and Rezaei (2000: 157) have explained that the arrangement of processions in Ardabil was aimed at creating unity among divided boroughs. The processions were re-scheduled over six days during the first ten days of Muharram. Each day, one of the boroughs runs its procession through all the other five boroughs. On the first three days, Heydari boroughs run their procession, and then the Nemati boroughs do so on the following days. The processions manifest the cohesion and integrity of all boroughs and the end of Heydari–Nemati divisions. Yet in this instance, the schedule also reinforces the traditional division. Even today, the Muharram unions self-identify based on the traditional Heydari and Nemati identities, quietly preserving the old constitution of urban society. For example, during my fieldwork in Ardabil I had a conversation with a person at the shrine of Sheikh Safi. I asked him which part of Ardabil his family was from and he replied that his family was from X locality. As I could not recall whether this was a Heydari or Nemati area, I asked him about the social affiliation. He was a young person, in his late twenties, so I was not surprised when he asked: 'What are Heydari and Nemati?' I asked him on what day of Muharram his locality ran their procession. His reply answered the original question, and I was able to tell him that his locality used to be Nemati.

The processions in Ardabil and Dezful are organized very differently; however, the processions in both cities create a performed space in which the past and present urban constitutions are entwined. The processions' schedule/temporality is as important as the spatial organization of procession to produce the performed space. In other words, the performed space is produced/manifested through the tempo-spatial orchestration of the processions, and is not just the result of new procession routes. As stated, the new processions both mediate the unification of traditional rival moieties and honour the traditional social divisions. The question is why and how people continue to associate themselves with the traditional identities after such a long time. Despite the transformation of urban society, the localities and Muharram unions remain fundamental components of urban society and social identity.

Dezful, like other Iranian cities, has grown extensively since the 1950s and the Heydari–Nemati division has gradually been forgotten. Although the urban population was mostly still living in the old city during the 1950s and the 1960s, this balance shifted in the following decades. The urban population increased sharply and people moved from older boroughs to modern neighbourhoods. The modern parts of the city are clearly distinguishable from the old city by their spatial configurations and the lifestyle of their residents. Slowly but surely, the old city suffered, as its needs were neglected, and became undesirable. However, the Muharram rituals bond the old and new city, keeping the old city alive in two key ways.

First, although many Muharram unions are established in modern residential areas, it is still very common for people to join the union of old localities for the commemoration of the Ashura tragedy. By doing so, they maintain their social affiliation with their locality of origin. The first and second generations of many families still practise their affiliation with old localities during Muharram. For example, Mr Karami (interviewed in September 2005) explained that 'still 70-80% of people and even the second generation are participating in the Muharram rituals of their old localities'. On the same issue, Mr Majdi stated that 'the traditional customs of Muharram are still practised; all guys of each localities, wherever they are living, come back to their original locality on the days of Taso'a and Ashura, and run their processions in the name of those localities' (interviewed in February 2006, Dezful). During my fieldwork, when I was in a procession as part of my participatory observation in 2006, I encountered an old friend who said: 'Oh you also came back from London for Muharram', and then introduced me to someone who was in his company and had just arrived from South Korea for the Muharram commemoration. In other words, while people may live in the new part of the city or even other cities, they commonly return to their original locality during Muharram as a way of defining their social identity. The old city may be undesirable for residency, but during Muharram it stands out as the source of social identities.

Second, as has been explained, the re-arranged processions preserve the idea of traditional Heydari–Nemati division, since the processions are scheduled based on identifying the unions as either Heydari or Nemati. Nowadays, even Muharram unions that represent the modern localities associate themselves with one or other of the traditional moieties to see when they should have their processions. To that end, the new unions identify as Heydari or Nemati based on the social affiliation of their founder – whether they belonged to an old Heydari or Nemati locality. In practice, this often works very well, as the new residential areas are transplant colonies of the old localities. Moreover, interviewees explained that new localities are identified as Heydari or Nemati by extending the old Heydari–Nemati border throughout the new city. As mentioned in chapter three, Simetri Street (today known as Shariati Street) sits on the old Heydari–Nemati border (Map 5.5). These two methods of demarcating the old and new city during Muharram illustrate a very interesting social phenomenon. While the modern structure was physically superimposed on the old city structure, the old city is still socially dominant in the Ashura commemoration. In other words, the modern state restructured the city by means of new streets and a masterplan but the old city determines the social structure by means of the Muharram processions.

The processions may be organized through the new streets, but all interviewees associated the old city with the most emotional and impactful parts of the processions. For example, Y. Karami (interviewed in September 2005, Dezful), who returns every year to his old locality for Muharram, has specified the top five emotional moments in their processions. As Map 5.6 shows, all these locations are associated with places in the old city. Although I do not attempt to articulate why such emotional moments are experienced throughout the old city, it is still relevant to refer back to a note in my fieldwork diary:

> Ashura night, Dezful, Iran, Feb. 2006
>
> I was always wondering why processions through old-narrow alleys of the old city become more emotional, and by far cannot be compared with the procession in wide and new streets. The processions through new streets have no dynamic, most of the time processionists want to just pass the streets to get to the actual part of processions in the old city. In contrast with the wide and straight streets, the density and dynamic spaces in the old city create a tempo in processions; at every turn of broken alleys, your feeling is changed. The procession constantly moves from narrow and tight alleys, where you feel the pressure of the crowd, into an open space of a local square, when you feel the relief from the pressure and can delightfully breathe fresh air. Interestingly, as even the old thoroughfares are narrow, a small group of 5–10 friends can make a circle within the procession, then emotionally rock each other for chest-beating or reciting dirge!! While such a group of friends frequently became very emotional in narrow alleys, passionate moments are very rarely expressed in a wide street.

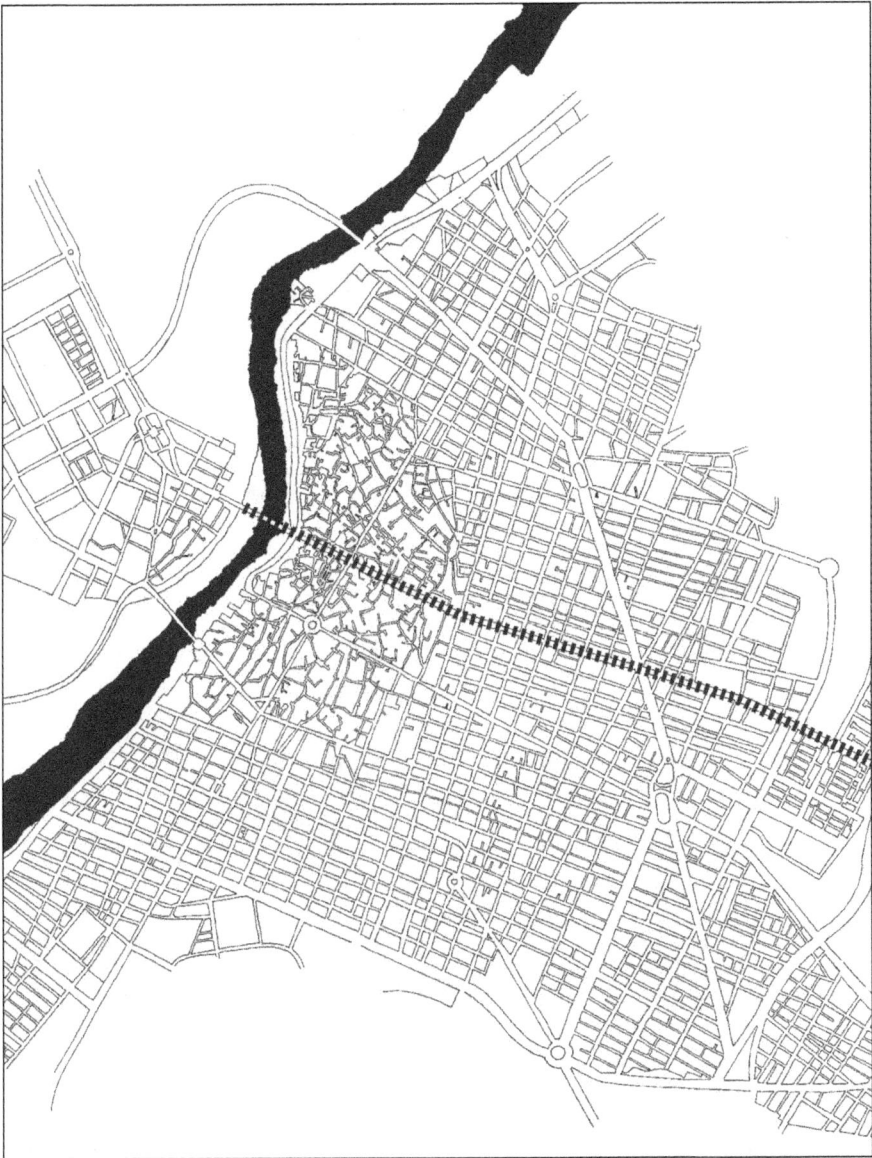

**MAP 5.5** The traditional Heydari–Nemati border in the modern city. Dezful, 1990s. Map by the author.

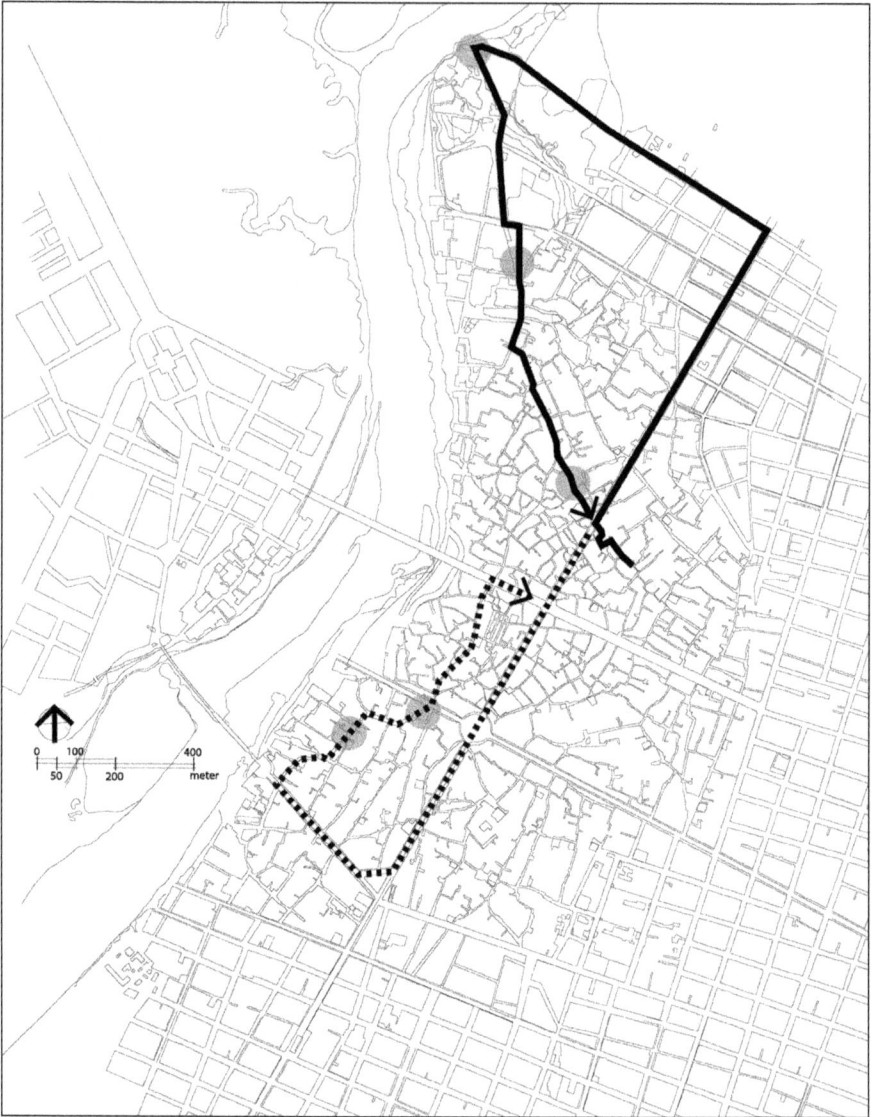

**MAP 5.6** The most emotional locations in processions based on Karami's narrative. The procession of Ashura morning (solid line), Ashura afternoon (dashed line). The background map shows the city during the early 1980s. Map by the author.

The intense emotional moments that occur in the old thoroughfares are a temporary experience of the Muharram processions. Yet these common experiences have a perpetual effect on the urban experience, even though the old city has lost its significance in everyday urban life. The processions disperse throughout the old city structure, highlighting it in the collective mental map of the city during Muharram when the old structures and localities regain their socially important positions. This echoes what Turner (1969) has noted about the temporal position of individuals during a liminal/anti-structural status. The everyday social relations of power are temporarily altered during an anti-structural status where individuals gain a social status that is very different from their everyday social positions. I am borrowing Turner's idea to articulate the position of the old city during the liminal time of Muharram. The old city temporarily gains an important position in the social space of the city during Muharram; however, this temporary status has a lasting influence on the social perception and mental map of the city.

The modern state drastically changed the physical shape of Iranian cities by superimposing a regular structure upon them (see chapter four). Elsewhere, I have analysed the drastic physical intervention of the modern state in Dezful (Masoudi Nejad, 2013) and explained that the construction of new streets throughout the old city was not simply a cutting away of the organic urban fabric. This intervention entirely transformed the configuration of urban structures, in which the old city structure retained no spatial significance and even became spatially segregated from other parts of the city. This is partially why the old city became an undesirable residential area. The configuration of the old city was physically transfigured and fragmented by modern interventions. Despite this, during the liminal time of Muharram the historical structure of the old city is highlighted and experienced through the processions, shaping the social and mental space of the city. In other words, the modern city structure, as a built space/environment, dominates the physical configuration of the city as it is experienced on a daily basis. However, the old city manifests itself as a lived structure that is collectively experienced during Muharram. The spatial organization of Muharram processions reveals a much more complex relationship between the physical, social and mental realms of the city. Therefore, any urban planners and designers who do not explore the liminal time of rituals will fail to capture the totality of the city.

The city has changed since the early 1950s, yet the spatial pattern of the Muharram processions has generally remained as it has been since the early 1950s. Nevertheless, the significant increase in the population of participants and numbers of Muharram unions has recently caused difficulties in some parts of the procession routes. As ever, if two unions find themselves face to face at a junction, tensions increase because each group wants priority over the other. Considering that these days a union could be comprised of tens of thousands of people, such an incident creates a very difficult situation. During my 2006 fieldwork, the city authorities (mainly the police) wanted to minimize the problems by changing some parts of the procession routes. They introduced some alterations in procession routes, regardless of the social meaning of the routes. People accepted the changes in socially neutral routes through the new streets. However, they did not tolerate any change to the essential parts of the routes, those that ran throughout the old city. As the police wanted to impose its plan, serious disagreements and tension arose during Ashura afternoon in 2006 and the plan was scrapped. Interestingly, the unions reached an agreement to alter part of the procession routes that in fact put more emphasis on the old city.

Urban society is not fixed and rigid, but an ever-changing system. Like other Iranian cities, Dezful has grown fast and has become a destination for rural-urban migration since the 1979 revolution. Moreover, Dezful as a border-city was heavily bombed and affected during the 1980s Iran-Iraq War. As extensively discussed in previous chapters, the Muharram commemoration is a social practice, a means of performing and mediating social changes. Yet why have there been no significant changes to the Dezful Muharram procession routes over the last sixty years,[3] and why do people resist any major change to the spatial organization of the processions? One reason is that the procession is only one of many Muharram rituals, and the spatial organization of processions is only one dimension of Muharram processions. As discussed in chapter two, there were many rituals in Dezful that died out mainly after the Iranian revolution of 1979. The Muharram procession itself is composed of many sub-rituals, rites and symbols, many of which have changed over time. For example, before the revolution men commonly went shirtless while performing chest-beating in the processions. After the revolution however, such bodily gestures became culturally unacceptable and gradually men started wearing black or dark clothes during the processions. While the spatial organization of processions has not changed, there are many other aspects of the rituals that exhibit social changes. In the next chapter, an investigation of the (re)invention of the symbolic shawl exchange during Muharram will help to demonstrate how social changes are reflected in the Muharram rites.

The historical observations throughout this chapter, along with chapters three and four, show that 'the spatial organization' of Muharram processions only changed when the constitution of urban society was fundamentally transformed. This occurred in Dezful in the 1950s, when the traditionally divided urban society transformed into an integrated system. The social transformation was highlighted by the rituals and established via the re-arrangement of processions. The spatial organization of Muharram processions will probably not remain as it is forever; it is conceivable that the procession routes will eventually change. As the city of Dezful grows quickly, both in terms of physical size and population, the urban society transmutes and fractures further. Socially, the fragmentation is due to the demographic diversity of the urban population, which has emerged in part because of the migration of nomadic communities into the city, communities that have no connection to the city's social history. If the fragmentation of urban society increases, then changes in the spatial organization of the processions are to be expected. One hypothesis is that a more fragmented urban society may result in multiple procession systems. While the procession routes established in the 1950s may remain the source of authentic social identity for those communities that associate themselves with the social history of the city, those communities lacking a social affiliation with the city's history may gradually invent their own processions. Moreover, the physical growth of the city might necessitate the establishment of multiple procession systems. The distance from the heart of Muharram processions, i.e. the old city, is an issue for many new residential areas. Currently, there are new areas that have Muharram unions and hold commemorative rituals at their community places; however, as they are too far from the old city they cannot hold a procession. As these unions are not yet socially established, the residents of these areas join the processions of other unions with whom they maintain a social affiliation. It is a matter of time to see how these parts of the city will define and practise their social identity during Muharram.

## Practising Past and Present through Performed Topological Space

The discussions throughout this chapter show that the annual commemoration of the tragic battle of Karbala constitutes alternative social modes of producing space, thereby creating a performed space in which the city's social past and present entwine. The performed space is neither contingent on the built space/environment, nor the equivalent of the spatial organization of processions, i.e. the assemblage of all procession routes. Rather, the performed space manifests itself through the spatio-temporal orchestration of Muharram processions. The performed space not only entwines the past and present social constitutions, but also retains the core of the old city structure as a lived structure. The built environment is a spatial system that is geometrical by nature; it can be described by usual geometric drawings that illustrate shapes, forms, angles and sizes. However, the performed space appears as a spatio-temporal occurrence that cannot be articulated by Cartesian geometry. I describe it as a 'topological space', a conceptual idea that helps to formulate the manifold realms of performed space.

The root of topology lies in an essay by Leonhard Euler (1741) that he published in response to a popular puzzle challenge to find a route in the city of Königsberg (now Kaliningrad):

> The East Prussian city of Königsberg (now Kaliningrad) occupies both banks of the River Pregel and an island, Kneiphof, which lies in the river at a point where it branches into two parts. There were seven bridges that spanned the various sections of the river, and the problem posed was this: could a person devise a path through Königsberg so that one could cross each of the seven bridges only once and return home? (Alexanderson, 2006: 567)

As Euler stated in his essay, the question seems to be geometrical, but in fact it does not require the measurement of distances, nor did calculation help at all. He argued that, instead, the concern was what he called 'the geometry of position', an innovative method which has been developed into graph theories and topology. As Biggs et al. (1999) explain, this well-known story in mathematics textbooks indicates that whereas many branches of mathematics were motivated by fundamental problems of calculation, graph theories were often developed in response to popular questions. However, what I would like to emphasize here is that this well-known story implies the topological nature of arranging a route throughout a city when distance is not the issue. This naturally brings to mind the idea of a procession route, which is not aimed at achieving the shortest path between two locations (see chapter three).

Geometry is preoccupied with form, shape, size, distance, inside/outside and far/near. But topology is about relationships and continuity in a system that configures parts into a whole. Moreover, while geometry describes one-, two- or three-dimensional systems, topology is aimed at formulating manifolds, e.g. 'n'-dimensional systems. The term 'topological space' was coined by Felix Hausdorff in 1922 (Shields, 2012: 47), and the Dutch artist Morris Escher's drawing are well known because of the visual tricks that he employed to represent topological space in two-dimensional geometrical drawings. A Möbius strip, the simplest of topological systems, is often used to illustrate topological space (Figure 5.1). A model of a Möbius strip is made by taking a paper strip and giving it a twist, and then joining the ends of the strip together to form a loop. If you move along the strip and return to your starting point, you have traversed on both sides of the strip without crossing or jumping over its surface. In other words, while you are on one side of the strip, you are spontaneously on the other side. We may geometrically distinguish each part/side of a topological space but they are the extension of each other. We can move from one side, dimension or realm to another in a topological space without realizing such a shift.

**FIGURE 5.1** Möbius Strip. Photograph by the author.

This is related to spontaneously experiencing or being in different realms or domains, as metaphorically illustrated in Escher's 'Three Worlds'. The title of this lithograph, that depicts a lake, refers to three worlds: (1) the surface of the water on which leaves float; (2) the world above the surface, the forest, that is observable through the reflection on the surface of water; (3) and the world below the surface, represented by a large fish swimming just below the water's surface. This image knits together the three realms, all of which inform the concept of performed space, a spatio-temporal occurrence in which the past and present social constitution of the city are discursively entwined.

Topology developed as a field of mathematics that is widely employed in the rigorous study of communication networks like the Internet, social networks, as well as urban networks. For example, I have used the space syntax method to topologically analyse the transformation of Iranian cities (Masoudi Nejad, 2013). However, I was overwhelmed by the diversity of disciplines that have recently taken topological approaches (from philosophy, music and theatre to mathematics) when I attended a conference that focused on the topological approach to cultural changes in Barcelona in 2009. Celia Lury (2013), one of the conference organizers, explains that the conceptual language of topology has recently been taken up in social and cultural theory, a trend that Shields (2012) calls a 'topological turn'. Marres (2012) even points out that it is hard to overestimate the importance of topology in social and cultural studies. The topological approach helps to articulate multi-domain social experience. For example, Latour has explained that topological ideas dismantle the idea that technology and society occupy different domains, and helps to develop the concept of 'assemblage' by which social, technical and natural entities are composed (Latour, 1988; Lury, 2013: 128). Generally, scholars have paid more attention to topology as a metaphorical language, and not as a rigorous analytical method in social science and cultural studies. The result has been a 'topological insight' to comprehending socio-spatial phenomena in social science.

To give an example, Shields (2012) notes how the topological approach helps one to understand the geography of a global era when distance has lost its conventional meaning. Because of the economic ease of travel and the speed of communications, our world is shrinking, leading to negation of space (Virilio, 1986: 133). Moreover, during the 1990s, scholars including Appadurai (1990), Cohen (1997) and Scholte (2000) suggested that globalization de-territorializes our landscape. However, trans-local networks that are topological in nature and in which the metric distance has lost its conventional meaning dominate the landscape of the global era. Shields argued that 'it is not a matter of negation of space but a change to conventional understandings and practices of space, a topological shift which involves both time and space: new cultural topology' (Shields, 2012: 49). Moreover, Shields has revisited the well-known social theories, including Giddens' or Harvey's time-space, under the light of topological insight. He reminds us that these theories have intertwined two different domains by conceptually employing topological ideas without directly announcing them as such. In this landscape, Lury (2013: 128) states that cultural change is increasingly becoming topological. She argues that this new reality calls not only for the use of topology as a conceptual language or theoretical framework, but also for the need to investigate the emergence of a topological culture. While I agree with Lury, the study of Muharram processions shows that socio-cultural practices are not becoming topological, but have been topological.

The notion of relative space theoretically envisages the production of performed space through Muharram processions, and the conceptual language of topology helps to formulate the integral manifold aspects of such a space. The traditional Muharram processions were articulated without such theoretical complexities (in chapter three), explaining that Muharram processions create a space in which social relations are maintained, practised and negotiated. However, the study of urban transformation and the re-arrangement of processions (in this chapter and in chapter four) calls for a theoretical framework that takes into account the complexity of the re-arranged processions. Lefebvre's idea of 'space as a social product' advances the understanding of Muharram processions as a medium to produce socially performed space. However, the conceptual language of topology makes it theoretically conceivable to formulate the performed space as a manifold system, in which spatial and temporal folds are not inter-related, but rather entwined. On one hand, the performed space is the result of the spatio-temporal orchestration of Muharram processions. On the other hand, the performed space offers the possibility of discursively practising the past and present of the city. Casting the performed space of Muharram as a topological space defines and integrates the extremely complex heterogeneous aspects of such a space.

Lefebvre's idea of history suggests that a historical passage is involved in breaking from one social mode into another. However, the study of Muharram processions suggests that the passage from the traditional urban constitution to the contemporary urban setting is not about breaking out from the past or even continuing the social past. The past and present are rather topologically intertwining in the performed space.

## Conclusion

This chapter has analysed the spatial connotations of Muharram processions that were re-arranged to signify urban transformation. These discussions revealed that the Iranian urban transformation is far more complex than what is often described when just focusing on what the modern Iranian state implemented. The Iranian Modernization was a project executed by the modern Pahlavi dynasty, but the urban and social transformation has developed beyond the aims of the deterministic Modernization projects. Of course, the social transformation was the result of the Iranian Modernization project. However, the procedure and the ways in which the changes unfolded are far from what the project engineers intended. This chapter illustrates the complexity of social transformation through an exploration of the spatial aspects of Muharram processions.

The significance of proposing the idea of performed space as topological space is more than a theoretical development in urban studies. Despite its theoretical complexity, the performed space of Muharram commemoration reveals a few simple but rather crucial points that advance the ways in which the city and its transformation are articulated. First, urban studies must not limit its investigations to the everyday status of the city. The liminal time of rituals is important because it produces not only a space for the intensive social interaction during rituals, but also an alternative social mode of space production that differs from the everyday social mode of production. As yet, we have a very limited knowledge about this social mode of space production, partly since the spatial curiosities in ritual studies have predominantly focused on the ritual in sacred places, and very little attention has been paid to spatially articulating the ritual (also see chapter one). Second, the perception and conception of a city are not always a reflection of the built environment. Instead, the social and mental perception of the hidden city structure is experienced through the processions. While such lived structures cannot be captured in the spatial pattern of everyday life and the morphology of urban structures, it is experienced through the collective performance that shapes the social and mental dimensions of the city.

## NOTES

1. As Safari has noted, the boroughs were later named Tabaar, Uchdokaan, Pir-abdolmalek, Unchi-maydan, Cheshmeh-bashi and Shikh Qabaghi respectively.
2. Asghar-zadeh (interviewed in March 2006 in Ardabil) has referred to oral narratives that he received and explained that the city governor, named Ali Bahadori, made a conciliation between Heydari and Nemati parties and established the new procession schedule that is still followed today. However, he did not give a date for this during the interview. This would date back to the late Qajar or early Pahlavi era, when a violent period was reported by Safari (1974) and Kasravi (1974: 195–97). Safari reported that by the late 1890s Heydari–Nemati tension escalated and caused serious violence between localities during Muharram, when each part of the city was supported by nomadic tribes. In response to the violence, a united council was established in 1908 (Safari, 1974: 200–202). Safari's testimony shows that the violence did not end in 1908; however, he did not specify when the violence took place and when the processions were re-arranged.
3. This is also the case in the city of Ardabil, where the spatial organization of processions has not changed for about a century.

CHAPTER 6

# Reinventing Muharram Rites

This chapter looks at the reinvention of the shawl exchange ritual and how in the late 2000s shawls are worn in a new way in Dezful. The new style of wearing shawls is not only visually fascinating but also an innovative social practice. This chapter departs from the 'spatial dynamics' of Muharram processions and contributes to an articulation of the dynamics of Muharram commemoration in general. The previous chapters examined the rearrangement of procession routes in the early 1950s in Dezful, an initiative that enabled conciliation between traditional rival parts of the city, known as Heydari and Nemati. Since the early 1950s, the procession arrangement has not changed. Why has the spatial organization of this socially representational practice not changed throughout what can be considered a very dynamic period in many other respects? Based on historical observations, I argue that 'the spatial organization' of processions will not change unless the constitution of urban society is fundamentally transformed. Although the configuration of procession routes has not changed in the past half-century, the landscape of Muharram remembrance has changed to reflect the social dynamics of the period. This chapter examines the dynamics of Muharram commemoration by focusing on the reinvention of the shawl exchange and shawl wearing.

The Muharram procession includes a repertoire of rites, symbolic gestures, social interactions and exchanges, all of which are in constant flux. In Iran, none of the Muharram rituals, including the procession, have ever solely been about the Ashura tragedy. They are charged with social agendas that serve to drive the dynamics of the rituals. This chapter is not about the dynamics of all the rites and performances associated with Muharram procession. The focus is on the changes in the ritual of exchanging shawls, a rite that signifies social recognition and friendship between individuals

**FIGURE 6.1** Ashura day, Dezful, February 2006. Photograph by the author.

and communities. This rite has evolved from a welcoming exchange and symbolic social recognition into an extraordinary fashion performance in contemporary Dezful. Instead of donning one or two shawls around their necks, individuals make a statement by wearing hundreds of shawls to proclaim their social status during Muharram. I read this initiative as a response to the situation in which some Muharram rites gradually diminished and many others were suppressed by the Iranian Islamic state after the Iranian Revolution (1979). This reinvention shows the cultural resilience capacity of common people in sustaining the ability to express and practice their social identity.

What makes the invention of the new style of wearing shawls particularly interesting is that the new custom was invented within a very short time. However, this spontaneous invention was well established and fully comprehended by everybody, since it was based upon the rite of exchanging shawls, which has a long history in Dezful. Luckily, this development unfolded during my fieldwork in 2006. However, the discussions in this chapter are not limited to my observations and interviews during my fieldwork. In order to fully articulate the process of this cultural initiative, this chapter looks at its broad historical and socio-political background. The discussion begins with a review of the traditional customs around the symbolic flag of the union, the symbolic exchange of friendship, and the practice of ritualized violence before the 1950s in Dezful. The second discussion looks at the dynamics of the Muharram commemoration landscape after the 1950s. This section also reviews the pressure placed on Muharram rituals by elites and authorities in the twentieth century, especially after the 1979 Revolution. The last section is predominantly based on my accounts and observations about the socially complex exchanging and wearing of shawls.

## Symbolism in Traditional Muharram Processions, from *Alams* to Shawls

Every Muharram union has an *alam* (flag) that symbolizes Hussein's standard in the battle of Karbala. Shi'i communities around the world have developed symbolic flags in diverse forms, shapes and sizes. In Dezful, the *alam* is mainly made of a long tree branch or trunk, dressed up and ornamented by shawls. The height of a Muharram union flag can be anywhere from six to nine metres, even up to twelve metres. As the symbolic flag represents Muharram unions, there has always been competition among localities to have the highest flag. The *alam* is often dressed in black shawls with a few colourful shawls at the very top, where a metal *panjeh*[1] is fitted. In the past, a few Muharram unions in Dezful differentiated their flags by dressing them in white or green shawls. In doing so these unions claimed a special status for themselves, as those unions were associated with sacred shrines or Friday Mosque. However, the number of distinguished flags has increased in recent times. This evidently shows that claiming such a status is part of social negotiation during Muharram, when every urban community tries, by all means, to claim social superiority.

Lifting and balancing the tall, heavy symbolic flag through processions symbolizes the struggle to keep Imam Hussein's standard flying in the battle of Karbala. The union flags used to be carried by groups of strong youths at the front of processions. There has always been competition among the youths to show their physical strength and skill in lifting and holding the symbolic flag. This competition is constituted in the rite of dancing the flag, known as *alam-yaraq* in Dezful (see also chapter two). This rite takes place in an open public space, often adjacent to the local religious community centre. The local youths show off their skills by lifting the flag and running around the local square to the rhythm of playing drums. In a more elaborate form of this rite in Dezful, the music is played by a small band, including a couple of drums and a *sorna*, a woodwind instrument. The rite is often practised in the late evening and naturally attracts many spectators. The most skilful person in lifting and balancing the flag is known as the locality's *alam-dar* (the flag-holder), an honourable position in the local Muharram union.

Traditionally, the symbolic union flag was carried by a group of flag-holders who were led by the appointed flag-holder throughout the processions.
The flag-holder of the locality oversees the flag and collects donations to pre-
pare the flag for Muharram. The few female interviewees I spoke with made
some very interesting points about the role of the flag-holder, points that
were never mentioned by my predominantly male interviewees. My interviews with Fatemeh-sultan Fathi and Hajar Karami were semi-structured,
like the other interviews; however, the discussion followed different topics
compared to my interviews with men. Fatemeh-sultan was in her late seventies and Hajar was in her early seventies when I interviewed them in 2006.
They both came from well-off families. One was from a Heydari locality
and the other from a Nemati locality. Interestingly, they both described the
flag-holder as a kind of social figure, and explained that when Muharram was
approaching the flag-holder began contacting wealthy families and collecting fabrics to adorn the top of the symbolic flag. Both women explained that
having a small stock of fabrics at home used to be a sign of wealth. Therefore,
the flag-holder visited the house of wealthy families in the locality to solicit
and collect precious fabrics for the symbolic flag. One of the interviewees
also noted that if a family kept fabrics for an expected baby, they would lend
some of the fabrics to be blessed by the flag.

The social interactions of the flag-holder with families in localities for
collecting donations or borrowing fabric shows that this position was not
based solely on physical ability. He could keep his position over time if he
had the ability to gain social trust within the community. In other words,
youths traditionally compete and show off their physical ability in order to
join the circle of flag-holders of their locality; however, the flag-holder must
also have social abilities in order to hold this privileged position. By missing
this fine social point, many scholars consider the rite of flag lifting (or similar
performances) as 'the rite of masculinity'[2] (Torab, 2007). There is no doubt
that these practices involve physical ability. However, these rites mediate
far more complex social interactions and negotiations through which individuals claim, assert, and maintain an important social position, such as the
flag-holder, during Muharram. Therefore, I argue against the scholarly pre-
occupation with applying academic discourses/jargons that do not advance
our understanding about these socially complex rites and practices. In the
absence of deep ethnographic fieldwork, such academic preoccupations can
lead to a misreading or a reductionist reading of these socially complex rites.

Traditionally, the unions carried processions toward neighbouring localities, or passed through localities during the final procession of Ashura day.
Visiting and passing through another locality demonstrated the social intimacy and friendship between the two localities.[3] These visits were welcomed
with symbolic gestures such as exchanging shawls. Commonly, the seniors

and union leaders, the dirge singer, and the flag-holders were honoured by a shawl. These symbolic exchanges registered the friendship between the two communities and also demonstrated the social status of those individuals who had a key role in representing their community during Muharram.

The processions were never free from tension and violence. Muharram rituals, like many other rituals, channel violence and, to some degree, justify it as part of alternative norms during the liminal time of ritual. René Girard (1977) has argued that rituals emerged from a foundation of primal violence. He has even argued that 'violence, in every cultural order, is always the true subject of every ritual or institutional structure' (Girard, 2003: 210). Historically, there were many occasions when tensions arose between localities over a dispute between the landlord families who governed the city boroughs. However, Muharram was always the time when disputes and tensions intensified among communities (see chapter three). When a procession entered the territory of another locality, the procession was either welcomed with symbolic gestures or violently challenged. Therefore, those who were in the front of the procession, such as the flag-holders, had to be physically strong and ready for fighting. Historically, the most serious tension and fighting occurred if a procession crossed the Heydari–Nemati border that traditionally divided Iranian cities into two rival parts. If a procession crossed this border, it was considered an incursion and attack. Those communities that saw their territory under attack violently challenged the unwelcome procession. The strangers' symbolic flag would be broken and their drums would be torn apart to keep the invading procession silent and defeated.[4] This ritualized violence was part of social competition among urban communities and an assertion of social superiority.

The social solidarity among communities was partly the result of ritualized violence against the 'other' Muharram unions (e.g. see Bell, 1997: 16). Although the engagement of individuals in street fights was socially disgraceful, ritualized violence during the liminal time of Muharram was perceived differently. Those brave front processionists who were involved in ritualized violence were proud of their role in proclaiming the dignity and the superiority of their community. These individuals were privileged with liminal social status within their community during Muharram, a social status that they would not have otherwise enjoyed in their everyday lives.

As I extensively discussed in previous chapters and elsewhere (Masoudi Nejad, 2014, 2015), although it is often argued that religious processions escalate urban violence, these rituals also mediate communal harmony and social conciliation. In fact, many disputes between communities were often settled during Muharram. If two communities reached a conciliation then they would welcome each other's processions with symbolic gestures such as honouring individuals in the front of processions with shawls. The process of reaching conciliations often involves behind-the-scenes negotiations between influential members of localities. The front processionists with physical capability played an important role in maintaining social conciliation and friendship with other localities. Therefore, their liminal social status during Muharram is not based on ritualized violence, but on their contribution to maintaining the social dignity of their community through fighting or friendship.

The social landscape of Muharram commemoration fundamentally changed in the early 1950s in Dezful, when the Heydari–Nemati division was abolished and the long-term enmity between the two urban parties ended. This historic social conciliation between the two moieties was initiated and established through Muharram rituals.[5] The processions that were organized in two separate territories were re-arranged to mediate symbolic visits between Heydari and Nemati localities. Now the processions are welcome when they pass through the territory of an old rival. Every host locality has a stand or kiosk placed along the procession route that greets and welcomes visiting processions. The host localities offer snacks and drinks to processionists, and sometimes animals are sacrificed as a blessing gesture. The rite of exchanging shawls remains a symbolic practice to signify friendships between localities. Of course, the Muharram observances are not entirely free from tension even today. However, as the re-arranged processions are socially aimed at demonstrating friendship between old rivals, the ritualized violence has gradually lost its social function. In this new landscape, those front processionists who were ready for fighting are now friendly with their counterparts and interact with them through the symbolic gesture of exchanging shawls, which conveys respect to the person honoured by the shawl.

## The Dynamics of Muharram Rites in the Post-1950s and the Revolution of 1979

There were numerous Muharram rituals and rites in which youths were in the limelight. The rite of *alam-yaraq* (the flag dance), the rite of *choo-zani* (playing wood), and *shemshail-sopar* (sword-and-shield) were three of the popular rites, among others, which were held in Dezful. Since the 1950s, when ritualized violence began to gradually disappear from the Muharram landscape, these rites became even more important in facilitating the practice of youth social identity. The rite of playing wood is a kind of participatory ceremonial dance that dramatically narrates the battle of Karbala. In this performance, participants hold and beat two logs of wood, about 15 cm long, while they jump and move in a circle. They bounce and move to the beat that they play. With each jump the participants turn, face the person next to them, and beat one another's wooden logs. The rite of sword-and-shield was a fighting performance using a sword or, alternatively, a bamboo stick wherein a group of participants fought each other while a small band of drummers played a heroic melody. Although this rite was a more realistic performance, it incorporated dancing and was performed by skilled participants.[6] These performances naturally attracted a crowd of spectators. The last time that I personally observed these two rites in Dezful was in the very early 1980s.

A wide range of rites and performances, from the rite of lifting *alam* and exchanging shawls to ritualized violence and the rite of playing wood, contribute to creating and stimulating the liminal status of Muharram. The commemoration of the Ashura tragedy, like other rituals and festivals, is carried out during a liminal state where social norms are altered or ignored (van Gennep, 1960). More importantly, social relations are defined according to an alternative social structure, articulated by Turner as 'anti-structure' (Turner, 1969). In this circumstance, individuals have a temporal or liminal social status that is not defined by an individual's everyday social class/position. During Muharram, an uninfluential individual can become a very important person in his locality due to his skill in lifting *alam*, playing music, or fighting to claim the superiority of his community. Although individuals from across social classes became key figures in their local Muharram unions, interviews with socially disadvantaged individuals indicate the significance of Muharram in satisfying this group. The liminal period gives these individuals social satisfaction and privilege due to their positive contribution to their community. However, it was not just the ritualized violence that faded from the landscape of Muharram commemoration in the post-1950s. Many other rites were diminished or suppressed by cultural and political forces after the Revolution of 1979.

Traditionally, the union's *alam* (symbolic flag) was carried in the front of the procession by a group of flag-holders, each of whom carried the symbolic flag for some distance. As unions became bigger and jammed the narrow alleys of the old city, the procession took much longer to reach the final destination. After the 1950s, the symbolic flags also became taller and heavier in a new symbolic competition between the unions of localities that wanted to symbolically manifest their superiority. This makes carrying the symbolic flags throughout very crowded processions a difficult and very risky practice. Should the flag-holder lose control, the tall and heavy flag falls into the crowd, leaving a group of casualties. Moreover, interviewees who talked about this subject also noted that certain features of the modern city, such as electrical wires stretched across streets and alleys, made it difficult to carry very tall symbolic flags throughout the processions. This rite gradually became a less integral part of Muharram processions.[7]

**FIGURE 6.2** The last few *alams* at the Shrine of Roodband on the morning of
Ashura day. Dezful, February 2006. Photograph by the author.

More recently, the union's flags have been carried to the shrine of
Roodband very early on the morning of Ashura day, often before sunrise.
Since the 1950s, this shrine has been the destination of all processions on
Ashura morning in Dezful. However, the symbolic flags are carried much
earlier than the beginning of the procession. The procession of *alams* became
an independent ritual of the very early morning when few spectators were
around to observe it. Each *alam* is carried by a small group of 10-12 men.
They often lay the *alam* on their shoulders and carry it to Roodband cemetery, near the shrine. When they arrive at the cemetery they lift and hold
the *alam* upright, and walk or run with it towards the shrine to the rhythm
of music played by a drummer. All of the *alams* are placed at the shrine and
only later, when each union's procession arrives at the shrine, are the *alams*
removed. The diminishment of carrying the symbolic flag through the procession was a natural and gradual change. Many other rites were suppressed
after the 1979 Revolution.

Although the Pahlavi era is associated with the suppression of Muharram
rituals, the 1979 Revolution had a greater impact on the rites. Previously,
men performed chest-beating in the processions while topless. After the revolution, people began questioning this norm. The argument was that this was
not acceptable according to Islamic teachings given that many procession
spectators were women. Since then, men in the procession have dressed in

black shirts. A more important change was linked to the fact that the Iranian Islamic state is headed by a religious figure, entangling political and religious authorities in a theocracy. In contrast to the previous Shi'i dynasties, i.e. the Safavids (r. 1501–1722), the Qajars (r. 1789–1925), and the Pahlavis (r. 1925–1979),[8] the Islamic state claimed direct authority over religious matters, such as approving some Muharram rituals and outlawing others. Right from the beginning, the Islamic state, well aware of Muharram commemoration as a powerful social institution, began controlling this annual event. While the Islamic state has supported Muharram commemoration, it has also imposed a certain agenda on it and made decisions on which rituals and practices are legitimate. Many rituals and performances believed to be illegitimate have been suppressed.

For example, the first Iranian supreme leader, Ayatullah S. Ruhollah Khomeini, disapproved of Muharram flagellation and issued several official religious decrees/opinions (*estefta-aat*). In these he emphasized limiting flagellation at the 'current time', fearing that the practice would spread a negative image around the world and discredit the Islamic state. In response to a religious question about flagellation, he replied: 'If it does not harm, it will be no impediment. But in the current time, do not practice it' (Khomeini, 2013a: 581). Later in 1981 he disapproved of flagellation in general, without any conditions (Khomeini, 2013b: 644–45). The second Iranian supreme leader, Ayatullah S. Ali Khamenei, also disapproved flagellation on religious grounds by stating that this practice was not considered to be the manifestation of sorrow, as it had no background at the time of the Shi'i *imams*, and it created a negative perception of the religion.[9] Although there are many high ranked Shi'i clergy who hold a different view and opinion about practising flagellation (e.g. see Masoudi Nejad, 2017), the state policy obviously follows and promotes the supreme leaders' religious statements.

As previously discussed, there are very diverse local Muharram rituals performed around the country. This made it impossible for the Iranian Islamic state or any single religious authority to make statements about all Muharram rituals. Therefore, local authorities, influential local Shi'i clergies, and more importantly the Komiyteh Enghalab Eslami (the revolutionary police) independently made decisions about local rituals and imposed their policies during the early 1980s. The common argument for outlawing and banning local rituals was that these rites and performances had nothing to do with Shi'i sorrow, and served more for entertainment. In Dezful, the state authorities abandoned many local rituals, such as the rite of *choo-zani* (playing wood) and *shemshail-sopar* (sword-and-shield) during the early 1980s. For years, the Dezful authorities also banned playing *sorna*, a blown wooden instrument, and heavily controlled Muharram events to impose these regulations. These local policies suddenly changed the landscape of Muharram observance in Dezful, and created a hostile situation for common people in a religious society where their social life was defined through Muharram rituals. Many interviewees spoke nostalgically about their role in banned performances. Although today official authorities may take a more relaxed approach toward the traditional performances, many rites – including the two aforementioned ones – were never revived.

The heart of Islamic state policy on Muharram rituals was a denial of the very nature of rituals and the historical fact that the Muharram commemoration has never solely been aimed at a religious agenda. Since the Safavids,[10] the Muharram rituals have shaped the Iranian 'public sphere' (Rahimi, 2004). The rituals facilitated religious agendas, manifested local culture, expressed social identity and included socio-political negotiations, public entertainment, and much more. Iranians have actively developed all kinds of rituals to commemorate Muharram by appropriating folklore performance arts (dance and music) based on the vernacular culture of religious society around the country. The rite of *bill-zani* (playing shovels), was incorporated into Muharram processions and reflects the agricultural culture of Birjand.[11] The multiple socio-cultural purposes and meanings are a common ground for rituals and festivals, and are not unique to the Muharram rituals. Schechner (1993), who studies performance arts in its broadest definition, has even argued that performance arts reach a pinnacle when religious rituals and entertainment are entwined in a performance. This idea expresses very well the nature of the Muharram passion play (*t'azyeh*) during the nineteenth-century Qajar era, which Chelkowski (2005) recognized as the most advanced and powerful form of Iranian drama. Although the Muharram passion play is aimed at narrating the tragedy of Karbala, it also became 'the' entertaining performance of the late Qajar era (Bayzaei, 2000: 114 &121). Despite the fact that religious establishments often objected to the play, the popularity of the play totally dominated the landscape of Muharram commemoration during the second half of the nineteenth century (e.g. Bayzaei, 2000: 120–21; Flandin, 1851). The Qajars were passionate patrons of Muharram rituals, a policy that greatly contributed to their popularity. This not only granted them the support of Shi'i establishments to legitimize their political authority, but also increased their social popularity in a deeply religious society. However, they had a fragile relationship with Shi'i establishments that sometimes mobilized the masses against the rule of the Qajars during the political turbulence of the nineteenth century (e.g. see Algar, 1969). Aghaie (2005) has argued that the Qajars tactically controlled the social power of Shi'i establishments by sponsoring Muharram rituals such as the Muharram passion play. These examples show that the landscape of Muharram was produced through complex socio-cultural and political processes over which religious establishments did not have full and direct control.

The liminal period of Muharram is the time when everyday norms are altered or ignored (van Gennep, 1960). Muharram provides a space in which individuals could experience a kind of freedom from the restraints of religious-social discipline and norms. For example, extreme gender segregation is relaxed during Muharram and people have an opportunity to mix with the opposite gender in public spaces. In other words, Muharram rituals blur or relax many of the roles and norms of religious society that are normally obeyed in the everyday. In his memoir, Haj Sayyah extensively criticizes Iranian society, including the landscape of Muharram commemoration in the late Qajar era. However, his account captures the liminal status in Tehran. He writes that 'the month of Muharram and Safar that are namely the months of mourn, actually are the month of out-and-about, seeing and being seen, freedom, misdemeanour and flirting, greedy, exhibiting luxury, and showing off especially at the Tekyeh-i Dowlat' (Sayyah, 1967: 87–88). Later he explains that there are no public entertainment events in Tehran and music is not allowed in public spaces in Iran. People are depressed by the restrictions that religious teachings impose on the public. He notes that 'The only escaping-way, which no one can object public [entertaining] events, is to name it after religious pious and devotion. The entertainment should be concealed in religious dress as this is the only escaping-way; [therefore] there are excessive bombasts and new innovations in this way' (Sayyah, 1967: 91). What Sayyah describes resonates in contemporary Iran. The Iranian cities are turned into a ritual arena during Muharram, when devotional practices, social interactions, and even religiously unacceptable behaviours are simultaneously manifested in public spaces. I recall that during the late 1980s, one of the darkest periods for public life in Iran, the atmosphere in some Muharram unions in Dezful pushed the boundaries so much that they were called 'discoes', while the evening performances held by unions were heavily controlled and watched by authorities.

Sayyah's memoir represents the increase in criticisms of Muharram rituals in the late nineteenth century. By the time of the Constitutional Revolution (1905–1911), secular and religious intellectuals increasingly criticized the ways in which common people commemorated the tragedy of Karbala. The position of these intellectuals can be seen as the foundation for the policy of the Pahlavis and the Islamic state after the revolution (1979) on Muharram rituals. The common ground that linked all these political and intellectual authorities was to deny the complex social role of Muharram rituals. The religious establishments, as well as religious intellectuals, considered the commemoration to be solely a religious practice and have always discouraged or disapproved practices that do not register this or challenge their authority in any form. On the other hand, the secular intellectuals rejected Muharram events altogether. They ignorantly dismissed the social significance of Muharram rituals, and considered them as the cause and the sign of social and cultural backwardness. This discourse is well expressed by Iranian intellectuals of the early twentieth century, such as Kasravi, who struggled against established religious values in traditional Iranian society. The secular intellectuals generally focused on the historical facts of the political dispute leading to the battle of Karbala, replacing Shi'i narratives with historical facts. In other words, this discourse demythologizes the tragedy of Karbala as the Shi'i myth, around which all Muharram rituals are developed, and ultimately aimed at making Muharram rituals meaningless.

Due to secular intellectual discourse and the Pahlavi state policy of discouraging Muharram rituals, the educated middle class commonly distanced themselves from religious rituals during the Pahlavi era. However, the grassroots of Iranian society never lost their deep connection to Muharram rituals because of the significance of the rituals in their social lives. As Sayyed Ghasem Ya-Husseini has mentioned, Reza Shah brutally suppressed and banned the public manifestation of Muharram rituals. However, when he was removed from power in 1941, people responded by overwhelmingly reviving all outlawed rituals, including the more irrational practices of self-flagellation (Ya-Husseini, 1992). As a religious intellectual, Ya-Husseini refused rituals such as the flagellation and argued that secular and Marxist intellectuals heavily attacked religious culture all together, by pointing their fingers at irrational practices such as flagellation. He made this argument in his introduction to *Azadari-haye Na-Mashro* (Amin, 1992),[12] a book that was initially translated and published by Jalal Al-e-Ahmad in 1953. Al-e-Ahmad was a prominent intellectual figure who aimed to challenge religious rituals like flagellation. Although this book received a negative backlash from religious communities in Tehran, it signified a new religious discourse that gradually rose to challenge orthodox religious norms and culture.

During the Pahlavi era, secular discourse predominantly influenced the position of the educated urban middle class on Muharram rituals. This changed with the rise of Dr Ali Shariati (d. 1977), one of the most influential religious-intellectual figures of the late 1960s. He actively produced a new reading of Shi'i Islam to mobilize new generations of educated middle classes against the tyranny of the Pahlavi monarch. To that end, Shariati focused on the battle of Karbala as the eternal battle between right and wrong, to produce a revolutionary paradigm. He argued that Ashura is about the entirety of history and human responsibility in history, therefore he claimed that the Shi'i philosophy of history is superior to the deterministic philosophy of dialectical materialism (Shariati, 2001: 130).[13] He argued that the essence of the Shi'i paradigm and the historic lesson of Hussein's uprising is eternal duty in the struggle for justice. This reading strongly reflects the Shi'i idea of the Ashura tragedy as meta-history (see chapter two). However, Shariati (1971) heavily condemned Muharram rituals as an important part of his revolutionary reading of Shi'i Islam. He believed that these rituals created a passive society that accepted cultural and political establishments.

Shariati claimed that the Safavids (r. 1501–1722) invented a reading of Shi'i Islam to fulfil their political authority, turning the revolutionary Shi'i Islam into a teaching that focuses on passive mourning over the tragedy of Ashura. He even argued that Muharram rituals were imported by the Safavids from Christian Europe, and that the rituals that have no roots in either Iranian or Shi'i culture (Shariati, 1971: 223–24). Clearly, there is very little evidence to support Shariati's reading of Muharram ritual history as a rootless practice in Shi'i history and Iran. There is evidence that links Muharram flagellation to similar rituals in the Italian Renaissance (see Nakash, 1993). However, the Muharram rituals developed through a complex socio-political and cultural process over a long period across the Shi'i world from Egypt to Iran, India and beyond. These rituals were dispersed around the Shi'i world, constantly (re)invented and diffused into local culture (see chapter two). Moreover, historians have shown that many Muharram performances are based on Iranian pre-Islamic practices, most famously the mourning ritual of Sog-e Siavash that had striking similarities to the commemoration of the Ashura tragedy (Bayzaei, 2000: 30, 55; e.g. see Yarshater, 1979). Shariati's classification of Muharram rituals as a baseless public festival has little evidentiary support. The arguments of his fiery sermons, published as *The Alavid Shiism and the Safavid Shiism*,[14] should be understood as part of his grand political project to produce a revolutionary reading of Shi'i Islam. This reading was aimed at undermining traditional Shi'i establishments that Shariati believed indirectly supported the political establishment of the Pahlavi. Unquestionably, Shariati was one of the greatest socio-political activists of twentieth-century in Iran, who creatively produced a reading of Islam that convinced and mobilized the educated urban middle classes against the Pahlavi monarchy. Yet his approach was problematic in its emphasis of the Ashura tragedy as a Shi'i myth and articulation of the battle of Karbala as meta-history, while refusing Muharram rituals and ignoring inherent interconnection between myth, creeds and rituals (see also chapters one and two). Nonetheless, Shariati has deeply influenced and shaped the religious intellectual discourse in condemning many Muharram rituals as a set of fabricated practices that have nothing to do with the true message of Hussein's uprising. This argument was echoed by state authorities after the 1979 Revolution and was used to diminish and suppress many Muharram rituals, such as the rite of *choozani* (playing wood) in Dezful. Above all, Shariati's approach contributed to dividing the Muharram rituals of the religious elites from those of the common people.

This historical review depicts the pressurized landscape of Muharram rituals under the influence of political and religious authorities and intellectual elites. Today the Iranian Islamic state policy promotes the symbolism of Ashura as a Shi'i myth and Muharram rituals as solely religious practices, an agenda strongly promoted by state media. Conversely, online social media predominantly features the secular discourse of de-mythicizing the Ashura tragedy. The religious and secular agendas for Muharram rituals may be oppositional but they both deny the social reality of rituals and further contract the liminal social space offered to common people in the Muharram rituals. Interestingly, the contemporary struggle between elites and common people over Muharram public performances echoes the historical landscape of performance arts during the early Islamic era. Bayzaei shows that while common people find a space for their social life through all kinds of public spectacles and performances, educated elites have never taken those performance arts to be serious and important. They did not see these performances as worthy of study or careful recording (2000: 52). The result is a limited number of historical testimonies and reports on Muharram rituals, while these rituals have dominated the public sphere since the Safavid era. These limited historical reports are almost entirely European-authored, without which we would have very little idea about the rituals even during the mid-nineteenth century. Even by the late nineteenth century, it was predominantly Europeans officials and diplomats who reported and recorded the details of Muharram rituals in Tehran.

Political elites have fulfilled their authority through Muharram commemoration. However, the liminal time of Muharram produces a space that has been very important for the social life of powerless people. Therefore, when large numbers of rites and rituals either diminished or were suppressed after the 1979 Revolution, common people constantly (re)invented new costumes and rites that helped them to express their social identity in public spaces. Meanwhile, religious educated elites have predominantly tried to 'purify' the observance of Ashura, and dismissed the cultural significance of common people's initiatives.

## The Invention of a New Rite

Today, the landscape of Muharram commemoration in Dezful is free from ritualized violence and many traditional performances and rites have disappeared from public spaces. Although the state policy in regulating traditional Muharram rituals is much more relaxed, the post-revolution policy permanently extinguished many rites. Although these changes socially disempowered people, the people have exhibited a great cultural resilience in claiming and maintaining their social status during Muharram by inventing new symbolic gestures, such as wearing hundreds of shawls.

As previously discussed, the exchanging of shawls to honour important members of Muharram unions has a long history in Dezful. This symbolic exchange became more common after the social conciliation of the 1950s. In more recent times, it has also become common practice for someone to donate tens of shawls to a local community's Muharram union. These shawls were either distributed among processionists of the local community, or more commonly they were used to symbolically welcome the procession of other localities. While exchanging shawls was very common, it was practised on a limited scale and recipients of shawls were often key union figures. Therefore, the scale of exchanging shawls during the first days of Muharram in 2006 surprised me. At all Muharram events, I observed that people widely gave shawls to others as a sign of friendship. As ever, the key individuals of unions were honoured by shawls, but this gesture was extensively practised among friends too. I was particularly surprised that I too received many shawls during events at which I did participatory observation. This was my hometown, thus some of the shawls were given by my old friends who had not seen me in a long time. In a few instances strangers honoured me with shawls. It seemed to be a way of showing appreciation to someone who was visiting their locality and producing a photo-documentary.

After a few days of receiving some shawls, I learned from the behaviour of others that I should wear my shawls all the time, as my social decoration. I was happy to do so as the shawls conveyed upon me the status of a local participant and not an outside observer. On one of the days, I received too many shawls and weirdly, I felt socially proud. I describe it as a weird feeling since my initial assumption was that I would not be involved in this social exchange. While I was walking back home, a little boy approached me and asked if he could have one of my shawls. I asked him to choose one, and I dropped it over his neck. He happily and proudly ran back to his mum. This simple interaction pulled me into the social game of exchanging shawls. Within a few days, the exchange of shawls soared and spread like a firestorm. People extensively practised honouring their friends and the senior members of unions with shawls.

By the 9th of Muharram, when the first major procession in Dezful takes place,[15] the reinvented exchanging and wearing of shawls was not only recognized by everyone but was also fully established. Usually people have one shawl but by then, many had more than a few. Those individuals who claim an important social position in their union now distinguish themselves from the crowds by wearing not five or ten but dozens and hundreds of colourful shawls. Traditionally, these individuals led the procession, carried the symbolic flag of their union, and were ready to fight for the superiority of their

**FIGURE 6.3**  Handing a friend a shawl during a procession in Dezful, February 2006. Photograph by the author.

locality. Quite clearly, these individuals are honoured by many during the first days of Muharram. However, the mountain of shawls does not necessarily mean that they received them one by one. This spectacle is an invented statement to declare their liminal social status. These individuals predominantly used to practise their social identity through physically demanding rites. Now, the mass of shawls has transformed their physical body into a 'social body',[16] symbolically manifesting their social identity.

I was curious about the development and establishment of such a symbolic exchange within such a short time, and assumed that this had developed gradually over several years. When I asked my family members and friends about it, they all said that this was the first time that wearing shawls in this way was so popular in the city. This innovation took place so quickly in part because it has its roots in the cultural symbolism of the shawl, which has a long historical precedent. The reinvention of a practice based on local cultural capital demonstrates an impressive capacity for cultural resilience.

This new Muharram fashion is a body statement based on immaterial social values associated with shawls made from very cheap fabric. The accumulation of hundreds of colourful shawls creates a unique aesthetic form that certainly contributes to the popularity of this fashion. I would argue that the popularity of this Muharram fashion is based on associating social and aesthetic values with shawls that have minimal material value. Modern high fashion is an industry that is quintessentially based on the constant invention of new aesthetic styles to distinguish privileged social classes by bodily and symbolically representing their economic capital in public spaces (Bourdieu, 1993). Although Western/modern fashion is a cultural institution (e.g. see Entwistle, 2015), it is ultimately driven by the capitalist logic of the fashion industry. On the contrary, wearing hundreds of shawls is a fashion of the common people whose invention is socially driven. This new style of wearing shawls particularly signifies the liminal social status of certain individuals who gain social privilege only during Muharram. While everybody can afford to wear hundreds of shawls, only those individuals who claim a special status for themselves in their Muharram union will make such a body statement. This new body statement was invented by the younger generation. However, as the 'social body', not the physical body, signifies the liminal status, many senior members of unions also employed it.

As a part of my participatory observation, I joined the Ashura morning procession of a locality that was historically located in a Nemati part of the city. The people of this locality used to be known for their willingness to use violence during Muharram rituals in order to claim superiority over other localities before the 1950s. For some distance, I followed the most influential member of this union, who was constantly honoured by shawls throughout the procession. He was walking at the front of the procession in an extremely charismatic manner, while he was surrounded by a group of men acting like his bodyguards. They were not really protecting him from harm, but were creating a space to show that he was a VIP. This man might be one of the best examples of the individuals I have been focusing on in this chapter. Raised in a poor working-class family, he asserted his social status and identity through Muharram rituals. He is well known across the city for his active engagement in ritualized violence during Muharram rituals that occurred before the 1950s. He was also allegedly involved in gang activities. Despite his background, he became a social conciliator and was financially better off due to 1960s-era economic development that improved the financial status of urban families in Iran.[17] He was in his late seventies by the time of my observation (in 2006), and now belongs to a social class different from his family background. Nonetheless, it is still during Muharram when he really defines and practises his social identity. He is not a member of the social or economic elite class; however, he is the most influential figure in the Muharram union of his locality. His social significance is derived from the fact that the personal relationship between him and his counterpart in another locality determines the relationship between the two unions.

As discussed in previous chapters, each locality runs their processions through different localities, a symbolic practice to maintain social intimacy between communities. The way in which the influential figures of each locality are welcomed throughout the procession by host localities is very important in maintaining mutual friendship between communities. While I followed the aforementioned influential figure, he was constantly honoured with symbolic gestures, such as sacrificing animals and exchanging shawls. He regularly passed the received shawls to the men who surrounded him. It was a practical matter – he could not keep all the shawls on his person. However, passing the shawls to his companions was also part of his charisma. By doing so, he not only manifested his relationship with the other members of his community but he symbolically extended his social body as defined by the men surrounding him. This reveals that the wearing of humble shawls unfolds into a complex social and body practice.

## Conclusion

This chapter departs from a conceptualization of the 'spatial dynamics' of Muharram rituals. It shows how common people contribute to the socio-cultural resilience mechanism that keeps Muharram commemoration relevant to a changing contemporary urban society. This resilience capability is crucial for the social sustainability of the urban community in an environment where their ability to manifest their social identity is weakened by the diminishment and suppression of many rituals. The initiation of a new style of wearing shawls cannot be considered a major change in the landscape of Muharram rituals; however, its cultural significance should not be underestimated. This new Muharram custom was a spontaneous initiative that demands a full investigation of its wider historical background. This costume spectacle did not emerge without context; its roots are in the long history of exchanging shawls in Dezful. Consequently, I describe the process as a (re) invention, not an invention.

The subject of this chapter was not only the (re)invention of a rite, but also the extinction of rites and rituals. Even within the relatively short period of history that this chapter reviewed, many rites gradually died out due to social changes or were suppressed by the political authorities. For example, ritualized violence disappeared from the landscape of Muharram when the social conciliation of 1950s changed urban social conditions in Dezful. This led the Muharram unions to compete with each other in more symbolic ways, such as having a taller symbolic flag (*alam*) that was carried in the front of processions. This symbolic competition went too far and made the flags too tall and heavy to be carried through very crowded processions. Therefore, carrying symbolic flags was excluded from Muharram processions. While some rites and customs gradually died out, the religious-political authorities in Dezful suppressed many others, such as the rite of playing wood.

The extinction of rituals creates the necessity for invention and reinvention of rituals. Interestingly, the historical review in this chapter showed that the common people were the driving force behind (re)inventing rituals, sustaining Muharram as a public space for performing their liminal social status. Intellectual and political elites played a destructive role during the late twentieth century by squeezing the social space that Muharram offers.

The common people understand the social significance of the liminal time of Muharram, when they can ignore everyday norms and claim a temporal social privilege that they do not have throughout the year. In this circumstance, marginalized people are empowered since the structure of urban society is altered during Muharram. As Victor Turner (1969) explains, the anti-structure social order during the liminal time of rituals plays a critical role in sustaining the social constitution as it facilitates the common experience of an intense alternative social solidarity (*communitas*) and a feeling of great social equality. When the extinction of rituals undermines the liminal status of Muharram, the capacity for inventing new rites is a cultural resilience ability that sustains social life for urban communities and the relevance of Muharram commemoration in contemporary urban society.

I would like to consider the struggle between the common people, elites and authorities as part of the social negotiation that takes place during Muharram. In fact, even secular intellectuals who challenge Muharram rituals energize social negotiations during the liminal time of Muharram. What clearly distinguishes the position of the common people from that of the elites and authorities (both secular and religious) is that the people have never conceived of Muharram rituals as a singularly religious practice. Secular elites refuse the commemoration of the Ashura tragedy, claiming that it is a backward religious custom and is irrelevant to the modern day, and religious intellectuals and establishments reduce it to only a religious practice. These approaches actively diminished Muharram rituals during the twentieth century. The Iranian Islamic state has supported Muharram commemoration since the 1979 Revolution but in claiming direct authority over religious matters, the state outlawed and suppressed many rites and rituals. The people showed their resilience capability by (re)inventing new rites and customs in order to maintain Muharram in the public sphere, a place where they can express their social identity.

It is rather problematic to generalize the findings of this very particular case study and apply them to all new rites. However, this study has shown that the process of (re)inventing wearing shawls is not stimulated by religious agendas, and religious elites and authorities make no contributions to its development nor have any control over it. Nonetheless, it is a valid general claim that this study illustrates that the common people form the core of the resilience mechanism that has preserved Muharram as a grand socio-religious ritual throughout the turbulent contemporary history of Iran.

## NOTES

1. *Panjeh* means hand and pentagonal. The five fingers of this abstract metal hand signify five persons: the Prophet Mohammad and the four most important members of his family – his son-in-law Ali, his daughter Fatima and his grandsons Hassan and Hussein.
2. For example, Torab has argued: 'These performances were no doubt intended to be impressive, with women as an audience enabling men to show off their masculinity through competitive displays of the heavy battle standards, the shedding of blood through flagellation' (Torab, 2007: 147).
3. See chapter three on the social logic of procession routes.
4. This subject is extensively discussed in chapter three.
5. This has been extensively discussed in chapters four and five.
6. Also discussed in chapter two.
7. Although the symbolic flags are no longer carried in the front of the procession, some unions may carry an *'alamat* through the procession. *'Alamat*, meaning sign, is also a kind of symbolic flag that has no historical background in Dezful. It has a background in cities in the centre of Iran and was introduced to Dezful in the late 1960s. An *'Alamat* is about two metres tall, but it is a very wide and heavy symbolic flag that is mainly dressed in black shawls, and is heavily decorated (see Figure 6.2, which shows an *'alamat* in the middle of the crowd).
8. Although the Pahlavi dynasty took on a secular policy, it was constitutionally a Shi'i dynasty and only a Shi'i Muslim could be appointed as the king.
9. See 'Practical law of Islam' (Khamenei, n.d.). The statement is made in response to question no. 1460. On the English version of the webpage, it is cited as question no. 1450.
10. This dynasty established Shi'i Islam as the official religion of the country in the sixteenth century.
11. In this rite, a group of participants hold shovels up high, then at emotional moments in the procession, they jump and turn, bashing other shovels, an act that imitates the soundscape of the battle of Karbala (for more see chapter two).
12. This Arabic book was originally entitled *al-Tanzyeh al-Amale al-Shabih*, authored by Ayatollah Sayyed Mohsen Amin Jabal Ameli.
13. This book contains a series of sermons that he delivered during 1969–1970.
14. This book, like most of his books, is a transcription of sermons on the topic.
15. The social conciliation among localities in the 1950s was ritually signified by the re-arrangement of Muharram processions in three main sessions to establish and maintain friendship among urban localities (for more, see chapter five).
16. Although I am inspired by Douglas (1973) to employ physical and social bodies, it is clear that physical body here does not refer to the biological body as referenced by Douglas.
17. See chapter four.

# AN URBAN-SPATIAL APPROACH TO MUHARRAM RITUALS

This book has investigated the spatial dynamics of Muharram rituals, by which Shi'i Muslims observe the tragedy of Ashura day, when Hussein and his companions were brutally slaughtered in Karbala in the seventh century. This historic tragedy transcended into meta-history and greatly contributed to establishing the Shi'i–Sunni division and shaping Shi'i creeds and rituals. This book has registered Muharram rituals as a religious practice, but refused the conventional frameworks of sacred–profane or religious–secular dichotomies. Muharram rituals are heavily charged with social and political agendas. Although this is a religious commemoration, the social and political agendas have evidently driven the evolution of Muharram rituals throughout history. Muharram rituals, like other rituals, have manifold aspects and cannot be limited or reduced to a single agenda. Therefore, although this study has mainly focused on the urban-spatial aspects of Muharram rituals, the rituals are investigated within their broad religious, social and political landscapes.

The motivations of this book are to shift attention away from the place of ritual to the spatial aspects of ritual, and to investigate the dynamics of Muharram rituals as part of urban processes. The key argument here is that Muharram rituals produce 'ritual space'. Understanding the production of ritual space and its dynamics furthers the articulation of urban transformation processes. 'Ritual space' is considered as a kind of 'social space' (Lefebvre, 1991). Following Lefebvre's seminal book, *The Production of Social Space*, Marxist and postmodern scholars, from Harvey to Soja, have made splendid theoretical contributions to the notion of social space and the study of urban dynamics. These contributions were predominantly made by investigating everyday life and social negotiations that are based on 'class struggle'. What differentiates 'ritual space' from conventional 'social space' is that ritual space is produced through social interactions during the liminal status of ritual. In this status, the strong sense of social solidarity is defined according to 'the anti-structure of *communitas*' (Turner, 1969); and social negotiations are driven by community struggle, not class struggle.[1] Therefore, the social logic of space production during the rituals diverges from Lefebvre's focus: the social mode of space production based on everyday life, driven by class struggle.

The theoretical characteristics of ritual space have barely been studied. On the one hand, ritual studies often addresses the location and the place of ritual, thus the idea of ritual space remains theoretically under-developed.[2] On the other hand, urban studies commonly neglects the significance of social interactions during the liminal time of rituals. By bridging these gaps, this book contributes to both ritual and urban studies. While each chapter addresses a specific question about the social and spatial logic of Muharram rituals and their evolution, this brief concluding chapter formulates the idea of 'ritual space' on a theoretical level.

## The Spatial Components of Ritual

'The spatial manifestation' and 'the spatial organization' of Muharram rituals are formulated as the two components of 'the spatial constitution' of the rituals. The concept of the spatial manifestation of ritual is developed according to two interrelated attention shifts in ritual studies. First, there is the shift of attention from the place to the spatiality of rituals. Second, there is the shift from articulating rituals based on action theory to considering rituals as intrinsically spatial performances.[3] This shifts theoretical focus from the idea of place to that of space. My general argument is that the location and place of ritual are part of ritual orchestration. However, singular focus on the place of ritual obscures the necessity of exploring how rituals spatially manifest.

The observation of diverse Shi'i rituals shows that Muharram performances are either spatially dispersed or manifested in a concentrated form. For example, the Ashura tragedy can be observed by a street procession that is spatially dispersed, or commemorated at the mourning service session that is spatially concentrated. These two forms of spatial manifestations play a crucial role in determining how a ritual functions socially and politically. The spatially concentrated rituals often serve to create social solidarity and maintain social bonds among community members. However, spatially dispersed rituals facilitate social interactions and negotiations with others. Muharram processions can mediate social intimacy or tension between communities, defining or disputing socio-spatial borders and territories in the urban landscape. The idea of spatial manifestation of rituals not only helps one to understand the complex social implications of rituals, but also provides a new platform to investigate the historical evolution of diverse Shi'i rituals.

The shift of focus from actions that are performed during rituals to the spatial manifestations of rituals creates a new approach to the history of Shi'i rituals, i.e. 'the spatial history of Muharram rituals'. Conventionally, Muharram rituals were catalogued based on what actions were performed – e.g. passion play, flagellation – and historians investigated when and where each ritual was initiated. The problem of focusing on actions occurs on both theoretical and practical levels. On the one hand, David Parkin (1992) shows that articulating rituals as actions does not solve the ritual–myth ambiguity. On the other hand, Shi'i Muslims around the world have appropriated all kinds of local/indigenous performances to commemorate the Ashura tragedy. Even within the geography of Iran, it is impractical to make a list of all performances that are practised during Muharram. The focus on 'the spatial manifestation' of Muharram rituals has two advantages. First, it explains that performing the very same action – such as lifting a symbolic coffin (*nakhl*) – can be spatially manifested in concentrated or dispersed forms, leading to entirely different social implications. Second, this approach offers an alternative to the descriptive reading of Muharram ritual history and provides an analytical history of the evolution of Muharram rituals.

The appropriation of local performances for Muharram commemoration was a mechanism to invent Muharram rituals. However, the spatial history of Muharram rituals reveals that the evolution of concentrated rituals into dispersed rituals – and vice versa – was the most important mechanism for (re)inventing Shi'i rituals. This mechanism was predominantly driven by political forces that either supported or suppressed the commemoration of the Karbala tragedy. Further investigation in chapter six shows that the (re)invention of rituals was mostly the result of social and political agendas. Religious agendas and Shi'i establishments had very little control over this complex cultural process.

The social and spatial logic of Muharram processions are extensively studied in chapters three, four and five, and articulate 'the spatial organization' of processions in the Iranian city of Dezful. The traditional Muharram rituals in general and processions in particular served urban communities (localities) in creating, maintaining, and performing social solidarity and negotiating their position in the broad social landscape of the city. More importantly, the spatial organization of processions produced a space which demonstrated not only social cohesions and relations but also the division of cities into Heydari and Nemati moieties. As discussed in chapter three, Muharram rituals appear to be the best prism through which the traditional social constitution of Iranian cities can be captured.

The physical configuration of old Iranian cities, characterized by organic and irregular forms, exhibit their very broad socio-political and cultural landscape. However, despite the commonly accepted claim, this organic structure does not reflect the social make-up of traditional urban society. For example, the border of the traditional locality (*mahalleh*) cannot be easily mapped, let alone captured through the configuration of urban structure. This is partly due to the rigidity of a city's physical shape and the social fluidity of the locality, which was the most fundamental element of old Iranian cities. A 'locality' generally refers to a group of people who are socially and spatially bound; it is a socio-spatial territory that often includes more than one neighbourhood. The social bonds among people and neighbourhoods that make up a locality have always been subject to negotiations and change, as has the territory of localities. In chapter three, I also explained other problems in defining and capturing the idea of locality based on the built environment or the configuration of city structures. Nonetheless, I was still surprised when I realized that the shape of old Iranian cities does not even project the Heydari–Nemati division, a major socio-spatial division by which the traditional cities were arranged.[4] In contrast, not only have Muharram processions been extremely reflexive to social dynamics, but they are also an active part of social negotiations that constantly change the socio-spatial pattern of the city. It is fair to state that while the built environment does not project the socio-spatial make-up of urban society, Muharram processions produce spaces through which we can comprehend the socio-spatial complexity of the traditional Iranian city.

'The spatial organization' of Muharram processions changed as the result of urban transformation. But the spatial organization of processions did not passively reflect rapid changes during the time of modern transformation. In Dezful, Muharram rituals were an active part of a tense and violent process through which the traditional urban society transitioned into modern times. The re-arrangement of processions was not only a medium to end violence between urban localities, but also ritually established a new urban constitution that was no longer based on Heydari and Nemati moieties. I formulate the re-arrangement of procession routes as a ritual in its own right and call it 'the rite of urban passage'. This rite implies a major socio-political transformation in the city, but does not have a religious connotation, addressing the fact that this ritual has always been charged with socio-political agendas.

The spatial dynamism of Muharram rituals is driven by two parallel processes: (a) the spatial evolution of ritual manifestation and (b) the transformation of the spatial organization of rituals. These are two parallel processes that drive the dynamics of 'the spatial constitution' of Muharram rituals, but the two are not necessarily interrelated. The socio-political forces that can cause the transformation of the spatial organization of rituals do not necessarily make an impact on the spatial manifestation of rituals. I must emphasize that this statement addresses the 'spatial' dynamic of rituals, not the dynamism of Muharram rituals in general. As discussed in chapters two and six, the cultural process of localizing the idea of Muharram observance and the reinvention of local performances to commemorate the Muharram tragedy have an important role in shaping the general landscape of Muharram rituals.

## Ritual Space: From Lefebvre's Social Space to a Performed Topological Space

Lefebvre's idea of social space is one of the theoretical foundations upon which this book is developed. His famous proposition reads: '(social) space is a (social) production' (Lefebvre, 1991: 26). In *The Production of Space*, he explains that the social mode of producing space is defined by and evolves through social interactions and negotiations across the three folds of space: lived, perceived and conceived space. In this process, social space is not just a passive production, it is an active part of defining the social mode of producing space. Lefebvre has argued: 'We are confronted not by one social space but by many – indeed, by an unlimited multiplicity or uncountable set social space which we refer to generically as social space' (1991: 86). He explains that social spaces are not things, and that they differ from natural or physical spaces since 'they are not simply juxtaposed, they may be intercalated, combined, superimposed – they may even sometimes collide' (Lefebvre, 1991: 88). Social spaces not only entwine with each other, but they also superimpose themselves over the built environment, impacting the way we experience and live in a city.

   In *The Production of Space*, Lefebvre aimed at bridging and integrating metaphorical, epistemological, mental and practical ideas of space, an initiative that made a great contribution to conceptions of space. There are two reasons why Lefebvre's legacy made a tremendous impact on urban studies and urban design/planning. First, the introduction of the idea of social space in the early 1970 was timely[5]: the school of Modernism was in crisis and seriously questioned. Jane Jacob's book, *The Death and Life of Great American Cities* (1961), is one of the most famous expressions of waning belief in the positivist approach of Modernist architects that reduced cities and urban spaces into socially meaningless functional zones. Second, by revealing that the city is a complex landscape of 'social spaces', and not the result of architectural practices, Lefebvre theoretically exposed the reasons why Modernism failed. He attacked Modernist architects such as Le Corbusier, who claimed to shape human relations by designing the

built environment (Lefebvre, 1996: 98). In fact, Modernism was a successful approach on the conventional architectural scale. However, Modernist
architects not only failed in their claims to create an ideal society by
designing 'new cities' or major residential areas, but also failed to even
offer socially meaningful public spaces. By introducing the idea of social
space, Lefebvre made a great contribution to establishing the 'spatial
turn' in social science that has changed how cities and urban societies are
studied and analysed. Lefebvre's legacy has also impacted urban design as
an academic discipline, though it would not have such impact on urban
design as a professional practice. The professional practitioners may use
Lefebvrian/postmodern jargon, but they still predominantly believe in
their role and power to shape city and society. Ironically, while Lefebvre
and the left-leaning scholars made the most important contributions to
urban studies in the second half of the twentieth century, the professional
practice of urban design is still dominated by right-leaning political ideologies such as neo-liberalism.

The idea of 'ritual space' in this book is influenced by ritual and spatial theories such as those of Turner, Parkin and Lefebvre. However, the
concept of ritual space is different from its intellectual ancestors. 'Ritual
space' is a kind of social space that is produced through the performance
of a ritual. What differentiates 'ritual space' from Lefebvre's social space is
that it is produced under the liminal status of ritual, when everyday norms
are altered, the force of class struggle is clearly weakened, and 'community
struggle' drives the social motivations and agendas. In other words, ritual
space is the result of a liminal/temporal social mode of producing space that
has not been seriously investigated by Marxist or postmodern scholars who
mainly focus on everyday life.

'Ritual space' is manifested in religious places and public space or dispersed throughout the city. However, as it coexists through performance of
ritual, it is spatially constituted according to 'the spatial manifestation' and
'the spatial organization' of ritual. In other words, ritual space is spatially
constituted based on the ritual per se, not the place of ritual. Although 'ritual
space' is transitory and exists through the performance of processions, and
since such space is collectively performed, produced and experienced in a
city, it has a perpetual impact on the ways in which the city is perceived,
conceived and lived. As discussed (especially in chapter five), my argument
is that the collective and emotional experience of ritual space impacts the
perception and mental map of the city. 'Ritual space' can still be articulated
within Lefebvre's framework of social space. However, the analyses of the
spatial organization of Muharram processions, particularly the re-arranged
contemporary processions, reveal a complexity that calls for further theoretical articulation.

The Modernization project permanently changed Iranian society. The modern state objectively engineered and transfigured the face of Iranian cities, a physical alteration that did not necessarily correspond to social changes. In other words, although the physical transformation of the city implies social changes, they did not reflect or project the nature of each other. Unsurprisingly, Muharram rituals appear as an active part of urban transformation. The end of urban division indicates the passage of the traditional city into a new era, a passage that was mediated, ritualized, and established by the re-arrangement of procession routes. This historic event signifies a critical turning point in the history of Muharram processions and Iranian cities. Granted, this turning point did not occur at the same time in all Iranian cities. For example, there was a few decades between the re-arrangement of Muharram processions in Dezful and Ardabil. This indicates that the re-arrangement of processions occurred only when the social transformation unfolded, and it was not engineered by the modern state. If the spatial organization of traditional processions was not complex enough, the re-arranged (or contemporary) processions exhibit far more social and spatial complexity.

As discussed in chapter five, I must emphasize again that the spatial organization of processions is not merely about individual processions – it is about the configuration of all processions across the city. The traditional organization of processions can be predominantly explained based on mapping all procession routes. However, the 're-arranged' processions in Dezful and Ardabil do not simply show a spatial pattern, since their organization is the result of the spatio-temporal orchestration of processions. In order to reflect the new urban constitution, the main/final processions of localities are no longer carried out on Ashura day, but they are scheduled at different times. For example, the major processions in Dezful are arranged in three major routes and scheduled in three sessions during the two days of Taso'a and Ashura, the 9th and 10th of Muharram. All localities run their procession toward a shrine/cemetery in the north of the old city on Ashura morning, representing the unity of all urban communities. Nemati localities have a dedicated session to carry their procession throughout Heydari parts of the city on Taso'a afternoon; then in return, Heydari localities carry their processions through Nemati territory on Ashura afternoon. These two sessions are aimed at expressing friendship between the two parts of the city, signifying the end of enmity between two traditional rivals. In this new arrangement, processions are still about practising and manifesting the social identity of localities and their intimacy with other urban communities. However, the new ritual arrangement confirms the end of the Heydari–Nemati era by leaving behind this historical division and moving into a new era. In other words, the re-arranged processions create a ritual space in which the new social order is manifested and practised.

The re-arranged processions are not merely about the new social constitution, they produce a ritual space in which the idea of urban past is also
preserved, manifested, and practised. The re-arranged processions signify
the end of the Heydari–Nemati era. However, the schedule of processions
is still based on identifying localities either as Heydari or Nemati. After
more than a half-century since the processions were re-arranged in Dezful,
the Heydari–Nemati division is a social legend, and there is no awareness
about the traditional division in the everyday life of the city. However,
the traditional socio-spatial division is still performed through Muharram
processions, since urban communities must associate their social identity
to either Heydari or Nemati in order to follow the procession schedule. In
other words, Muharram processions entwine the city's past and present.
As discussed in chapter five, what makes such complex ritual space even
more fascinating is that the procession not only entwines the 'social' past
and present of the city. The spatial organization of the procession also
reconstructs the old morphological structure of the city, which disinte-
grated in the superimposition of the modern grid network of streets upon
the old city. The re-arranged processions are mainly organized throughout
the old city, which was neglected by modern urban planners and is now
a spatially segregated part of the city. However, Muharram processions
reconstruct and highlight the old city structure as a lived and performed
space, a space that people collectively perform and experience every year
via the processions. Indeed, the Muharram processions produce a manifold space in which the city's past and present are discursively practised
and unfolded.[6] Therefore, I argue that Muharram rituals produce a space
that can be articulated as a 'performed topological space', a space I call,
more simply, 'ritual space'.

Lefebvre's idea of history suggests that historical passage is involved
with breaking from one social mode of producing space into another.
In this framework, produced social space reflects its own era. The
study of Muharram rituals, however, suggests that the passage from the
traditional urban constitution to the contemporary urban setting is not
about breaking from the past or continuing the social past. The past
and present of the city are topologically intertwined in 'ritual space',
allowing for the seamless performance and experience of both states
during the liminal time of ritual. In contrast with geometrical space, in
topological space different sides, folds or realms are not separated but
are seamless extensions of each other. Therefore, our experience of ritual
space is simultaneously related to all folds of such space. The conceptual
framework of topological space not only formulates the idea of ritual
space produced through the re-arranged processions, but also clearly
differs from the idea of space as introduced by Lefebvre.

## Contributions to Urban and Ritual Studies

This book explores the history of Muharram rituals in its broad landscape in chapter two. However, the discussions throughout the other chapters predominantly deal with the spatial dynamics of rituals in the specific social history and geography of Iran. For example, the members of the studied urban society are Shi'i Muslims and the rituals are practised in a religiously homogenized context. Moreover, although the Pahlavi dynasty did not support the commemoration of the Ashura tragedy and even (unsuccessfully) tried to remove it from public spaces, this modern monarchy was constitutionally a Shi'i dynasty. Therefore, the idea is not to generalize the findings of this research as a universal principle that can be applied to the dynamic of Muharram rituals in other contexts, such as colonial India, or in Iraq under the Sunni/secular/military rule of Saddam Hussein. Nonetheless, this research can advance the study of not only Muharram rituals in different socio-political and cultural contexts, but also ritual studies in general. This contribution is not based on the findings in Iranian cities, but aims at showing the significance of spatial approaches in ritual studies.

The contribution of this research to urban studies is based on the point that the city is not merely the production of everyday social interactions. It is produced through layers of social interactions in different statuses, including the liminal time of ritual when community struggle (not class struggle) drives social negotiations and tensions. Therefore, the social landscape of the city has to be comprehended according to both everyday and liminal statuses. Moreover, the spatial articulation of ritual makes it conceptually possible to position ritual as the keystone of a framework in urban studies. This research framework is a new window that offers a fresh outlook on the city and its dynamics through the lens of rituals. This shows the significance of investigating rituals in research about cities. Ultimately, this study depicts ritual as a part of urban processes by which urban communities constantly negotiate and influence city evolution. This reveals that the problem of the twentieth century and contemporary new cities is not just their shape and their socially meaningless zones, but more importantly the absence of rituals. A city or settlement without rituals and festivals that mediate intensive social interactions and negotiations is not a city; it is a necropolis with no past or future.

### NOTES

1. See Introduction.
2. See chapter one.
3. Discussed in chapters one and two.

4. Though in comparison to localities, the Heydari–Nemati division is certainly more easily mapped.
5. *The Production of Space* was originally published in 1971.
6. For more discussion, see chapter five.

# BIBLIOGRAPHY

Abrahamian, Ervand. 1982. *Iran Between Two Revolutions*. Princeton Studies on the Near East. Princeton, NJ: Princeton University Press.

Afary, J. 2003. 'Shi`i Narratives of Karbala and Christian Rites of Penance: Michel Foucault and the Culture of the Iranian Revolution, 1978–1979', *Radical History Review* 2003(86): 7–35.

Aghaie, Kamran Scot. 2005. *The Martyrs of Karbala: Shi'i Symbols and Rituals in Modern Iran*. Publications on the Near East, University of Washington. Seattle, SA: University of Washington Press.

Alexander, Christopher, Sara Ishikawa, Murray Silverstein, Max Jacobson, Ingrid Fiksdahl-King and Shlomo Angel. 1978. *A Pattern Language: Towns, Buildings, Construction*. New York: Oxford University Press.

Alexanderson, Gerald L. 2006. 'About the Cover: Euler and Königsberg's Bridges: A Historical View', *Bulletin of the American Mathematical Society* 43(4): 567–73.

Algar, Hamid. 1969. *Religion and State in Iran, 1785–1906: The Role of the Ulama in the Qajar Period*. Berkeley, CA: University of California Press.

Amin, Mohsen. 1992. *Azadari-Haye Na-Mashro* [Illegitimate mourning ceremonies]. Translated by Jalal Al-e-Ahamad. Bushehr: Darya.

Ansari, Ali Massoud. 2003. *Modern Iran Since 1921: The Pahlavis and After*. Harlow: Longman.

Appadurai, Arjun. 1990. 'Disjuncture and Difference in the Global Cultural Economy', *Theory, Culture & Society* 7(2–3): 279–93.

Asad, Talal. 1993. *Genealogies of Religion: Discipline and Reasons of Power in Christianity and Islam*. Baltimore, MD and London: Johns Hopkins University Press.

Ashraf, Ahmad. 1969. 'Historical Obstacles to the Development of a Bourgeoisie in Iran', *Iranian Studies* 2(2–3): 54–79.

———. 1988. 'Bazaar-Mosque Alliance: The Social Basis of Revolts and Revolutions', *International Journal of Politics, Culture, and Society* 1(4): 538–67.

Ayoub, M. 1978. *Redemptive Suffering in Islam: A Study of the Devotional aspects of `Āshūrā in Twelver Shī`ism*. Religion and Society 10. The Hague: Mouton.

———. 1987. 'Ashura', edited by E. Yarshater. *Encyclopaedia Iranica*. London: Routledge & K. Paul.

———. 1988. 'Diverse Religious Practices', in Seyyed Hossein Nasr, Hamid Dabashi and Seyyed Vali Reza Nasr (eds), *Shi'ism: Doctrines, Thought, and Spirituality*. Albany, NY: State University of New York Press, pp. 258–59.

Azimi, Fakhreddin. 2004. 'Unseating Mosaddeq, The Configuration and Role of Domestic Forces', in Mark J. Gasiorowski and Malcolm Byrne (eds), *Mohammad Mosaddeq and the 1953 Coup in Iran*. Modern Intellectual and Political History of the Middle East. Syracuse, NY: Syracuse University Press, pp. 27–101.

Azkaei, Parviz. 1985. 'Dastan-i Jumhory-i Hamedan [The story of the republic of Hamedan]', *Ayandeh* 10: 833–39.

Bahar, Muhammad Taqī. 1944. *Tarikh Mukhtasar Ahzab Siyasi Iran: Inqiraz Qajariyeh* [The brief history of Iranian political parties: The downfall of Qajar]. Vol. 1. Tehran: Amir Kabir.

Baktash, Mayel. 1979. 'Ta'ziyeh and Its Philosophy', in Peter Chelkowski (ed.), *Ta'ziyeh: Ritual and Drama in Iran*. New York: New York University Press and Soroush Press, pp. 95–120.

Banani, Amin. 1961. *The Modernization of Iran, 1921–1941*. Stanford, CA: Stanford University Press.

Barabadi, Sayed Ahmad, Gholam Hussaien Shoeibi, Masomeh Homaei and Maryam Vali-Dad. 2002. *Mardum-Shenasi-e Maracem Azadari Mah-e Moharaam Dar Shahrestan Birjand* [Anthropology of ceremonies of lament of the month of Moharam in the city of Birjand]. Tehran: Markaz-e Nashr va Tahghighat-e Ghalam-e Ashena.

Barbaro, Giosofat, Henry Edward John Stanley, Charles Grey, William Thomas and Eugene Armand Roy. 2010. 'Narrative Most Noble Vincentio d'Alessandri', in *Travels to Tana and Persia, and A Narrative of Italian Travels in Persia in the 15th and 16th Centuries*. Cambridge Library Collection – Hakluyt First Series. Cambridge: Cambridge University Press.

Bayat, Asef. 2010. *Life as Politics: How Ordinary People Change the Middle East*. Stanford, CA: Stanford University Press.

Bayzaei, Bahram. 2000. *Namayesh Dar Iran* [Theatre in Iran]. Tehran: Intisharat Roshangaran va Mutaleat Zanan.

Bell, C.M. 1992. *Ritual Theory, Ritual Practice*. New York: Oxford University Press.

———. 1997. *Ritual: Perspectives and Dimensions*. New York: Oxford University Press.

Biggs, Norman L., E. Keith Lloyd and Robin J. Wilson. 1999. *Graph Theory 1736–1936*. Oxford: Clarendon Press.

Blank, Jonah. 2001. *Mullahs on the Mainframe: Islam and Modernity Among the Daudi Bohras*. Chicago, IL: University of Chicago Press.

Bloch, Maurice. 1986. *From Blessing to Violence: History and Ideology in the Circumcision Ritual of the Merina of Madagascar*. Cambridge Studies in Social Anthropology, no. 61. Cambridge: Cambridge University Press.

Bolokbashi, A. 2001. *Nakhl Gardani*. Tehran: Daftar-i Pajuhesh-haye Farhangi.

Bonine, Michael. 1989. 'BAZAR, General', edited by E. Yarshater. *Encyclopaedia Iranica*. London: Routledge & K. Paul, http://www.iranicaonline.org/articles/bazar-i.

Bosworth, C.E., C. Hillenbrand and L.P Elwell-Sutton (eds). 1983. *Qajar Iran: Political, Social and Cultural Change, 1800-1925*. Edinburgh: Edinburgh University Press.

Bourdieu, Pierre. 1993. *The Field of Cultural Production: Essays on Art and Literature*. Cambridge: Polity Press.

Bowie, Fiona. 2000. *The Anthropology of Religion: An Introduction*. Oxford: Blackwell.

Bozorgnia, Zohreh. 2004. 'Tekyeh and Hussainiyeh', *Memar* 27 (November): 100–106.

———. 2006. *Tekyeh-Ha va Husseiniyeh-Haye Iran* [Iranian Tekyehs and Husseiniyehs]. Tehran: Sofiyan.

Calhoun, Craig J. 2002. *Dictionary of the Social Sciences*. Oxford: Oxford University Press.

Calmard, J. 1996. 'The Consolidation of Safavid Shi'ism: Folklore and Popular Religion', in Charles Melville (ed.), *Safavid Persia: The History and Politics of an Islamic Society*. Pembroke Persian Papers 4. London: I.B. Tauris, pp. 139–90.

Campbell, Tom. 1981. *Seven Theories of Human Society*. London: Clarendon Press.

Canetti, Elias. 1962. *Crowds and Power*. London: Gollancz.

Chardin, John. 1671. *Le Couronnement De Soleïmaan Troisième Roy De Perse, Et Cequi S'est Passé De Plus Memorable Dans Les Deux Premières Années De Son Regne*. Paris.

———. 1993. *Safarnāmah-I Shārdan: Matn-I Kāmil*. Tehran: Tūs.

Chehabi, Houchang E. 2004. 'Dress Codes for Men in Turkey and Iran', in Turaj Atabaki and Erik Jan Zurcher (eds), *Men of Order: Authoritarian Modernization under Atatürk and Reza Shah*. Library of Modern Middle East Studies 21. London: I.B. Tauris, pp. 209–38.

Chelkowski, Peter J. 1988. 'Diverse Religous Practices', in Seyyed Hossein Nasr, Hamid Dabashi, and Seyyed Vali Reza Nasr (eds), *Shi'ism: Doctrines, Thought, and Spirituality*. Albany, NY: State University of New York Press, pp. 262–67.

———. 2005. 'Time Out of Memory: Taziyeh, the Total Drama', *TDR/The Drama Review* 49(4): 15–27.

Cohen, Robin. 1997. *Global Diasporas: An Introduction*. London: UCL Press.

Cronin, Stephanie. 2003. 'Riza Shah and the Paradoxes of Military Modernization in Iran, 1921–1941', in Stephanie Cronin (ed), *The Making of Modern Iran: State and Society under Riza Shah (1921–1941)*. New York and London: Routledge Curzon, pp 37–64.

Crow, Douglas Karim. 1986. 'The Death of Al-Husayn b. 'Ali and Early Shi'i Views of the Imamate', *Al-Serat* 12(1): 71–116.

———. 2008. 'The Death of Al-Husayn b. 'Ali and Early Shi'i Views of the Imamate', in Paul Luft and Colin Turner (eds), *Shi'ism: Critical Concepts in Islamic Studies*. London and New York: Routledge, pp. 1:52–91.

Curzon, George Nathaniel Curzon. 1892. *Persia and the Persian Question*. London: Longmans, Green & Co.

Da'ei Dezfoli, Seyyed Abdullah. Undated [original 1826]. *Tazkerat Al-Akhbar va Majm'a Al-Abrar*. Ahwaz: Alamshah Library and Bookshop.

Darkatanian, Gholamreza. 2009. 'Saale Hezbi Dar Dezful Be Ravayet Asnad [The year of party in Dezful by the narrative of Documents]', *Faslnameyeh Motale'at Tarikhi* 24 (Spring): 79–107.

Dieulafoy, Jane. 1887. *La Perse, La Chaldée Et La Susiane: Relation De Voyage*. Paris: Hachette.

Douglas, Mary. 1973. *Natural Symbols: Explorations in Cosmology*. Pelican Anthropology Library. Harmondsworth: Penguin.

Durkheim, Emile. 1963. *Primitive Classification*. London: Cohen & West.

———. 1995. *The Elementary Forms of the Religious Life*. London: Free Press.

Ehlers, Eckart and Willem Floor. 1993. 'Urban Change in Iran, 1920–1941', *Iranian Studies* 26(3–4): 251–75.

Eliade, Mircea. 1959. *The Sacred and the Profane: The Nature of Religion*. New York: Harcourt Brace Jovanovich.

Entwistle, Joanne. 2015. *The Fashioned Body: Fashion, Dress and Social Theory*. Cambridge: John Wiley & Sons.

Esfahani, Hadi Salehi and M. Hashem Pesaran. 2009. 'The Iranian Economy in the Twentieth Century: A Global Perspective', *Iranian Studies* 42(2): 177–211.

Euler, L. 1741. 'Solutio Problematis Ad Geometriam Situs Pertinentis', *Commentarii Academiae Scientiarum Imperialis Petropolitanae* 7(1–10): 128–40.

Falsafi, Nasr Allah. 1985. *Zindagani-i Shah Abbas Avval*. 3rd edn. Tehran: Elmi.

Faqihi, Ali Asghar. 1978. *Al-I Bouyah Va Awza-i Zaman-i Ishan: Ba Nimoudari Az Zindig-i Mardum Dar On Asr* [Buyids and the condition of their era]. Tehran: Intishārāt-i Saba.

Feyerabend, Paul K. 1993. *Against Method*. 3rd edn. London and New York: Verso.

Fischer, Michael M.J. 1980. *Iran: From Religious Dispute to Revolution*. Harvard Studies in Cultural Anthropology 3. Cambridge, MA: Harvard University Press.

Flandin, Eugène. 1851. *Voyage en Perse pendant les années 1840 et 1841*. Gide et Jule Baudry.

Floor, Willem M. 1987. *Justarha-Ei Az Tarikh-i Ijtima-Ei Iran Dar Asr-i Qajar* [The inquests of social history of Iran in the Qajar Era]. Translated by Abu al-Qasim Sirri. Tehran: Toos.

———. 1998. *A Fiscal History of Iran in the Safavid and Qajar Periods, 1500–1925*. Persian Studies Series 17. New York: Bibliotheca Persica Press.

Fustel De Coulanges, Numa Denis. 2001. *The Ancient City: A Study on the Religion, Laws, and Institutions of Greece and Rome*. Kitchener: Batoche Books.

Gennep, Arnold van. 1960. *The Rites of Passage*. London: Routledge & K. Paul.

Ghaffari, S. Ghaffar. 2005. *Yadegar Man* [My memoir]. Dezful: Afham.

Giddens, Anthony. 1979. *Central Problems in Social Theory: Action, Structure and Contradiction in Social Analysis*. London: Macmillan.

———. 1984. *The Constitution of Society: Outline of the Theory of Structuration*. Oxford: Polity.

Girard, René. 1977. *Violence and the Sacred*. Translated by Patrick Gregory. Baltimore, MD and London: Johns Hopkins University Press.

———. 2003. *Things Hidden Since the Foundation of the World*. Translated by Stephen Bann and Michael Metteer. London and New York: Continuum.

Gluckman, Max. 1962. 'Les Rites de Passage', in Max Gluckman (ed.), *Essays on the Ritual of Social Relations*. Manchester: Manchester University Press, pp. 1–52.

———. 1963. *Order and Rebellion in Tribal Africa: Collected Essays with an Autobiographical Introduction*. New York: Free Press.

Goffman, Erving. 1956. *The Presentation of Self in Everyday Life*. Edinburgh: University of Edinburgh.

———. 1961. *Encounters: Two Studies in the Sociology of Interaction*. Indianapolis, IN: Bobbs-Merrill.

———. 1966. *Behavior in Public Places: Notes on the Social Organization of Gatherings*. New York: Free Press.

———. 1967. *Interaction Ritual: Essays on Face-to-Face Behaviour*. New York: Doubleday.

Good, Mary-Jo Delvecchio and Byron J. Good. 1988. 'Ritual, the State, and the Transformation of Emotional Discourse in Iranian Society', *Culture, Medicine and Psychiatry* 12(1): 43–63.

Gouvea, Antonio de. 1646. *Relation Des Grandes Gverres Et Victoires Obtenvues Par Le Roy De Perse Cha Abbas Contre Les Emperevrs De Tvrqvie Mahomet Et Achmet Son Fils: En Svite Dv Voyage De Qvelqves Religieux De l'Ordre Des Hermites De S. Augustin Enuoyez En Perse Par Le Roy Catholique Dom Philippe Second, Roy De Portugal*. Roven [i.e. Rouen]: Nicolas Loyselet.

Graf, F. 1998 'Ritual', in S. Hornblower and A. Spawforth (eds.), *The Oxford Companion to Classical Civilization*. Oxford: Oxford University Press.

Green, Arnold H. 1988. 'The History of Libraries in the Arab World: A Diffusionist Model', *Libraries & Culture* 23(4): 454–73.

Gregory, Derek and John Urry (eds). 1985. *Social Relations and Spatial Structures*. Critical Human Geography. Basingstoke: Macmillan.

Habibi, Mohsen. 1996. *Az Shaar Ta Sharestan, Tahli-e Tarikhi Az Mafahoom Shahr va Simaye Kalbadi Aan* [From Shaar to Sharestan: The historical analysis of the concepts of the city and its physical manifestation]. Tehran: University of Tehran Press.

Haider, Najam Iftikhar. 2011. *The Origins of the Shī'a: Identity, Ritual, and Sacred Space in Eighth-Century Kūfa*. Cambridge Studies in Islamic Civilization. New York: Cambridge University Press.

Haqani, M. 2002. 'Muharram Az Negah-i Tarikh va Tasvir [Muharram from the viewpoint of history and image]', *Tarikh-i Moaaser Iran* 6: 493–545.

Haqiqat, Abd al-Rafi. 1968. *Tārikh-i Nahzatha-Yi Fikri-i Iraniaan: Ta Payan-i Qarn-i Sevoum Hijri* [The history of Iran's intellectual movements, until the end of 10th Century]. Tehran: Intisharat-i Farhang.

Harvey, David. 1973. *Social Justice and the City*. London: Edward Arnold.

———. 1990. *The Condition of Postmodernity: An Enquiry into the Origins of Cultural Change*. Oxford: Basil Blackwell.

Howard, I.K.A. 1990. *The History of Al-Tabari Vol. 19: The Caliphate of Yazid b. Mu'awiyah A.D. 680-683/A.H. 60-64*. New York: SUNY Press.

Howarth, Toby M. 2005. *The Twelver Shî'a as a Muslim Minority in India: Pulpit of Tears*. Routledge Persian and Shî'î Studies Series. London: Routledge.

Hubert, Henri and Marcel Mauss. 1981. *Sacrifice: Its Nature and Function*. Chicago, IL: University of Chicago Press.

Hussain, A.J. 2005. 'The Mourning of History and the History of Mourning: The Evolution of Ritual Commemoration of the Battle of Karbala', *Comparative Studies of South Asia, Africa and the Middle East* 25(1): 78–88.

Imam, Sayyed Muhammad Ali. 2003. *Maghalati Darbareyeh Tarikh Jographiyayeh Dezful* [Essays on the historical geography of Dezful]. Dezful: Darol-moemenin.

Inglehart, Ronald. 1997. *Modernization and Postmodernization: Cultural, Economic and Political Change in 43 Societies*. Princeton, NJ and Chichester: Princeton University Press.

Jacobs, Jane. 1961. *The Death and Life of Great American Cities*. New York: Random House Inc.

Jafariyan, Rasul. 2001. *Tarikh-i Tashayoue Dar Iran, Az Aghaz Ta Qarn-i Dahoom Hejri* [The history of Shi'a in Iran, from the beginning to ninth century]. Qom: Ansarian.

Jenab bol-lahi, M.S. 2000. 'Rabeteye Makan-Garayee va Vefagh-e Ejtemaei Dar Ayeen-Haye Sogvari Moharam [The relation between place and social solidarity in the rite of lament of Moharam]', in B. Aytollahzadeh-Shirazi (ed.), *Majoomeyee Maghalat Nokhostin Hamayesh Moharaam va Farhang Mardoom Iran, Tehran, 1376* [Proceedings of the first congress of Moharaam and Iranian folk, Tehran 1997]. Tehran: Miras-i Farhangi Keshvar, pp. 135–45.

Kagaya, K. 1990. 'Doo-Dastegi Ejtemaei va Mazhabi Dar Iran [Social and religious duality in Iran]', *Ayandeh* 15: 733–39.

Kamali Dezfuli, Seyyed Ali. 2005. *Kamali Nameh* [The epistle of Kamali]. Edited by Habib-bullah Naziri Dezfuli. Qom: Hozoor Publishing Institute.

Kampfer, E. 1981. *Safarnamah-e Kampfer*. Translated by Kaykavos Jahandari. Tehran: Shirkat Sahami Enteshat Kharazmi.

Kasravi, Ahmad. 1944. *Shi'igari*. Tehran: Payman.

———. 1974. *Tarikh-i Mashrute-Ye Iran* [History of the Iranian Constitutional Revolution]. Tehran: Amir Kabir.

Katouzian, Homa. 2000. *State and Society in Iran: The Eclipse of the Qajars and the Emergence of the Pahlavis*. London: I.B. Tauris.

———. 2003. *Iranian History and Politics: The Dialectic of State and Society*. RoutledgeCurzon/BIPS Persian Studies Series. London: RoutledgeCurzon.

———. 2004. 'Mosaddeq's Government in Iranian History, Arbitrary Rule, Democracy, and the 1953 Coup', in Mark J. Gasiorowski and Malcolm Byrne (eds), *Mohammad Mosaddeq and the 1953 Coup in Iran*. Modern Intellectual and Political History of the Middle East. Syracuse, NY: Syracuse University Press, pp. 1–26.

Keyes, Charles F. 1975. 'Buddhist Pilgrimage Centers and the Twelve-Year Cycle: Northern Thai Moral Orders in Space and Time', *History of Religions* 15(1): 71–89.

Khamenei, S. Ali. n.d. 'Practical Laws of Islam', www. leader.ir. Accessed 22 August 2017. http://www.leader.ir/en/book/23.

Khomeini, Rohullah. 2013a. *Estefta-Aat Imam Khomeini*. Vol. 3. 9 vols. Tehran: The Institute of Arrangement and Publishing Imam Khomeini's Works.

———. 2013b. *Estefta-Aat Imam Khomeini*. Vol. 8. 9 vols. Tehran: The Institute of Arrangement and Publishing Imam Khomeini's Works.

Kiani, Mustafa. 2005. *Memari Dawreyeh Pahlavi Avval: Digarguni Andishah-Ha, Paydayish Va Shaklgiriye Memari Doureye Bist Saleh-Ye Moaser Iran 1299–1320* [The first Pahlavi architecture]. Tehran: The Institute for Iranian Contemporary Historical Studies.

Korom, Frank J. 1994. 'Memory, Innovation, and Emergent Ethnicity: The Creolization of an Indo-Trinidadian Performance', *Diaspora: A Journal of Transnational Studies* 3(2): 135–55.

———. 2003. *Hosay Trinidad: Muharram Performances in an Indo-Caribbean Diaspora*. Philadelphia, PA: University of Pennsylvania Press.

Kreinath, Jens. 2004. 'Theorethical Afterthoughts', in Jens Kreinath, Constance Hartunge and Annette Deschner (eds), *The Dynamics of Changing Rituals: The Transformation of Religious Rituals within Their Social and Cultural Context*. New York: Peter Lang, pp. 267–82.

Kreinath, Jens, Constance Hartunge and Annette Deschner (eds). 2004. 'Introduction', in *The Dynamics of Changing Rituals: The Transformation of Religious Rituals within Their Social and Cultural Context*. New York: Peter Lang, pp. 1–8.

Lockhart, Laurence. 1960. *Persian Cities*. London: Luzac & Company Ltd.

Lambton, Ann K.S. 1953. *Landlord and Peasant in Persia: A Study of Land Tenure and Land Revenue Administration*. London, New York and Toronto: Oxford University Press.

———. 1969. *The Persian Land Reform, 1962–1966*. Oxford: Clarendon Press.

Latour, Bruno. 1988. *Science in Action: How to Follow Scientists and Engineers through Society*. Cambridge, MA: Harvard University Press.

Lefebvre, Henri. 1991. *The Production of Space*. Oxford: Blackwell.

———. 1996. *Writings on Cities*. Cambridge, MA: Blackwell Publishers.

Lévi-Strauss, Claude. 1963. *Structural Anthropology*. New York: Basic Books.

Lewis, G. 1980. *Day of Shining Red: An Essay an Understanding Ritual*. Cambridge Studies in Social Anthropology 27. Cambridge: Cambridge University Press.

Livingstone, E.A. (ed.). 2006. *The Concise Oxford Dictionary of the Christian Church*. 2nd edn. Oxford: Oxford University Press. http://www.oxfordreference.com/view/10.1093/acref/9780198614425.001.0001/acref-9780198614425.

Lury, Celia. 2013. 'Topological Sense-Making: Walking the Mobius Strip from Cultural Topology to Topological Culture', *Space and Culture* 16(2): 128–32.

Maddox, G. 2008. 'Religion and Politics', in B. Galligan and W. Roberts (eds), *The Oxford Companion to Australian Politics*. Oxford Companions Series. Oxford: Oxford University Press.

Madelung, Wilferd. 1988. *Religious Trends in Early Islamic Iran*. Columbia Lectures on Iranian Studies, no. 4. Albany, NY: Persian Heritage Foundation.

Mahmoodzade, Azim. 2002. 'Tahlil Ravani Roydad-Haye Saale Hezbi Dar Dzful [Psychological analyses of incidents in the party year in Dezful]', in Muhammad Reza Radfar and Azim Mahmoodzade (eds), *Dezful in Nationalization of Oil Industry, The Party Year*. Dezful: Afham, pp. 75–132.

Makki, Hussain. 1989. *Khaterat Siasi Hussein Makki* [Hussein Makki's political memoir]. Tehran: Elmi.

———. 1982. *Tarikh Bist Saleyeh Iran*. Vol. 4. 8 vols. Tehran: Amir Kabir.

Malcolm, John. 1829. *The History of Persia: From the Most Early Period to the Present Time. Containing an Account of the Religion, Government, Usages, and Character of the Inhabitants of That Kingdom*. Vol. 2. 2 vols. London: John Murray.

Marres, Noortje. 2012. 'On Some Uses and Abuses of Topology in the Social Analysis of Technology (Or the Problem with Smart Meters)', *Theory, Culture & Society* 29(4–5): 288–310.

Masoudi Nejad, Reza. 2012. 'Practising Fractal Shi'i Identities through Muharram Rituals in Mumbai', *Diversities* 14(2): 103–17.

———. 2013. 'The Discursive Manifestation of Past and Present Through the Spatial Organization of the Ashura Procession', *Space and Culture* 16(2): 133–60.

———. 2014. 'Religious Procession as a Mediator for Social Intimacy: Building Communal Harmony in Dharavi after the 1992 Mumbai Riot', in Kosta Mathey and Silvia Matuk (eds), *Community-Based Urban Violence Prevention: Innovative Approaches in Africa, Latin America, Asia and the Arab Region*. Bielefeld: Transcript Verlag, pp. 265–78.

———. 2015a. 'Urban Violence, the Muharram Processions and the Transformation of Iranian Urban Society, the Case of Dezful', in Nelida Fuccaro, Ulrike Freitag, Claudia Ghrawi, and Nora Lafi (eds), *Urban Violence in the Middle East: Changing Cityscapes in the Transition from Empire to Nation State*. New York: Berghahn Books, pp. 91–110.

———. 2015b. 'The Muharram Procession of Mumbai: From Seafront to Cemetery', in Peter Van deer Veer (ed.), *Handbook of Religion and the Asian City: Aspiration and Urbanization in the Twenty-First Century*. Oakland, CA: University of California Press, pp. 89–109.

———. 2017a. 'The Ritual and Built Initiatives of the Iranians in Bombay', in Gabriele Vom Bruck and Charles Tripp (eds.), *Precarious Belonging: Being Shi'i in Non-Shi'i*

*Worlds*. London: Centre for Academic Shia Studies, pp. 61–125. https://eprints.soas. ac.uk/21741/.

———. 2017b. 'Performed Ritual Space: Manifestation of Ritual Space through Flagellation in Mumbai Muharram', *Journal of Ritual Studies* 31(1): 1–15.

Matthee, Rudi. 2006. '"Sister Shi'a States? Safavid Iran and the Deccan in the 16th Century". Deccan Studies, 2/2 (2004), pp. 44–72', *Abstracta Iranica. Revue bibliographique pour le domaine irano-aryen* Volume 27 (September).

Mazaheri, M.H. 2006. 'Rasaneh-Ye Shi-eh; Sougvari Shi'aian Iran Az Aghaz Ta Pish Az Piroozi Engelab Eslami [Shi'i media; mourning of Iranian Shi'a from the beginning to the Islamic Revolution]', *Akhbar-i Adyan* 18: 40–47.

Mazzaoui, M.M. 1979. 'Shi'ism and Ashura in South Lebanon', in Peter J Chelkowski (ed.), *Ta'ziyeh, Ritual and Drama in Iran*. New York University Studies in Near Eastern Civilization 7. New York: New York University Press, pp. 228–37.

Mirjafari, H. 1979. 'The Haydarî-Ni´matî Conflicts in Iran'. Translated by John R. Perry. *Iranian Studies* 12: 135–62.

Modelski, George. 2003. *World Cities: -3000 to 2000*. Washington, DC: FAROS2000.

Moghadam, Fatemeh E. 1996. *From Land Reform to Revolution: The Political Economy of Agricultural Development in Iran 1962–1979*. Library of Modern Middle East Studies 4. London: I.B. Tauris.

Monfared, Afsaneh. n.d. 'Tekyeh', *Daneshnamyeh Jahan Islam* [The encyclopaedia of the Islamic world]. Moasesyeh Dayerat al-Maref al-feghat al-Eslami. Accessed 23 September 2016.

Moore, Sally Falk and Barbara G. Myerhoff. 1977. *Secular Ritual*. Assen: Uitgeverij Van Gorcum.

Morris, Brian. 1987. *Anthropological Studies of Religion: An Introductory Text*. Cambridge: Cambridge University Press.

Motadel, David. 2013. 'Iran and the Aryan Myth', in Ali M. Ansari (ed.), *Perceptions of Iran: History, Myths and Nationalism from Medieval Persia to the Islamic Republic*. London: I.B. Tauris, pp. 119–45.

Motamedi, S.H. 1999. *Azadari Sonati Shiayan* [The traditional Shi'i mourning]. Vol. 1. Qom: Asr-i Zohor.

Mottahedeh, Roy P. 1986. *The Mantle of the Prophet: Learning and Power in Modern Iran*. London: Chatto & Windus.

Najm mol-Molk, Haj Abdul al-Ghaffar. 1962. *Safarnamehye Khuzestan* [Khuzestan travelogue]. Tehran: Elmi.

Najmabadi, Afsaneh. 1987. *Land Reform and Social Change in Iran*. Salt Lake City, UT: University of Utah Press.

Nakash, Yitzhak. 1993. 'An Attempt to Trace the Origin of the Rituals of 'Āshūrā'', *Die Welt des Islams*, New Series, 33(2): 161–81.

Newman, Andrew J. 2012. 'The Origins of the Shi'a: Identity, Ritual, and Sacred Space in Eighth-Century Kufa (Review)', *Journal of Shi'a Islamic Studies* 5(2): 195–200.

Nozari, E. 2006. *Tarikh-i Ijtema-Ye Iran; Az Aghaz to Mashroutiat* [Social history of Iran, from the beginning to the Constitutional Revolution]. Tehran: Khujasteh.

Odenthal, Andreas. 2004. 'Ritual between Tradition and Change: The Paradigm Shift of the Second Vatican Council's Liturgical Reform', in Jens Kreinath, Constance Hartunge and Annette Deschner (eds), *The Dynamics of Changing Rituals: The*

*Transformation of Religious Rituals within Their Social and Cultural Context*. New York: Peter Lang, pp. 211–20.

Pappe, Ilan. 2005. *The Modern Middle East*. London: Routledge.

Parkin, David. 1991. *Sacred Void: Spatial Images of Work and Ritual among the Giriama of Kenya*. Cambridge Studies in Social and Cultural Anthropology 80. Cambridge: Cambridge University Press.

———. 1992. 'Ritual as Spatial Direction and Bodily Division', in D. de Coppet (ed.), *Understanding Rituals*. London and New York: Routledge, pp. 11–25.

Parsadust, Manuchihr. 1996. *Shāh Ismāʿīl-I Avval: Pādshāhī Bā Aṣr'hā-Yi Dīrpāy Dar Īrān Va Īrānī* [Shah Ismael the First]. S.l.: Shirkat-i Sihāmī-i Intishār.

Perry, John R. 1999. 'Toward a Theory of Iranian Urban Moieties: The Haydariyyah and Nicmatiyyah Revisited', *Iranian Studies* 32(1): 51–70.

Platvoet, Jan G. 2004. 'Ritual as War: On the Need to De-Westernize the Concept', in Jens Kreinath, Constance Hartunge and Annette Deschner (eds), *The Dynamics of Changing Rituals: The Transformation of Religious Rituals within Their Social and Cultural Context*. New York: Peter Lang, pp. 243–66.

Pooya, S.A. 2000. 'Justari Darbareyeh Nakhl va Nakhl-Bardari Dar Yazd, Ba Ta-Kid Bar Nakhl-e Tarikhi-e Amir-Chakhmagh ÜAn Study about Nakhl and Nakhl-Bardari in Yazd]', in *Majmoeh-Ye Maghalat-e Nokhostin Hamayesh Moharaam va Farhang-e Mardom Iran, Urdibehesht 1376* [Proceedings of the first congress of Moharam and Iranian folk, Tehran 1997]. Tehran: Pajouheshkadeh Mardom Shenasi, pp. 107–20.

Poulantzas, Nicos. 1973. *Political Power and Social Classes*. London: Sheed and Ward.

Radfar, Muhammad Reza. 2002. 'Dezful Dar Meli Shodan Sanat-i Naft [Dezful in the nationalization of the oil industry]', in Muhammad Reza Radfar and Azim Mahmoodzade (eds), *Dezful in Nationalization of Oil Industry, The Party Year*. Dezful: Afham, pp. 10–72.

Rahimi, Babak. 2004. *Between Carnival and Mourning: The Muharram Rituals and the Emergence of the Early Modern Iranian Public Sphere in the Safavi Period, 1590–1641 C.E.* Florence: S.n.

———. 2011. *Theater State and the Formation of Early Modern Public Sphere in Iran: Studies on Safavid Muharram Rituals, 1590–1641 CE*. Iran Studies 5. Leiden and Boston, MA: Brill.

Rappaport, Roy A. 1968. *Pigs for the Ancestors: Ritual in the Ecology of a New Guinea People*. New Haven, CT and London: Yale University Press.

———. 1979. *Ecology, Meaning, and Religion*. Richmond, CA: North Atlantic Books.

Ravandi, Murtaza. 1979. *Tārikh-i Tahavoulat-i Ijtima-i* [The history of social changes]. Tehran: Jibi.

Rezaei, M. 2000. 'Daramadi Bar Sonat Azadari Mah-e Moharam Dar Ardebil [An introduction to the tradition of lament of the month of Moharam in Ardebil]', in Majoomeyee Maghalat Nokhostin Hamayesh Moharaam va Farhang Mardoom Iran, Tehran, 1376 [Proceedings of the first congress of Moharaam and Iranian folk, Tehran 1997]. Tehran: Miras Farhangi Keshvar, pp. 147–64.

Rizvi, Saiyid Athar Abbas. 1986. *A Socio-Intellectual History of the Isnā ʾAsharī Shīʿīs in India*. Vol. 2. 2 vols. New Delhi: Munshiram Manoharlal.

Russell, Bertrand. 1961. *History of Western Philosophy: And Its Connection with Political and Social Circumstances from the Earliest Times to the Present Day*. 2nd edn. London: Routledge.

Saeidi, Horiyeh. 1999. 'Mashrotyyat Dar Dezful [The constitution in Dezful]', *Tarikh-i Moaaser Iran* 3(10): 305–18.

Safari, Baba. 1974. *Ardabil Dar Gozaargah Tarikh* [Ardabil through the passage of history]. Vol. 1. Tehran: Chapkhaneye Bahman.

Salmanzadeh, Cyrus. 1976. 'The Impact of Agrarian Reform Measures on Village Social Structure in Rural Dezfoul, Iran, with Specific Reference to Required Developments in Extension Work'. PhD. Reading, UK: University of Reading.

Salmanzadeh, Cyrus and Gwyn E. Jones. 1979. 'An Approach to the Micro Analysis of the Land Reform Program in Southwestern Iran', *Land Economics* 55(1): 108–27.

Sanders, Paula A. 1994. *Ritual, Politics, and the City in Fatimid Cairo*. Albany, NY: State University of New York Press.

Sayyah, Hamid. 1967. *Khaterat Haj Sayyah Ya Doran Khoof va Vahshat* [Haj Sayyah's memoir or the era of fear and horror]. Edited by Sayfullah Golkar. Tehran: Amir Kabir.

Schechner, R. 1994. 'Ritual and Performance', in Tim Ingold (ed.), *Companion Encyclopedia of Anthropology*. London and New York: Routledge, pp. 613–47.

Schechner, Richard. 1988. *Performance Theory*. Rev. and expanded edn. New York: Routledge.

———. 1993. *The Future of Ritual: Writings on Culture and Performance*. London: Routledge.

Scholte, Jan Aart. 2000. *Globalization: A Critical Introduction*. Basingstoke: Palgrave.

Shariati, Ali. 1971. *Tashayyue Alivi va Tashayyue Safavi* [The Alavid Shiism and the Safavid Shiism]. Vol. 9. Collection of Works. Tehran: Entesharat Husseinyeh Arshad.

———. 2001. *Hussein Vares Adam* [Hussein the heir of Adam]. Collections of Works. Tehran: Qalam.

Shields, Rob. 2012. 'Cultural Topology: The Seven Bridges of Königsburg, 1736', *Theory, Culture & Society* 29(4–5): 43–57.

Smith, Jonathan Z. 1982. *Imagining Religion: From Babylon to Jonestown*. Chicago, IL: University of Chicago Press.

———. 1987. *To Take Place: Toward Theory in Ritual*. Chicago Studies in the History of Judaism. Chicago, IL: University of Chicago Press.

Soja, Edward W. 1989. *Postmodern Geographies: The Reassertion of Space in Critical Social Theory*. London: Verso.

Stausberg, Michael. 2004. 'Patterns of Ritual Change among Parsi-Zoroastrians in Recent Times', in Jens Kreinath, Constance Hartunge and Annette Deschner (eds), *The Dynamics of Changing Rituals: The Transformation of Religious Rituals within Their Social and Cultural Context*. New York: Peter Lang, pp. 233–42.

Tabari, Muḥammad ibn Jarir. 1997. *The Community Divided*. SUNY Series in Near Eastern Studies. New York: State University of New York Press.

Tabatabaei, Muhammad Husayn. 1975. *Shi'ite Islam*. Translated by Seyyed Hossein Nasr.

Tambiah, S.J. 1979. *A Performative Approach to Ritual*. London: Oxford University Press.

Tavasoli, Mahmood. 1987. 'Husseiniyeh-Ha, Takaya, and Mosalla-Ha [Husseiniyehs, Tekyehs and Mosallas]', in Muhammad Yusef Kiani (ed.), *Memmari Iran, Doryeh Eslami* [Iranian architecture: Islamic era]. Tehran: Vezarat Ershard Eslami, pp. 1: 81–89.

Tavernier, Jean Baptiste. 1684. *Collections of Travels Through Turkey into Persia, and the East-Indies, Giving an Account of the Present State of Those Countries: Being the Travels of Monsieur Tavernier, Bernier, and Other Great Men: Adorned with Many Copper Plates*. London: Moses Pitt.

——. 1957. *Safarnameh-Ye Taverniyeh*. Translated by Abu Turab Noori and Hamid Shirani. 2nd edn. Iṣfahān: Sanai.

Thompson, P.R. 1998. 'The Voice of the Past', in Robert Perks and Alistair Thomson (eds), *The Oral History Reader*. London: Routledge, pp. 21–28.

Torab, Azam. 2007. *Performing Islam: Gender and Ritual in Iran*. Woman and Gender: The Middle East and the Islamic World. Leiden: Brill.

Turner, Victor. 1967. *The Forest of Symbols: Aspects of Ndembu Ritual*. Ithaca, NY and London: Cornell University Press.

——. 1968. *The Drums of Affliction: A Study of Religious Processes among the Ndembu of Zambia*. Oxford: Clarendon Press and International African Institute.

——. 1969. *The Ritual Process: Structure and Anti-Structure*. London: Routledge & K. Paul.

——. 1974. *Dramas, Fields, and Metaphors: Symbolic Action in Human Society*. Symbol, Myth and Ritual Series. Ithaca, NY and London: Cornell University Press.

——. 1975. *Revelation and Divination in Ndembu Ritual*. Ithaca, NY: Cornell University Press.

——. 1979. 'Frame, Flow and Reflection: Ritual and Drama as Public Liminality', *Japanese Journal of Religious Studies* 6(4): 465–99.

——. 1982. *From Ritual to Theatre: The Human Seriousness of Play*. Performance Studies Series. New York: Performing Arts Journal Publications.

Van der Veer, Peter. 1994. *Religious Nationalism: Hindus and Muslims in India*. Berkeley, CA: University of California Press.

—— (ed.). 2015. *Handbook of Religion and the Asian City: Aspiration and Urbanization in the Twenty-First Century*. Oakland, CA: University of California Press.

Virilio, Paul. 1986. *Speed and Politics: An Essay on Dromology*. Semiotext(e) Foreign Agents Series. New York: Columbia University.

Waeiz Kashifi, Hussein. 1979. *Rowdat Al-Shuhada*. Tehran: Kitab-Forushi Islamiyah.

Warf, Barney. 2004. 'Nigel Thrift', in Phil Hubbard, Rob Kitchin and Gill Valentine (eds), *Key Thinkers on Space and Place*. London and Thousand Oaks: Sage, pp. 294–300.

Watt, W. Montgomery. 1960. 'Shi'ism under the Umayyads', *Journal of the Royal Asiatic Society of Great Britain and Ireland* 3/4 (October): 158–72.

White, Hayden. 2013. Hayden White and Ethan Kleinberg: A Conversation at Wesleyan's Center for the Humanities Interview by Ethan Kleinberg. Video. https://www.youtube.com/watch?v=ViG30Fkz2cI&t=30s. Accessed 13 November 2017.

——. 2014. 'Tears in the Fabric of the Past: New Theories of Narrative and History', presented at Tears in the Fabric of the Past: New Theories of Narrative and History, University of California Berkeley, November. https://www.youtube.com/watch?v=Mr5DgDvltwo. Accessed 13 November 2017.

White, Hayden V. 1975. *Metahistory: The Historical Imagination in Nineteenth-Century Europe*. Baltimore, MD: Johns Hopkins University Press.

Ya-Husseini, Sayyed Ghasem. 1992. 'Introduction', in Mohsen Amin, translated by Jalal Al-Ahamad (ed.), *Azadari-Haye Na-Mashro* [Illegimate mourning ceremonies]. Bushehr: Darya.

Yarshater, Ehsan. 1979. 'Ta'ziyeh and Pre-Islamic Mourning Rites in Iran', in Peter Chelkowski (ed.), *Ta'ziyeh: Ritual and Drama in Iran*. New York: New York University Press and Soroush Press, pp. 88–94.

Zandi, Hushang. 1969. *Majmoehye Qavanin va Muqarrarat Shahrdari-Ha va Khadamat Shahri* [The municipality legislations]. Tehran: Kharazmi.

# INDEX

www.ingramcontent.com/pod-product-compliance
Lightning Source LLC
Chambersburg PA
CBHW070929030426
42336CB00014BA/2603